W9-BMD-941

butter sugar flour eggs

butter sugar

flour eggs

whimsical irresistible desserts

gale gand, rick tramonto, and julia moskin

PHOTOGRAPHS BY kelly bugden

CLARKSON POTTER/PUBLISHERS
NEW YORK

Copyright © 1999 by Dynamic Duo, Inc., and Julia Moskin

Photographs copyright © 1999 by Kelly Bugden

All rights reserved. No part of this book may be reproduced
or transmitted in any form or by any means, electronic
or mechanical, including photocopying, recording, or by
any information storage and retrieval system, without
permission in writing from the publisher.

Published by Clarkson N. Potter, Inc., New York, New York
Member of the Crown Publishing Group.

Random House, Inc. New York, Toronto, London, Sydney, Auckland
www.randomhouse.com

CLARKSON N. POTTER is a trademark and POTTER and
colophon are registered trademarks of Random House, Inc.

Printed in the United States of America

Design by Constance Old

Library of Congress Cataloging-in-Publication Data
Gand, Gale.
    Butter sugar flour eggs / by Gale Gand, Rick Tramonto, and
Julia Moskin; photography by Kelly Budgen.—1st ed.
        p.   cm.
    Includes index.
    1. Desserts. 2. Baking. I. Tramonto, Rick. II. Moskin, Julia.
III. Title.
TX773.G33   1999
641.8'15—DC21   99-13858
                                CIP

ISBN 0-609-60420-1

10 9 8 7 6 5

This book is for our son, Giorgio Montana Gand Tramonto. Thank you for gracing our lives, eating our cooking, whisking the blintzes on Saturday mornings, helping us transform from daughter/son to mother/father, and sharing the joy of tenderness and feelings of peace, in and out of our kitchen.

And to Gale's fiery mother, Myrna Joan Grossman Gand, who was a great baker and a would-be writer—sorry you're not here to see that you passed on both talents. Thank you. You are terribly missed.

thanks from gale and rick

To our book people Julia Moskin, our culinary soulmate, thank you for putting our musings into words in a way that makes sense. You are brilliant! Roy Finamore for making a delicious book for us. Lauren Shakely and the team at Clarkson Potter, especially Chris Smith. Jane Dystel for always watching over us. Mary Ann Forness for testing half of the recipes and being willing to do 9:00 P.M. tastings. Mary Mullins for testing half of the recipes and driving chocolate cakes around in her non-air-conditioned car! Kelly Bugden, Roscoe Betsil, Jee Levin, and Charles Gold and Peri Wolfman.

To our friends and family Bob Gand for teaching more than most fathers do and tasting the first banana bread. Frank and Gloria Tramonto for their love. Lana Rae and Big Red Catering Company for undying support in oh-so many ways. Karen Katz, Gale's best friend, for peerless support and understanding that there was no playing the whole summer we wrote this. Grandma Elsie Grossman for gorgeous odors and endless baking. Gary and Joan Gand for their great appetite for our work. Aunt Greta and Uncle Robert Pearson for the first whisk and copper bowl. Marthe Hess, Muriel Hamon, Judy Anderson, Vinnie Rupert, Aunt Teresa Treuhaft. Marks and Spencer for good strong tea all through the night. And from Rick: My lord Jesus Christ for keeping me on the right road.

To our colleagues Muhammad Salahuddin for poetry and watching home plate. Larry Binstein and European Imports for cheeses that pleases. Marty Tiersky for vino that is keeno. Chef Greg Broman, our mentor, whether he likes it or not! Julia

Child for including Gale in her baking book and television series. Bobby Flay for fun in the sun with the kids. Bob and Wendy Payton, Rich Melman, Brasserie T investors and staff.

Mark Andelbradt, Barb Charal, Michael Fox, Wendy Glenn, Steve Ottmann, Charles Haskell, Kevin Brown, Bob Wattel, Jay Stieber, Scott Barton, all the staff at LEYE, all the staff at Tru, Emeril Lagasse, Jean-Georges Vongerichten, Nico Ladenis, Peter and Mary Weber, Maida Heatter, Albert Kumin, Pierre Gagnaire, Maurice Bernachon, Nancy Silverton, Lionel Poilâne, Gaston Lenôtre, Barbara Tropp, Emily Luchetti, John Mariani, and Bill Rice.

La Varenne Cooking School, Women Chefs and Restaurateurs, American Dairy Association, the Food Network for their support since the beginning, Sara Lee Bakeries, American Institute of Baking, James Beard House, Gateway 2000 Computers.

All our great purveyors who keep us ripe each day. Everyone who has let us into their kitchens to cook and experience the magic.

thanks from julia

To Gale Gand and Rick Tramonto for their recipes, faith, and stories worth writing about. To Jane Dystel, our tireless agent and hound dog, who barks and bites so we don't have to. To Roy Finamore for his great eye. To Chris Smith for his dry good humor. To my family for their kindness about the grape clafouti, and countless other things.

And most of all to Darren Kapelus, the single best ingredient in the mixing bowl of my life.

contents

introduction: We began this book with a single goal. We wanted to capture the sense of sweet abundance you feel when you walk into your favorite bakery. The glossy tarts, the pale ivory cheesecakes, the chunky cookies, the brightly colored birthday cakes, the darkly frosted éclairs, the holiday pies, the chocolate truffles— we wanted them all. But as we tried to pin that experience down, something strange happened. What really intrigued us wasn't the perfectly risen cake, or the flawless pie crust, or the picture-perfect meringues we could imagine in the cases. It was the stuff in the kitchen: the bricks of smooth creamy butter, the snowy mountains of sugar, the sacks of flour, the golden glow of fresh egg yolks, and the magic of stiffly whipped egg whites. It was the blocks of dark chocolate and bowls of melted chocolate, piles of lemons ready for zesting, and pale pink grapefruits and juicy peaches and ruby cherries and fat blackberries. It was shiny pecans and hard almonds and soft cream cheese, heady ginger and candied citron and everything else that makes baking so deeply, deeply satisfying.

We're in love with our own ingredients.

That's why this book is called *Butter Sugar Flour Eggs*, after the first and most important elements of any dessert recipe. If you've ever made so much as a batch of cookies, you know that that is where it all begins. Butter brings flavor and richness; Sugar lends sweetness and melting textures; Flour provides substance; and Eggs bring it all together. Afterward the flavorings take over: Chocolate, Citrus, Fruit, Nuts, Cheese, and Spices complete the dessert-making pantry. Most desserts have one strong, characteristic flavor or texture that sings louder than anything else, and that's how we decided which tribe they belonged to.

We hoped that you would like the idea of choosing a dessert not by technique, but by flavor, the way you choose desserts from a restaurant menu. At our restaurant, Brasserie T, no one ever says to us "What cake are you making tonight?" It's always "What do you have that's really chocolaty?" or "I love a good lemon dessert." There are "apple people" and "ginger people" among our regulars and our friends; some devotees will order anything with the word *caramel* in it. When imagining a

dessert as part of a menu, any good cook will think about flavor first.

As we began a recipe list, trying to include all the many desserts we have learned and loved, another strange thing happened. The ingredients began to come alive. They took over. They asserted their personalities, got up and walked around the pages of the book, put on clothes, and even came together in surprising new ways. Suave Chocolate learned to dance with rustic Fruit. Young Cheese was introduced to aggressive, warm Spice. We found that sometimes we wanted both Chocolate and Spice to come over for an exciting evening; often we just felt like relaxing with old friends Butter and Sugar. Fruit offered to help Eggs with her weight problem, and even old-fashioned Nuts learned a few new tricks.

We share these personalities with you so that you can experience baking the way we do. When you're in the kitchen with this book, we want you to feel that we're there with you, offering baking advice and experience. But we also want you to feel the presence of the wonderful ingredients that we're all lucky enough to cook with. We see each recipe as a dynamic new combination of ingredients. Our Purely Pound Cake, Sweet Tart Pastry, and Rainbow Sugar Cookies are all made from butter, sugar, flour, and eggs. But they are so different! We wanted to explore why. What happens if you add chocolate? Well, that's Brooklyn Blackout Cake. What happens if you take out the flour and add fruit? Harriet's Chewy Chocolate Pavé. What if you then get rid of the chocolate and add molasses and rum? Molasses-Rum-Raisin Cake.

But as we tried to put together a complete collection, we realized that certain desserts— pumpkin pie, for example—are so wedded to certain holidays that there is no separating them by flavor. Desserts are an important part of our holiday celebrations, and so a Holiday chapter went in. We also realized that a dessert isn't only about the finished dish: It can also be about the shiny teapot, the steaming espresso, the amber dessert wine, the frosty glass of milk alongside. So we added playful, optional suggestions about what you might drink with each dessert to make desserts more fun, full, filling, and fulfilling. Notes on how to make and choose the dessert drinks are collected at the end of the book. We also realized, thanks to our valiant recipe testers, that people cook very differently and there is a wide range of opinion about just what creaming butter and mixing batter and so on really mean. So we added a chapter of basic procedures, explaining what we do and why.

After "sifting" through all the flavor possibilities, we've included recipes for almost every kind of dessert, from rice pudding to cookies to pecan pie to chocolate éclairs. You'll learn the easiest methods for custards, strudels, phyllo dough, and even Baked Alaska. Unless you are a very experienced baker, we'd recommend sticking closely to the recipes at first. Baking is so precise in terms of chemistry (liquids, temperatures, reactions, sugars, proteins all working together) that even substituting one fruit for another can radically change your desserts. As you gain experience, you'll see certain patterns in the way sugar and eggs work together, or how much butter it takes to get flour to relax. Chocolate's temperamental behavior won't get to you anymore, and you'll appreciate the predictable qualities of nuts. You'll learn which personalities are best suited to yours.

In writing this book, we also got to see our own personalities in new ways. A pastry chef has to combine the skills of a jeweler, a physicist, a chemist, an artist, a perfumer, and an assembly-line worker. Any chef needs the patience of a saint, the nature knowledge of a botanist, the geometrical mind of a mathematician, and the construction know-how of an engineer. A writer must be an imaginary chef, a fly on the wall, an historian, and an archaeologist.

As we dug through recipes from every stratum of our cooking lives, we unearthed relics from England, French classics, Italian-American innovations, Hungarian family traditions, and personal favorites from far-flung lands like Cleveland in the 1930s; Rochester, New York, in the 1970s; and New York City in the 1980s. Many of our favorite desserts are the adult renditions of childhood treats like butterscotch pudding, taffy apples, and root beer floats, which you'll find throughout the book. We like to make them for people almost as much as we like eating them ourselves. Like nothing else, these flavors and textures remind us of the pleasures of home cooking. Together, all these recipes present our complete history, sung in the exuberant harmonies of butter, sugar, flour, eggs, chocolate, citrus, fruit, nuts, cheese, and spices.

We hope you'll sing along.

THE INFORMATION IN THIS SECTION MAY NOT BE NEWS TO YOU. But we've noticed that pastry chefs and home bakers all have their own independent ideas about things like whipping egg whites, creaming butter, and measuring flour. The following notes cover some basic methods that we use every day, in almost every recipe. We also used them in testing for the book, and following them will help ensure great results in your kitchen!

When **creaming butter,** remove your butter from the refrigerator 30 minutes beforehand. If starting with frozen butter, cut it into small

of confectioners' sugar contains more sugar than a cup of granulated sugar. When we say **sugar** we mean plain white granulated sugar. Other kinds are specified. If necessary, you can **make light brown sugar** by combining equal parts of granulated sugar and dark brown sugar.

When making a **caramel,** it's especially important to keep any sugar crystals away from the boiling caramel. Start by pouring the sugar into the center of a clean, dry, deep saucepan. Carefully pour the water around the sugar, trying not to splash any sugar onto the sides of the pan. Do not stir; gently draw your finger

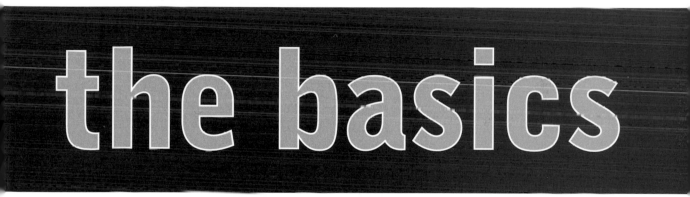

the basics

pieces and give it at least 45 minutes to warm up. Microwaving butter to warm it quickly doesn't really work; it goes from frozen butter directly to melted butter. What you want is cool butter. Butter has been correctly creamed when it is smooth, not when it is clumped up on your mixer beaters. If it clumps, it's still too cold; give it a few more minutes to soften. You want a soft, fluffy paste of cool butter, lighter than what you began with from the air you've mixed in. This is an integral step in many recipes, so don't skimp on it!

Substituting sugars is not a good idea in baking, which can be very precise. For example, light brown sugar and dark brown sugar are very different in their flavor and their effects, and a cup

through the center of the sugar twice, making a cross, to moisten it. Over medium high heat, bring to a boil without stirring. Cook without stirring, watching carefully, until amber-caramel in color, 10 to 20 minutes. To test the color as it cooks, use a wooden spoon (to prevent burning yourself) to drip a few drops of the caramel onto a white plate. If you need to test it more than once, use a clean spoon—do not put the same spoon back into the cooking caramel.

To measure flour, we use the dip-and-swipe method, scooping the flour up in a measuring cup and leveling it with a knife across the top. **Don't pour** flour into your measuring cup or tap or bang it to level it out. Swiping across the top means that you must use measuring cups that hold exactly the amount you are trying to measure. You can't accurately measure 1 cup of flour in a 4-cup measure, because you won't be able to swipe across the top.

All eggs in this book are grade large. When **separating eggs,** refrigerate the yolks after separating, but let the whites warm up to room temperature before whipping them. They will be stiffer and fluffier, and if you are folding them into temperature-sensitive ingredients like melted chocolate it's best if they are not cold. **Whip egg whites** in a completely clean, completely dry bowl: A speck of yolk, water, or grease can make it impossible to whip whites stiff. Whip egg whites at high speed in a large bowl, to get the most air into them. We always whip them to the soft peak stage, then add a little sugar for the final minute of whipping. The sugar dissolves and helps the egg whites stiffen and remain flexible. We use **raw egg yolks** very rarely, but when we do, we buy fresh cartons from a large market with good turnover (never a farmstand), we keep them cold the whole time we are working with them, and, of course, we do not serve them to anyone who is ill or immune-impaired.

To melt chocolate, we feel that the good old double-boiler method can't be beat. Start with chopped chocolate (see below) for even melting. The trick is to adjust the heat so that the water in the bottom is barely simmering, not bubbling or boiling. The simmer should be just visible; French cooks call this stage "smiling." Chocolate melted over barely simmering water will not scorch and will stay melted. If you don't have a double boiler, set a metal or glass bowl over a saucepan of water. The bottom of the bowl should not be touching the water. Never cover chocolate in a double boiler, even after it is melted. Drops of water might form on the lid, and if they drop into the chocolate, it may seize up. **Melt white chocolate** over very hot water, not barely simmering water; white chocolate scorches at a lower temperature.

Store chocolate at room temperature, not in the refrigerator. **To chop chocolate,** use a large heavy knife. Always have the chocolate at room temperature to prevent it from splintering and flying around; cold chocolate is too hard to cut, and the knife may slip and cut you. To chop chocolate in a food processor, chill the chocolate slightly and pulse it just until chopped. **To shave chocolate,** peel it off the block with a sharp vegetable peeler, or grate it on the large holes of a box grater. The first method gives you larger pieces, but in either case the chocolate will splinter somewhat. To prevent splintering, set the chocolate in a warm place for an hour.

Toasting nuts is a very important step to release the nuts' flavors. Spread whole or chopped nuts out on a baking sheet and put them in a preheated 350-degree oven (or toaster oven). Check them frequently after the first 5 minutes, shaking the pan occasionally to make sure they brown evenly. When they smell toasty and look slightly browned, after 10 to 20 minutes, remove them immediately and transfer to a bowl as they cook very quickly and can scorch after this point. Do not try to toast ground nuts.

Hazelnuts should be peeled after toasting, though you can buy pre-peeled ones now. If they come with a thin brown skin, toast them lightly, then wrap them in a dishtowel and let them sit for 15 minutes (the steam created in the towel will loosen the skins). Rub the nuts together in the towel to rub the skins off the nuts, and then pick out the nuts. Not every bit of skin will come off, but that's okay.

Before **chopping toasted nuts,** let them cool completely. Pulse them in a food processor or chop them coarsely with a very sharp knife. **Grinding nuts** is more tricky. Finely ground almonds, pecans, and walnuts can be bought at many supermarkets. At home, almonds can be pulsed until ground fine in a food processor. However, more oily nuts like walnuts can suddenly become pasty and greasy if processed too long. You can protect against this by grinding nuts with ¼ cup of the sugar in the recipe. The sugar absorbs the oils. Either blanched or plain almonds can be used in these recipes, unless specified otherwise.

When **mixing doughs and batters,** we often add dry and wet ingredients in alternating batches; we find that the mixture comes together faster and more smoothly, and it puts less strain on your mixer's motor and beaters. Stop fairly often to scrape down the sides of the bowl. When we warn you not to "overmix" the dough, it is to prevent the gluten in the flour from being activated by the heat and friction, which would make your dough stretchy and tough. When a recipe specifies "do not overmix," stop mixing as soon as the ingredients are blended. No flour or streaks should be visible.

Kneading dough for biscuits and cookies is different from kneading dough for breads. For the few breads in this book, you will be kneading in a mixer. Some of our biscuit and cookie doughs are kneaded by hand, but only lightly. You are trying to bring the dough together and smooth it out without warming it up too much; 5 to 10 "kneads" is plenty.

When **working with phyllo dough,** keep the box of phyllo refrigerated until you are ready to use it. If you buy it frozen, thaw it in the refrigerator the day before you are going to use it. When ready to use, unroll the pastry onto a work surface and keep it covered with a towel. You can lightly mist the towel with water if you have a spray bottle handy, but don't dampen the towel under the tap: It gets too wet, and the moisture causes the sheets to stick together.

When **choosing baking pans,** keep in mind that we used heavy aluminum cake pans and aluminum or glass pie pans for testing. Good non-stick pans are fine for most baking, but pie crusts will not brown as well in nonstick pans. If using glass baking pans, you may need to increase the cooking times given; just keep a closer eye on the baking.

To make a **hot-water bath,** or bain marie, line a 2-inch-deep (at least) roasting pan with paper towels or newspapers. This is to create a layer of water *under* the dish as well as around it; direct contact between the metal roasting pan and the baking dish would create a "hot spot" where they meet. Also, the paper will keep the dishes from sliding around. Arrange the dish or dishes in the roasting pan, leaving room between them and making sure they are not touching the sides of the pan. Then fill the pan with very hot tap water until it comes halfway up the sides of the dishes. Immediately place the pan in a preheated oven.

butter

"Butter is only as good as the cream
with which it is made."
Irma Rombauer and Marion Rombauer Becker

purely pound cake

lydia's austrian raspberry shortbread

millionaire's shortbread

sugar-crusted breton butter cake

giant's thumbprint butter cookies

brown butter tuiles

plain and perfect pie crust

crumbly pie crust

pâte brisée

sweet pastry

personality profile: Butter is a true aristocrat—and a modest one. Suave, obliging, and not in the least temperamental, butter smooths out rough edges and makes even the plainest companions sparkle. Butter is invited everywhere, but is rarely the center of attention; and though there are many pretenders to butter's high throne, there are no real challengers to its stature.

It's not much of an overstatement to say that there could be no baking without butter. Obviously, it's that wonderful creamery flavor that we love—but butter also slaves away as the workhorse of the pastry kitchen, in charge of some of the most elemental processes that turn mere ingredients into delightful desserts. Of course it adds a smooth gloss to custards, browns to nuttiness in cookies, softens cake batters into tenderness, and carries the taste of chocolate, lemon, and spice to the luscious point where they fill your mouth with flavor. But most important, butter is the ingredient that turns any dough from paste to pastry, magically flaking, crumbling, or puffing at the whim of the cook.

If, as a child, you learn what real butter tastes like, there is no going back. Americans used to cheerfully eat quantities of sweets like butterballs (butter creamed with confectioners' sugar and lemon juice, formed into balls, and chilled), shortbread, butterscotch, fudge, and fondant, thus developing a lifelong taste for the good stuff. In the Gand household circa 1965, when Gale was growing up in Deerfield, Illinois, butter was the fifth food group. Whole categories of food were seen as vehicles for butter: muffins, bagels, vegetables, bread, biscuits. Like many schoolchildren, Gale churned butter for the first time in history class, not a dairy barn, but she took to it right away. Soon she was making large batches at home, mixing it with sugar, and hiding the resulting paste in the back of the cupboard to eat by spoonfuls. No wonder she became a pastry chef!

The flavor of butter itself is highlighted in our recipes for pound cake (the ultimate *Butter Sugar Flour Eggs* recipe), Breton Butter Cake (a yeast dough layered with butter, in the French tradition), and Millionaire's Shortbread, which fuses classic butter shortbread with a butter-based caramel. Butter's ability to create irresistible textures shines in Lydia's Austrian Raspberry Shortbread, and the toasty flavor of brown butter is what makes our tuile cookies hauntingly good. And then we come to pastry.

Cold butter worked into flour—one of the many chemistry experiments that make up the bakers' craft—is a good basic description of pastry dough. Using cold butter is not a whim or a pretension; it's a must, and the key to good doughs. To be scientific, cold butter is an emulsification of water in fat; microscopic beads of water suspended in butterfat-rich cream. When this emulsification is lightly mixed with flour, the beads of water remain safely coated and separate from each other. But when the mixture is heated in the oven, each bead of water expands as it turns into steam, explodes out of its fat-and-flour coat like the Incredible Hulk, leaving the coat behind to melt into a flake of pastry. A pie crust, a tart shell, a wedge of shortbread—all are made up of stacked flakes of melted butter, air, and cooked flour.

Now, if the butter you begin with is warm, or if vegetable oil is used, the water is already gone, the emulsification is broken, and the flour starts to absorb the fat immediately, making an impossibly heavy dough. This is why you must start with cold butter and chill the dough after mixing (and chill it yet again during the rolling if the butter seems to be warming up). The butter must stay separate from the flour up until the baking, and this is why you can leave fairly large bits of unmixed butter in your pastry dough without fear.

Though pastry chefs may use very different techniques for blending and kneading different doughs, home cooks certainly don't need to know them all. For our purposes the basic, but flexible, doughs presented here are all you need. They vary mostly in how much sugar is used and what liquid (water, egg, or cream) is added.

Like most chefs, we confess to a certain amount of sneaky pleasure in the reports that margarine and hydrogenated vegetable shortening are not, after all, more healthy than butter. Both substances try to artificially re-create the makeup of butter by whipping water and air into oil, but for flavor purposes it simply does not work. You may not eat shortbread and pie every day, but when you are going to all the trouble of making a buttery dessert, you must use *real* butter. If you have pound cake only once a year, that's all the more reason to make it a good one.

We almost always use unsalted butter in baking, adding salt later in the recipe; we feel that this allows the clear butter flavor to come through, and you can control the amount of salt in the dish. Also, unsalted butter is likely to be fresher than salted, as the salt acts as a preservative. Where butter is concerned, fresher is always better. We used regular supermarket butter to test the recipes. European-style butter is delicious on toast, but since it contains less water than American butter, it is a difficult choice in baking and may make these recipes slightly greasier than they should be.

As far as measuring butter goes, we measure both by weight (in ounces) and by volume (in tablespoons). We don't measure in cups, feeling that mashing butter into a measuring cup is an unnecessary step that few people take anyway. One pound of butter equals 2 cups equals 4 sticks equals 32 tablespoons.

To sum up: Butter is one of the great reasons to be a cook. Now go have some fun.

purely pound cake

1 pound (4 sticks) unsalted butter, slightly softened
1 pound (2⅛ cups) sugar
1 pound (12) eggs, separated
¼ cup brandy
2 teaspoons rose water (optional)
¼ teaspoon nutmeg (⅛ teaspoon if freshly grated)
½ teaspoon salt
1 pound (3½ cups) all-purpose flour, sifted 3 times

Heat the oven to 325 degrees. Butter two 6-cup loaf pans and line them with parchment or wax paper.

Cream the butter in a mixer fitted with a whisk attachment (or using a hand mixer) until very light and fluffy, about 10 minutes. Add the sugar and cream together. Add the egg yolks 2 at a time, mixing well between additions. The mixture should be very fluffy.

Add the brandy, rose water, nutmeg, and salt and mix to incorporate. Working in 3 batches, add the flour, mixing just until combined and scraping down the bowl between additions.

Whip the egg whites in a clean, dry bowl until stiff but not dry. Add to the batter and mix well, until no streaks of egg white remain. If necessary, fold in the last few streaks by hand. Pour the batter into the pans and smooth the tops.

Bake until the cakes are golden brown and split on the top and a tester inserted in the center comes out clean (a few crumbs are okay), 70 to 80 minutes. Let cool in the pan on a rack for 30 minutes. Knock the cake out of the pan and let cool completely. Remove the parchment paper.

MAKES 2 CAKES

Nothing partners pound cake as well as fresh-brewed tea. Instead of putting jam on the cake or sugar in the tea, we like to stir a teaspoon of raspberry or strawberry jam into our tea, as they do in Eastern Europe.

Here they are: butter, sugar, flour, and eggs, a pound of each, baked into perfect harmony.

Gale's collection of antique and modern cookbooks holds countless recipes for pound cake, many of which aren't really pound cake at all. True pound cake is unleavened; baking soda and powder weren't widely available until the nineteenth century.

We use an eighteenth-century method that brings whipped egg whites on board for lightness. The flavorings—brandy and rose water—are from the 1917 WHITE HOUSE COOKBOOK, and they give the cake an elusive, antique perfume without imparting a strong flavor. For centuries before vanilla was generally available, or even known to the Western world, rose water and orange-blossom water were in constant use as flavorings in dessert cookery.

Since real pound cake has no leavening except the air worked in by creaming the butter, sifting the flour, and whipping the egg whites, don't skimp on those steps! Serve in thin slices, or toast it and top with fruit compotes or preserves such as the strawberry-rhubarb preserves on page 168. For a half-pound cake, simply cut the recipe in half. The full recipe makes two rather large loaves.

lydia's austrian raspberry shortbread

1 pound (4 sticks) unsalted butter, slightly softened
4 egg yolks
2 cups granulated sugar
4 cups all-purpose flour
2 teaspoons baking powder
¼ teaspoon salt
1 cup raspberry jam, at room temperature
¼ cup confectioners' sugar

When we were taking our baby steps as chefs, one of our favorite teachers was Lydia, queen of the soup pots at the Strathallen Hotel in Rochester, New York. She grew up in Austria, so, of course, she knew plenty about baking. When we got to work in the morning, we'd taste that day's "zoop" (as she'd say in her strong accent), then watch as she demonstrated family baking recipes like this one. Grating the frozen shortbread dough into the baking pan gives it a lighter, more open texture; adding a middle layer of raspberry jam makes it stunningly delicious. For a chocolate-raspberry shortbread, substitute 1 cup cocoa for 1 cup of the flour.

Photograph on page 148.

Cream the butter in a mixer fitted with a paddle attachment (or using a hand mixer) until soft and fluffy. Add the egg yolks and mix well.

Mix the granulated sugar, flour, baking powder, and salt together. Add to the butter and egg yolk mixture and mix just until incorporated and the dough starts to come together. Turn the dough out onto a floured work surface and form into two balls. Wrap each ball in plastic wrap and freeze at least 2 hours or overnight (or as long as a month, if you like).

Heat the oven to 350 degrees.

Remove one ball of dough from the freezer and coarsely grate it by hand or with the grating disk in a food processor into the bottom of a 9×13-inch baking pan or a 10-inch tart pan with a removable bottom (see photograph). Make sure the surface is covered evenly with shreds of dough.

With the back of a spoon or a flexible spatula, spread the jam over the surface, to within ½ inch of the edge all the way around. Remove the remaining dough from the freezer and coarsely grate it over the entire surface.

Bake until light golden brown, 30 to 40 minutes. As soon as the shortbread comes out of the oven, dust with confectioners' sugar. Cool on a wire rack, then cut in the pan with a serrated knife.

MAKES 12 TO 16 LARGE BARS

☞ *This rich, ladylike cookie demands a flowery tea; rose hip's light tartness is perfect here, and its pale pink color echoes the raspberry filling.*

millionaire's shortbread

8 ounces (2 sticks) unsalted butter, slightly softened
3 cups sugar
2¼ cups all-purpose flour
2 tablespoons cornstarch
½ cup water
2 tablespoons salted butter
½ cup heavy cream, heated to lukewarm
8 ounces semisweet chocolate
1½ teaspoons vegetable oil

Heat the oven to 350 degrees. Line a 9×13-inch baking pan with parchment or wax paper.

Cream the unsalted butter in a mixer fitted with a paddle attachment (or using a hand mixer) until soft. Add ½ cup of the sugar and mix until incorporated.

Mix the flour and cornstarch together. Add the dry ingredients to the butter mixture and mix at low speed just until the ingredients are incorporated and the dough comes together. Turn the dough out onto a floured work surface and knead it 5 to 10 times, to bring the dough together and smooth it out.

Reflour your work surface. Roll the dough out to fit the sheet pan. To transfer to the sheet pan, roll the dough up onto the rolling pin, lift it up, and unroll it into the pan. Using light strokes of the rolling pin, roll the dough evenly into the corners and edges of the pan, and roll out any bumps. (Or, press the rolled-out dough thoroughly into the pan with your fingers.) Prick the shortbread all over with a fork to prevent any buckling or shrinking.

Bake in the center of the oven for 15 minutes. After 15 minutes, rotate the pan and knock it once against the oven rack, to ensure even cooking and a flat surface. Bake 10 to 15 minutes more, until very lightly browned. Let cool on a wire rack in the pan.

While the shortbread is cooling, make the caramel: Pour the remaining 2½ cups sugar into the center of a deep saucepan. Carefully pour the water around the sugar, trying not to splash any sugar onto the sides of the pan. Do not stir; gently draw your finger through the center of the sugar twice, making a cross, to moisten it. Over medium-high heat, bring to a boil without stirring. Cook without stirring, watching carefully, until amber-caramel in color, 10 to 20 minutes. Immediately remove from the heat and stir in the salted butter with a wooden spoon. Slowly and

Scotland is not well known as a haunt of millionaires, but its shortbread is legendary. Besides, who needs to be a millionaire when anyone with a baking pan and a few basic ingredients can make authentic Scottish millionaire's shortbread? It's just like a delectable combination of a candy bar and a cookie. We discovered it while working in England and scouting for ideas for afternoon tea—a new cooking challenge for us. The original recipe appeared on a can of condensed milk, which was considered a great luxury when it was introduced to Britain. We prefer the real dairy flavor of caramel made with butter and cream.

In a proper three-course afternoon tea, sweets like Millionaire's Shortbread come after the sandwiches and the scones with cream and jam, as a sort of dessert. For plain shortbread, just ignore the chocolate-caramel topping and sprinkle the baked shortbread with 2 tablespoons of sugar as it comes out of the oven.

carefully pour in the lukewarm cream, stirring slowly but constantly. (It will bubble up and may splatter.) Pour over the baked shortbread and smooth the top. Place in the refrigerator, uncovered, to harden slightly.

When the caramel has set, make the chocolate topping: In the top of a double boiler (or in a mixing bowl) set over barely simmering water, melt the chocolate, stirring frequently. Stir in the vegetable oil. (This will make the chocolate less brittle when it hardens.) Pour over the cooled caramel and spread quickly with a spatula or the back of a spoon to cover the entire surface.

Let the chocolate set completely, then use a heavy knife to cut the shortbread into $1\frac{1}{2} \times 3$-inch bars. Store in an airtight container.

MAKES ABOUT 24 COOKIES

There's no better choice here than a pot of a classic English tea blend from India, such as Ty-Phoo.

sugar-crusted breton butter cake (KOUIGN-AMANN)

½ ounce fresh yeast or ¼ ounce (1 package) active dry yeast
¼ cup warm water
2¼ cups all-purpose flour
¼ teaspoon salt
About 10 tablespoons lukewarm water
8 tablespoons (1 stick) best-quality unsalted butter, cut into pieces
   and slightly softened
¼ cup granulated sugar
2 tablespoons confectioners' sugar

Dissolve the yeast in the warm water in a medium bowl. When dissolved, mix in ½ cup of the flour with your fingers, rubbing them together to break up any lumps. Cover with a very slightly damp towel and let rise in a warm place until doubled in bulk, about 30 minutes.

Combine the remaining 1¾ cups flour and the salt in a large bowl. Add the yeast mixture and mix together with the tips of your fingers. Gradually sprinkle in the lukewarm water, mixing with your fingers to make a pliable dough. If the water is all mixed in and the dough still seems dry, add another tablespoon of water. Knead until smooth, about 4 minutes. Return the dough to the large bowl, cover with the damp towel, and let rise in a warm place until doubled in bulk, about 1 hour.

Turn the dough out onto a floured work surface and dust the top of the dough with flour. Roll into a rectangle about the same size as a sheet of paper, 8½×11 inches. Turn the rectangle so that the narrow end faces you, as though you are preparing to write on the paper. Dot the lower two-thirds of the dough rectangle with the pieces of butter and sprinkle with the granulated sugar.

Working as though you are folding a letter, and folding the top down first, fold the dough in thirds. Roll the folded dough out into a rectangle, 8½×11 inches. Fold in thirds again in the same way, cover with the damp towel, and let rest 15 minutes. Roll into a rectangle again, fold in thirds, cover with the damp towel, and let rest 15 minutes. One last time, roll into a rectangle, fold in thirds, cover with the damp towel, and let rest 15 minutes.

Heat the oven to 400 degrees. Butter and flour a 9-inch round cake pan.

Kouign-amann means "bread and butter" in the native language of Brittany, on the west coast of northern France, but the butter definitely outweighs the bread in this extraordinary traditional cake. It's oozing with butter and crackly with sugar; no other seasonings are permitted to affect the flavors. Brittany is a rural part of France where time seems to stand still, especially in northern towns like Locronan; some of the best butter in France, lightly salted with Atlantic sea salt, is made there.

Yes, this cake is rich: A steady diet of kouign-amann is not recommended, even in Brittany. But when you happen on some particularly good fresh creamery butter, showcase its flavor by making—and then diving into—a kouign-amann. It's equally good for dessert or breakfast, and it lasts beautifully.

Note that both **warm** water (to wake up the yeast) and **lukewarm** water (to moisten the dough) are used in this recipe. Warm water feels distinctly warm to the touch; lukewarm water feels about the same as body temperature.

Photograph on page 138.

Roll the dough into a circle about 10 inches in diameter. Transfer to the pan and fold up the corners to fit the square into the round pan. Using a sharp knife or razor blade, make a crosshatch pattern across the top of the cake (like a tic-tac-toe board).

Bake 20 minutes, brushing the top every 5 minutes with the melted butter that oozes out from the cake. Sprinkle with the confectioners' sugar and continue baking (do not baste) until golden brown on the top but still moist inside, about 10 minutes more.

Let cool on a rack just until the crust is slightly hardened. Serve warm, cut into wedges.

MAKES 1 CAKE

Gale's Breton friend Muriel introduced her to the pleasures of Brittany, and Muriel's fondness for Earl Grey tea – as well as the tea's own citric, bergamot flavor – makes it the perfect choice for this rich cake.

giant's thumbprint butter cookies

8 ounces (2 sticks) unsalted butter, slightly softened
⅔ cup sugar
¼ vanilla bean, halved lengthwise, soft insides scraped out
⅛ teaspoon salt
2 cups plus 2 tablespoons all-purpose flour
¼ cup apricot, raspberry, or another jam of your choice

Heat the oven to 350 degrees. Butter 3 sheet pans, or use 1 pan and bake the cookies in 3 batches.

Cream the butter and sugar in a mixer fitted with a paddle attachment (or using a hand mixer) until fluffy. Add the vanilla scrapings and salt and mix until incorporated. Add the flour and mix at low speed until incorporated.

Using your hands, roll the dough into golf-ball-size balls and arrange them 2 inches apart on the cookie sheet, flattening them out a bit as you go. Using your thumb, press the top of each cookie to make a shallow well. Roll your thumb back and forth to widen the well. Using a small spoon, fill the wells with jam.

Bake until very lightly browned around the edges, 25 to 30 minutes. Let cool slightly on the pan, then transfer to a rack to finish cooling. Store in an airtight container.

MAKES 18 LARGE COOKIES

A drop or two of almond extract in a glass of cold milk gives it a light, delightful nuttiness that harmonizes beautifully with the buttery vanilla and fruit flavors.

Here's one of our favorite American butter traditions: Every summer as the Iowa State Fair begins, a butter **artiste** pulls on a parka and heads for a refrigerated shed full of fresh yellow butter to create the life-size Butter Cow that is the centerpiece of the fair. As the Butter Cow is to a butter pat, so are these cookies to ordinary thumbprint cookies: bigger, better, and altogether more buttery. If giants made thumbprint cookies, they would look like this.

These oversized cookies get their vanilla flavor from vanilla beans rather than from vanilla extract; the difference is a softer, but much clearer vanilla flavor. We like the specks of vanilla in the finished cookies.

brown butter tuiles

6 tablespoons unsalted butter
2 egg whites
¼ cup sugar
½ cup all-purpose flour
¼ teaspoon pure vanilla extract

Brown butter, or **beurre noisette** ("hazelnut butter"), is one of the easiest "chef tricks" a home cook can master. There are no hazelnuts involved; browning the milk solids in the butter deliciously transforms its flavor from milky-creamy to nutty-toasty.

The only real trick to browning butter is careful watching: no answering the phone, no drifting off to see the score of the game, and no checking your e-mail in the middle. That's because brown butter can become burned butter faster than you can say **"beurre noisette."**

Tuiles are a great dessert when you're having company: They are elegant and impressive, but light and appealing after a big dinner. Most important, you can make the batter and/or the cookies several days in advance (let the batter warm up before baking). They are a perfect counterpoint to ice creams like Sweet-Hot White Pepper Ice Cream (page 239), Honey-Lavender Ice Cream (page 46), or good store-bought ice cream or sorbet.

Photograph on page 160.

Heat the oven to 350 degrees.

Melt the butter in a heavy skillet over medium heat. After it melts, continue to cook the butter, watching carefully. It will foam and subside, then separate into golden butterfat and cloudy white milk solids. The milk solids will begin to brown. When they are lightly browned and the butter smells nutty and toasted, remove from the heat and set aside to cool slightly.

Whip the egg whites and sugar in a clean dry bowl until stiff and glossy. Add the flour, vanilla, and brown butter and mix at low speed until blended. The batter will beome thicker as the egg whites lose volume.

On 2 nonstick sheet pans, or pans lined with parchment paper, use a spatula or the back of a spoon to pour and spread the batter in very thin circles 8 inches in diameter. You will probably be able to fit only two tuiles per pan; they should be very thin, almost so thin that you can see the pan through them. Bake until light golden brown, 8 to 10 minutes. Using a spatula or your fingers, immediately lift the tuile off the pan. Holding it from above with the tips of your fingers, gently crumble the tuile from the center (see photograph). It should look like a fine handkerchief that's been dropped on the floor. Set aside to cool.

Repeat with the remaining batter. The batter may stiffen up as the butter cools; you can warm it briefly in the microwave, or set the bowl over hot water to keep the batter warm.

Store cooled tuiles in an airtight container, placing sheets of parchment or wax paper between the tuiles.

MAKES ABOUT 10 TUILES

They say that wine aged in old oak barrels develops the flavor of vanilla, and that's certainly true of well-aged Cognac. Its warm vanilla flavors make it a perfect partner for these tuiles.

plain and perfect pie crust

4½ cups sifted all-purpose flour
2 teaspoons salt
2 teaspoons sugar
12 ounces (3 sticks) cold unsalted butter, cut into pieces
½ cup ice water (strain out the ice just before using)
2 teaspoons red wine vinegar

Mix the flour, salt, and sugar in a mixer fitted with a paddle attachment (or using a hand mixer) for 1 minute. Add the butter and mix just until you have a crumbly, sandy mixture. You should still be able to see the pieces of butter.

Mix the water and vinegar together. With the mixer running at medium speed, drizzle in the water-vinegar mixture and mix just until a dough forms. You should still see small bits of butter.

Turn out onto a work surface, divide the dough in half, and shape into round, flat disks. Wrap separately in plastic wrap and refrigerate at least 30 minutes before using. *(Or, refrigerate up to 48 hours or freeze up to 1 month before using. If refrigerated more than 2 hours, let stand at room temperature 30 minutes before rolling out. If frozen, let thaw in the refrigerator overnight before rolling out.)*

When the time comes to roll out the dough, let the dough warm up for a few minutes at room temperature. Dust a work surface with just a few tablespoons of flour and keep some extra flour at hand. If you like, you can roll out the dough between two sheets of wax paper (flouring the bottom sheet and the top of the dough before rolling), which makes it much easier to transfer to the pan later on. However, you won't be able to check the progress of the dough as easily. It's entirely up to you.

Sprinkle a little flour on top of the dough and start rolling outward from the center with quick, light strokes. Don't worry if the edges split a bit; concentrate on getting a good circle going from the center. Lift up and rotate the dough ¼ turn every minute or so to help ensure even rolling. The dough should feel smooth and soft; some say it should feel like the inside of your forearm. If it gets sticky, sprinkle on a bit more flour, but don't do this more than two or three times; the dough will absorb too much flour. If it gets warm or limp, put it back in the fridge for 15 minutes to firm the butter up. Keep rolling until the circle is at least 2 inches

Somehow, the prospect of mixing and rolling a pie crust can bring even experienced bakers a twinge of anxiety. And for the uninitiated, just reading the recipe can make you break a sweat. Will my crust be "tough"? Will I "overwork" the dough? What does that mean? What if I have no "pie weights"? And just what are pie weights anyway?

Do not fear. This recipe comes from Gale's mother, Myrna, who "tested" it more times than we can count, by producing wonderful pies year after year. Sifting the flour is an important step, not for lightening so much as for measuring: It's the only way to ensure you're adding a precise amount of flour without weighing it. The vinegar, which leaves no taste behind, helps make the recipe foolproof, because it promotes the flakiness that is hard to achieve by mixing alone and helps prevent the gluten from developing. Gluten is what makes doughs stretchy, a good thing in breadmaking but not what you want in a pie crust since gluten causes shrinkage during the baking and a tough finished crust. "Overworked" dough has been mixed too long and has developed gluten.

Rolling out pie dough is most often the part of the process that has people gnashing their teeth. See our notes in the recipe.

larger than your pan (for example, 11 inches wide for a 9-inch pie pan), or 3 inches larger for deep-dish pies.

Set your pie or tart pan nearby. We always use heavy aluminum pans, because glass pans seem to bake the crust too fast. However, we know that the advantage of glass is that you can easily check the color of the crust. Again, it's up to you. Either choice will work.

To transfer the crust to the pan, we find it easiest to roll a finished crust up onto the rolling pin, then gently unroll it in the pan. Or, you can fold it gently in quarters, lift it up, position the center point at the center of the pan, and unfold it into the pan. If using wax paper, peel off the top layer, turn the crust over gently into the pan, and peel off the remaining paper. Make sure that the dough is allowed to settle completely into the pan.

Don't stretch and press the dough into the corners; stretched dough will likely shrink back when you bake it. Instead, lift the edges of the crust to let it settle down into the corners. If the dough tears a bit, don't be concerned; we'll patch it in a minute. Using scissors or a sharp knife, trim the dough to within ¾ inch of the rim. Use any extra scraps to patch the crust, pressing with your fingers (wet the scraps slightly if necessary), or set aside to make cookies.

FOR A SINGLE-CRUST PIE

Working around the rim, turn the crust under itself (*not* under the rim of the pan) to make a thick edge, pressing it firmly against the pan to reduce shrinkage. To decorate the rim, just press it all around with the back of a fork. For a slightly more advanced look, press the thumb and forefinger of one hand together. Use them to gently push the thick dough rim *inward*, while pushing *outward* with the forefinger of the other hand, so that they intersect in a "V" with the dough in between. Repeat all around the rim to make a zigzag edge. Chill 20 minutes before filling.

FOR A DOUBLE-CRUST PIE

Leave the edges of the bottom crust hanging over the rim. Roll out the second piece of dough into a circle about 11 inches in diameter. Line a sheet pan with parchment or wax paper. Roll the dough up onto the rolling pin, then unroll it onto the sheet pan. Chill while you fill the bottom crust.

When the bottom crust is filled, rest the top crust on top and pinch the edges together, trim to within 1 inch of the rim, and turn the edge under itself (not under the rim of the pan) all the way around. To decorate the rim, just press it all around with the back of a fork. For a slightly more advanced look, press the thumb and forefinger of one hand together. Use them to gently push the thick dough rim *inward*, while pushing *outward* with the forefinger of the other hand, so that they intersect in a "V" with the dough in between. Repeat all around the rim to make a zigzag edge. With the tip of a pair of scissors, snip 4 evenly spaced small vent holes in the top crust. Chill 20 minutes before baking.

FOR A PREBAKED PIE OR TART CRUST

Heat the oven to 375 degrees. Line the inside of the chilled crust with aluminum foil (don't turn it down over the rim, but leave the extra sticking up so that you have something to hold on to). Fill the foil all the way up to the top of the shell with pie weights, rice, or dried beans. (Pie weights are reusable metal or ceramic pellets that hold the crust in place as it bakes. You can buy them at cooking supply stores.) Bake 25 to 30 minutes, until dry and beginning to turn "blond." Lift the foil and weights out of the shell and bake another 10 to 15 minutes, checking frequently to prevent overbaking, until medium brown.

MAKES 2 CRUSTS; CAN BE HALVED

crumbly pie crust

1½ cups all-purpose flour
¼ cup sugar
8 tablespoons (1 stick) unsalted butter, cut into pieces and
   slightly softened
1 egg yolk

Any time you are suddenly struck by a pie craving, or if you're just not in the mood to mother a pie crust, crumbly pie crust is your best friend. You don't have to roll it out or weight it down, and it can't shrink or buckle. And the only tools you need to make it are your own hands.

Crumbly Pie Crust is sandier than a plain crust, and is also richer and sweeter in flavor—perfect for a simple tart like Raspberry Cream Tart (page 184) or whenever you're working with a creamy, not too-sweet filling. Gale makes large batches of this mixture and keeps it in the fridge for pie attacks; you can, too. The only trick to note: When pressing the crust into your pie pan, try to keep it the same thickness all the way around; don't let it thicken at the corners. Each corner should look like the point where a wall meets the floor: squared off, at a neat 90-degree angle.

Put the flour in a large bowl. Add the sugar and mix. Make a well in the center and place the butter pieces and egg yolk in the well. Using your fingers, work the butter and egg yolk together until well combined. Using your fingers, work the butter-egg mixture into the flour mixture until combined but still loose. The dough will be crumbly, but when you squeeze a handful in your hand it should hold together.

Sprinkle the dough into a 10-inch pie or tart pan. Press the dough firmly and evenly onto the bottom and sides of the pan, making sure not to let the crust thicken at the corners. It should make a clean right angle where the sides meet the bottom.

Chill the crust at least 30 minutes or, covered, up to 3 days.

Heat the oven to 400 degrees. Bake until light golden brown, 20 to 25 minutes. Let cool before filling.

MAKES 1 CRUST

pâte brisée

2¼ cups all-purpose flour
12 tablespoons (1½ sticks) unsalted butter, cut into pieces and
slightly softened
1 egg
Pinch of sugar
¾ teaspoon salt
1 tablespoon cold milk

Mound the flour on a work surface. Make a well in the center and place the butter, egg, sugar, salt, and milk in the well. Pinch the wet ingredients together with your right hand, then gradually draw the flour into the well with your left, mixing it into the wet ingredients with your right hand as you go.

Knead the dough by pushing it in sections against the work surface, pushing firmly down and away from you with the heel of your hand. Gather the dough back up, form it into a disk, wrap it in wax paper or plastic wrap, and chill it at least 2 hours before using. To roll out and prebake, follow the method for a single-crust pie on page 31.

MAKES 1 CRUST

This crust is Gale's version of a French pastry classic, the all-purpose equivalent of American pie dough, which in France is used for both sweet and savory pies and tarts. It is not sweet in itself, but we enrich the crust a bit with egg and milk, making it more tender. It is a good choice for tarts, especially those with sweet fillings. You can tell that it's a French recipe by the brief kneading at the end, which smooths the fat into the flour; the technique of pushing the dough down and away from you with the heel of the hand is called **fraisage.**

sweet pastry

1 cup all-purpose flour
¼ cup sugar
4 tablespoons cold unsalted butter, cut into pieces
1 egg yolk
1 teaspoon heavy cream
⅛ teaspoon vanilla extract

Pâte sucrée ("sugared pastry") is probably the simplest of the traditional French pastries to make, and fortunately it's one of the most delicious. Crumbly and melting, almost like shortbread, pâte sucrée is used in France for those glowing fruit tarts that look so fetching in the pâtisserie windows—and melt so quickly in your mouth. It's sweeter than pie crust, and because cream and egg yolks (not water) provide the liquid, the resulting crust is more flavorful.

Working the butter evenly into the dry ingredients is the key to this dough.

In a mixer fitted with a paddle attachment (or using a hand mixer), mix the flour and sugar.

Add the butter and mix until coarse and sandy.

Whisk the egg yolk, cream, and vanilla together. Add to the flour-butter mixture and mix at low speed just until combined.

Turn out onto a work surface and form into a disk. Wrap in plastic wrap and refrigerate for at least 60 minutes, until ready to use. Roll out as directed in the recipe.

MAKES 1 CRUST

sugar

"The best sugar is hard, solid, light,
exceeding white and sweet, glistring like snow."
Dr. Thomas Muffett

brown sugar shortbread

sharrow bay sticky toffee cake

butterscotch pudding

maple-iced angel food cake

honeycomb and honey-lavender ice cream with

 warm strawberry salad

sarah's oatmeal lace cookies

molasses-rum-raisin cake

rainbow sugar cookies

honey bunches

personality profile: Sugar is a seductive, temperamental mistress. She can be as smooth as honey, as homey as maple syrup, as warm as butterscotch—or she can be as hard as sugar crystals and as touchy as a saucepan full of caramel. If you treat her right, there's almost nothing she won't do. Apply just a little warmth, and she melts.

The cupfuls of snowy white sugar that we casually pour into cake batters, cookie doughs, and saucepans of caramel are truly an everyday miracle. For centuries, the home baker's repertoire included a range of sweeteners: Honey, sugarcane syrup (molasses), sorghum syrup, maple sugar, beets, corn, and carrots were all pressed into service. But as Dr. Muffett's sixteenth-century remark proves, pure white cane sugar has long been the most prized of all.

In medieval Europe, sugar was so precious that it was doled out as medicine, by pharmacists. As recently as the nineteenth century, cane sugar was an international form of currency. Only a century ago, American housewives had to chip their sugar off hard, rounded conical sugarloaves (hence the name Sugarloaf Mountain in Vermont), and grind it by hand or melt it down, skim out the many impurities it contained, and use the resulting clear syrup in cooking.

Today, white sugar is so plentiful that only health concerns—and occasional boredom with its one-dimensional flavor—prevent us from using it in everything. But sugar and butter are a remarkable flavor combination. That lovely paste is the basis for countless doughs, batters, and frostings. The combination takes on its most intriguing character when cooked down into a molten, satiny mass of caramel or butterscotch. Homemade Butterscotch Pudding and our tawny Sharrow Bay Sticky Toffee Cake take the combination to its ultimate expression. Caramelizing sugar is a great way to give it added dimension. For general instructions on caramelizing sugar, see page 13 in the Basics chapter.

We love the toasty flavor of light brown sugar, and you'll see it in many recipes throughout the book. Both light brown and dark brown sugar do contain molasses—the cane syrup that is extracted in the process of making sugar—but both are really white sugar in disguise. The molasses is added *back* to the sugar after the refining process, so the health benefits are negligible, but the flavor is much improved. Dark brown sugar has a strong molasses character, so we rarely use it. (Either kind can be warmed to softness in the microwave.) Light brown sugar adds its subtle warmth to recipes like our Brown Sugar Shortbread. We also like to go back to the old sweeteners and appreciate their unique flavors and properties. The result is recipes like Maple-Iced Angel Food Cake, which takes some of its sweetness from the nuttiness of maple, and Honey-Lavender Ice Cream, an aromatic infusion of earthy honey.

There is nothing quite like the flowery muskiness of honey. It's a great flavor when used carefully; we usually combine it with some sugar to keep the flavor delicate. Honey smells and tastes wonderfully *alive;* like yogurt, it contains active cultures (and, for this reason, should not be fed to newborn babies). The flavors of different honeys, like those of wines, depend on the local flora and fauna and can vary a great deal. Supermarket honeys are inoffensive blends of many kinds, but if you are lucky enough to come across lavender, orange-blossom, sunflower, or another single-strain honey, snap it up.

Molasses can be light or dark. We prefer the light, also known as cane syrup, for use in baking; blackstrap molasses is too bitter.

Given the precision of baking chemistry, it's not possible to give any blanket instructions about substituting one sweetener for another in our recipes. Each sweetener has its place.

Sweetness, whether it comes from ripe fruit, golden honey, white sugar, amber caramel, dark chocolate, or nutty brown sugar, is the one flavor element all of the recipes in this book have in common. The quest for sugar has influenced the twists and turns of history more than any other single food. It is an elemental flavor, with a whole area of the tongue dedicated to its appreciation, and is well worth exploring!

brown sugar shortbread

8 ounces (2 sticks) unsalted butter, slightly softened
½ cup light brown sugar, packed
2¼ cups all-purpose flour
2 tablespoons cornstarch
¼ teaspoon ground cinnamon
2 tablespoons granulated sugar

Heat the oven to 350 degrees. Line a 10×14½-inch sheet pan (with sides) with parchment or wax paper.

Cream the butter in a mixer fitted with a paddle attachment (or using a hand mixer) until soft and smooth. Add the brown sugar and mix until incorporated.

In a separate bowl, stir together the flour, cornstarch, and cinnamon. Add to the butter mixture and mix at low speed just until the ingredients are incorporated and the dough comes together. Turn the dough out onto a floured work surface and knead it 5 to 10 times, just to smooth the dough.

Reflour your work surface. Roll the dough out to fit the sheet pan. To transfer to the sheet pan, roll the dough up onto the rolling pin, lift it up, and unroll it into the pan. Using light strokes of the rolling pin, roll the dough evenly into the corners and edges of the pan, and roll out any bumps. (Or, press the rolled-out dough thoroughly into the pan with your fingers.) Prick the shortbread all over with a fork to prevent any buckling or shrinking.

Bake in the center of the oven for 15 minutes. After 15 minutes, rotate the pan and knock it once against the oven rack, to ensure even cooking and a flat surface. Bake 10 to 15 minutes more, until very lightly browned.

Immediately sprinkle the granulated sugar evenly over the surface. Let cool on a rack for 10 minutes, then cut into 1½×3 inch bars. Let cool completely in the pan, then store in an airtight container.

MAKES ABOUT 30 COOKIES

Brighten up the smooth flavors of shortbread with a spicy Latin American coffee, such as Colombian or Costa Rican.

You'll notice while baking from this book that Gale sneaks a bit of light brown sugar into almost everything she makes. White sugar, a peerless product in many ways, doesn't taste like anything but **sweet**. Using brown sugar, like toasting nuts before adding them to a recipe, adds another level of flavor. You won't think "This tastes like brown sugar." You'll simply think "This is the best shortbread I have ever had."

Homemade shortbread with ice cream is one of the coziest desserts you could possibly make. Though it used to be made throughout the land, almost no one bakes it at home anymore. It's a snap.

sharrow bay sticky toffee cake

FOR THE CAKE

12 ounces dried dates, pitted and coarsely chopped

2½ cups water

2 teaspoons baking soda

3¼ cups all-purpose flour

2 teaspoons baking powder

8 tablespoons (1 stick) unsalted butter, slightly softened

1⅔ cups granulated sugar

4 eggs

2 teaspoons pure vanilla extract

FOR THE SAUCE

2¼ cups light brown sugar, packed

7 tablespoons unsalted butter

1 cup half-and-half

1 teaspoon brandy

¼ teaspoon pure vanilla extract

TO FINISH THE DESSERT

1 cup chilled heavy cream

Heat the oven to 350 degrees. Line a 9×13-inch baking pan with parchment or wax paper.

MAKE THE CAKE

Combine the dates and water in a saucepan and bring to a boil over medium-high heat. Turn off the heat and gradually mix in the baking soda (it will foam up when you add it). Set aside.

Mix the flour and baking powder together.

Cream the butter in a mixer fitted with a whisk attachment (or using a hand mixer) until smooth and fluffy. Add the granulated sugar and mix until smooth. With the mixer running, add two of the eggs and mix. Add the remaining two eggs and the vanilla and mix.

Add about a third of the flour mixture and a third of the date mixture and mix. Repeat until all the flour mixture and date mixture are incorporated into the batter. The batter will be thin.

Pour the mixture into the pan and bake until firm and set in the center, about 40 minutes. Let cool completely in the pan.

Turn the cake out onto a sheet pan and peel off the parchment paper. *(The recipe can be made up to this point up to 2 days in*

Sticky toffee pudding (the English call all desserts "pudding") is a quintessential childhood dessert, with the same sweet and wonderfully sticky qualities as American butterscotch pudding or brownies. In fact, this is more like a cake than a true pudding. Sharrow Bay is a gorgeous country-house hotel in England's Lake District, the birthplace of this dessert. Sharrow Bay's version has become legendary among aficionados of all ages (like us).

This is an ideal fall and winter dessert, and a Gale Gand signature. People are sometimes suspicious of the dried dates in the recipe, but the baking soda actually seems to dissolve the dates into the cake, leaving behind a moist texture, deep tawny color, and haunting flavor. A dollop of whipped cream on top cuts the sweetness.

advance and refrigerated, covered. Bring to room temperature before serving.)

When ready to serve, preheat the oven to 400 degrees.

MAKE THE SAUCE

In a medium saucepan, bring the brown sugar, butter, half-and-half, and brandy to a boil over medium-high heat. Let simmer 3 minutes. Turn off the heat and mix in the vanilla.

Pour the sauce slowly and evenly over the top of the cake (you may not use all the sauce). Bake until the sauce is bubbly and the cake is heated through, about 5 minutes. Let cool briefly before serving.

Meanwhile, in a mixer fitted with a whip attachment (or using a hand mixer), whip the cream into soft peaks.

Cut the hot cake into squares and serve immediately, topped with whipped cream, and pass any remaining sauce at the table.

MAKES 8 TO 10 SERVINGS

An English childhood dessert calls for a comforting English child-hood drink like cambric tea, which is weak tea mixed with plenty of milk. (Cambric is a delicate fabric that is white and thin, rather like the tea.) Strong tea is good too.

butterscotch pudding

2¼ cups milk (not skim)
1 cup heavy cream
6 tablespoons unsalted butter
1¼ cups light brown sugar, packed
3 egg yolks
¼ cup cornstarch
¼ teaspoon salt
1½ teaspoons pure vanilla extract

Combine the milk and cream in a large saucepan and bring to a simmer over medium heat. Immediately turn off the heat and set aside.

Melt the butter in a large, heavy skillet over medium heat. Stir in the brown sugar, raise the heat to medium-high, and cook 5 to 7 minutes, stirring constantly, to caramelize the mixture. (You'll smell a characteristic nutty-caramel aroma when the butter browns, signaling that the mixture is ready.)

Whisking constantly, gradually add the butter–brown sugar mixture to the hot milk–cream mixture. If the mixture isn't smooth, blend for 20 seconds with a hand blender or pour through a fine sieve.

Put the egg yolks in a medium bowl. Whisk in about ½ cup of the hot milk mixture. Whisk in the cornstarch and salt until dissolved. Whisk the egg mixture back into the hot milk mixture in the saucepan.

Whisking constantly, cook over medium-high heat until thick and just boiling. When the mixture thickens, the whisk will leave trail marks on the bottom of the pot and the mixture will have a few large bubbles boiling up to the top.

Turn off the heat and whisk in the vanilla. Pour into 6 to 8 custard cups, ramekins, or mugs and chill, uncovered, at least 2 hours or overnight. Serve chilled.

MAKES 6 TO 8 SERVINGS

The warm flavor of butterscotch calls for an iced earthy, full-bodied coffee like Indonesian Java. To contrast the creaminess of the pudding, drink it black—maybe even with coffee ice cubes so it stays extra-strong.

Never made butterscotch pudding? Hmm. Well, do you remember the delicious feeling of mud squishing between your toes at the bottom of a cool creek on a hot summer day? That's just what a spoonful of this cool, thick concoction feels like. Butterscotch pudding is a glorious, richly satisfying dessert that we're determined to bring back to the American table. Butterscotch is a caramel-like blend of brown sugar and butter. After years of synthetic versions, many people think they don't like butterscotch pudding, but we're out to prove them all wrong with this recipe. Try it and see.

maple-iced angel food cake

FOR THE CAKE

1½ cups egg whites (from about 12 eggs), at room temperature
1¼ teaspoons cream of tartar
½ teaspoon salt
1¼ cups granulated sugar
1¼ cups sifted cake flour
1 teaspoon pure vanilla extract
3 tablespoons pure maple syrup

FOR THE ICING

¼ cup pure maple syrup
1 tablespoon egg white
1½ cups confectioners' sugar

Maple's nutty sweetness is a delectable counterpoint to the cloudlike sponge that is angel food cake. Ripe juicy berries are always nice with the fluffiness of angel food cake, and blackberries and maple make an especially fine combination. Real maple syrup has a very strong flavor (not surprising when you consider that it takes 80 gallons of sugar-maple sap to make 1 gallon of syrup) and this satisfying icing bears a resemblance to maple-sugar candy. The maple flavor in the cake is much lighter.

Photograph on page 141.

🥄

Root beer's complex flavor has maple undertones; serve it ice cold in frosted glasses, with a scoop of vanilla ice cream if you like.

Heat the oven to 375 degrees.

MAKE THE CAKE

Whip the egg whites in a mixer fitted with a whisk attachment (or using a hand mixer) until foamy. Add the cream of tartar and salt and continue whipping until soft peaks form. With the mixer running, gradually add 1 cup of the granulated sugar and continue whipping until the egg whites are stiff, about 30 seconds more.

Sift the remaining ¼ cup granulated sugar together with the sifted cake flour 3 times, to aerate the mixture. Fold into the egg whites, then fold in the vanilla and maple syrup.

Spoon the batter into an ungreased 9- or 10-inch tube pan, or 6 miniature ones. Smooth the top with the back of the spoon. Bake until light golden brown, 30 to 35 minutes. Cool by hanging the cake (in the pan) upside down around the neck of a bottle until it cools to room temperature. Run a long, sharp knife blade around the cake to loosen it, then knock the cake out onto a plate. The outside crumb of the cake will remain in the pan; exposing the white cake underneath.

MAKE THE ICING

Stir the ingredients together until smooth. Pour over the top of the cake and spread with a spatula, letting the glaze trickle down the sides. Let set for at least 30 minutes, or until the icing is hard, before serving. Slice with a serrated knife, using a sawing motion.

MAKES 1 LARGE OR 6 MINIATURE CAKES

honeycomb and honey-lavender ice cream with warm strawberry salad

FOR THE ICE CREAM

2 cups heavy cream

1 cup half-and-half

½ vanilla bean, split lengthwise

1 tablespoon fresh or dried lavender flowers (available at natural-food stores and herb shops)

⅓ cup honey

9 egg yolks

¼ cup sugar

1 cup crème fraîche or sour cream

FOR THE SALAD

1 cup raspberries

1 tablespoon sugar

16 large strawberries, green parts trimmed off

One piece honeycomb, about 4 inches x 1 inch

MAKE THE ICE CREAM

Heat the cream, half-and-half, vanilla bean, lavender, and honey in a large saucepan over medium heat, stirring occasionally to make sure the mixture doesn't scorch on the bottom. When it reaches a fast simmer (do not let it boil), turn off the heat and set aside to infuse for 10 to 15 minutes.

Whisk the egg yolks and sugar together.

Whisking constantly, slowly pour the still-hot cream mixture into the egg yolk mixture. Return the mixture to the saucepan and cook over medium heat, stirring constantly with a wooden spoon. At 160 degrees, the mixture will give off a puff of steam. When the mixture reaches 180 degrees it will be thickened and creamy, like eggnog. If you don't have a thermometer, test it by dipping a wooden spoon into the mixture. Run your finger down the back of the spoon. If the stripe remains clear, the mixture is ready; if the edges blur, the mixture is not quite thick enough yet. When it is ready, quickly remove it from the heat.

Meanwhile, half-fill a large bowl with ice water. Strain the mixture into a smaller bowl to smooth it and remove the vanilla bean and lavender. Whisk in the crème fraîche. Rest the smaller bowl in the ice water and let the mixture cool, stirring often, then freeze according to the directions of your ice-cream maker.

We first approached beehives on the wild English moor known as Dartmoor, near Sherlock Holmes' Baskerville Hall, and were fascinated to watch a beekeeper plunge his fist into a buzzing hive and pull out a chunk of warm comb. The taste was extraordinary. In small amounts, honeycomb (a combination of edible beeswax and honey, which the bees use to store and age the honey) enhances cereals, hot biscuits, and this dessert. If you can't find jars of honey that contain honeycomb, simply drizzle any good-quality honey over the dessert.

Strawberries and cream is a—perhaps **the**—classic English dessert combination. Since England is where we first encountered honeycomb, adding it to strawberries and cream was an easy decision. The warmed strawberry slices have the flavor of strawberry preserves. Lavender adds an herbal perfume to the ice cream—but plain old vanilla ice cream would be good, too.

Photograph on page 133.

MAKE THE SALAD

Puree the raspberries and sugar in a blender. Strain out the seeds and taste the puree for sweetness, adding more sugar if necessary. Divide the puree on 4 ovenproof plates and spread to evenly coat the bottom of each plate.

Thinly slice the strawberries and carefully fan them out on top of the raspberry puree, starting at the edge of the plate and spiraling in to the center. Use 4 berries per plate. *(The dessert can be made up to this point up to 8 hours in advance. Tightly cover each plate with plastic wrap and refrigerate until ready to serve. Remove the plastic wrap before baking.)*

Heat the oven to 450 degrees. Bake the strawberries 2 minutes, just until warmed. Remove from the oven and place a scoop of ice cream in the center of each plate (it will start to melt immediately). Cut the honeycomb into 4 pieces and place on top of the ice cream. Serve immediately.

MAKES 4 SERVINGS, WITH ICE CREAM LEFT OVER

The many delectable flavors here (strawberry, vanilla, lavender, honey) call for something light, festive, and fruity. Why not a Kir Royale (a drop of Cassis liqueur with Champagne poured over it)?

sarah's oatmeal lace cookies

1 cup all-purpose flour
½ teaspoon baking powder
1 cup sugar
1 cup rolled oats (not quick-cooking)
¼ cup heavy cream
¼ cup light corn syrup
8 ounces (2 sticks) unsalted butter, melted
2 tablespoons vanilla extract

Heat the oven to 350 degrees.

Mix the flour, baking powder, sugar, and oats in a mixer fitted with a whisk attachment (or using a hand mixer).

Mix the cream, corn syrup, melted butter, and vanilla together and add to the dry ingredients. Mix just until combined and set aside for 15 minutes.

Keeping in mind that the cookies will spread until completely flat, drop the batter by heaping teaspoons onto nonstick sheet pans, spacing them out evenly. You can fit 6 cookies on a 14×17-inch pan; bake them in batches if necessary.

Bake until golden brown, 8 to 10 minutes. Let cool 2 to 3 minutes in the pan, then use a spatula to transfer to wire racks to finish cooling. To store, layer the cookies with wax paper and store in an airtight container.

MAKES ABOUT 2 DOZEN COOKIES

These make a great afternoon snack with a glass of lemonade. For fancier occasions, add sprigs of fresh mint.

Gale has received plenty of awards and tributes for her desserts, but her very favorite might be the letter that she received one day from a nine-year-old named Sarah. "I am thinking I would like to become a chef," Sarah wrote. "I can already cook a little. My specials are oatmeal lace cookies and Swedish pancakes." Gale and Sarah started a correspondence, and when Gale hosted a birthday luncheon for Sarah at Brasserie T, Sarah returned the favor by parting with her signature recipe.

These are rather like tuiles, thin and brittle, and they spread a lot while baking: Give them plenty of space on the baking sheet.

molasses-rum-raisin cake

2 cups ground walnuts
⅔ cup plus 2 tablespoons sugar
1 cup all-purpose flour
1½ teaspoons baking powder
½ teaspoon salt
⅓ cup raisins
Freshly grated zest of 1 lemon
2 tablespoons dark rum
1 teaspoon pure vanilla extract
2 tablespoons dark molasses (not blackstrap)
½ cup vegetable oil
2 egg whites
Confectioners' sugar

Molasses and rum, both made from sugarcane, are a natural flavor pairing. (The vanilla in the recipe also hails from tropical climes.)

To make molasses, rum, and sugar, the syrup squeezed from the canes is gradually reduced to its component parts. First, the clear white sugar crystals are extracted. Next, the remaining brown syrup is boiled and the next stage of the product—the light molasses—is skimmed off. (This light molasses, when fermented, becomes rum.) After more boiling, the dark molasses is removed. And finally, the bitter blackstrap molasses remains. Blackstrap is only fractionally more health-giving than other molasses and we never use it in baking.

Because it contains no butter or egg yolks, this cake is extremely low in cholesterol and relatively low in fat. It tastes rich and spicy.

Heat the oven to 350 degrees. Butter and flour a 9-inch cake pan.

Combine the walnuts and ⅔ cup sugar. Set aside.

Sift the flour, baking powder, and salt together. Add the raisins and lemon zest and toss to coat.

Stir the rum, vanilla, molasses, and vegetable oil together and set aside.

In a mixer fitted with a whisk attachment, whip the egg whites until soft peaks form. Add the remaining 2 tablespoons sugar and whip until stiff and glossy. Fold in the ground walnut mixture.

Working in alternating batches, and folding after each addition, add the flour mixture and the oil mixture to the egg white mixture. Pour into the prepared pan and bake until the cake is slightly firm to the touch and a tester inserted in the center comes out clean (a few crumbs are okay), 30 to 40 minutes. Let cool in the pan, to keep the cake moist; it will fall a bit as it cools.

To serve, turn the cake out onto a platter upside down so that the bottom becomes a nice flat top. Dust with confectioners' sugar.

MAKES 1 CAKE

Ginger beer, which has both ginger and lime flavors, has the perfect tropical spice. A scoop of vanilla ice cream wouldn't hurt!

rainbow sugar cookies

FOR THE COOKIES

¾ cup granulated sugar

12 tablespoons (1½ sticks) unsalted butter, slightly softened

⅔ cup vegetable shortening

1 egg

¼ teaspoon pure vanilla extract

½ teaspoon baking powder

3½ cups all-purpose flour

FOR THE ICING

2 cups confectioners' sugar

2 to 3 tablespoons milk

½ teaspoon pure vanilla extract

4 colors of food coloring

Heat the oven to 350 degrees. Butter 2 sheet pans (or use 1 pan and bake the cookies in 2 batches).

MAKE THE COOKIES

Cream the granulated sugar, butter, and shortening in a mixer fitted with a paddle attachment (or using a hand mixer) until fluffy. Add the egg, vanilla, and baking powder and mix. Add the flour and mix. Shape the dough into a large flat disk, kneading briefly if necessary to bring the dough together. Wrap in plastic wrap and chill 1 to 2 hours.

On a lightly floured surface, roll out the dough ¼ inch thick. Using cookie cutters or empty coffee cans, cut out large round cookies about 4 inches in diameter. Transfer to the prepared pan. Bake until light golden, 20 to 25 minutes. Let cool completely on the sheet pan.

MAKE THE ICING

Stir the confectioners' sugar, 2 tablespoons milk, and the vanilla together until smooth. If still too thick to spread, add the remaining tablespoon of milk a little at a time until the icing is smooth and pourable, but thick enough to coat. Spoon ¼ cup of white icing into each of 4 small bowls. Color them 4 different colors (we like bright pink, green, yellow, and blue). Cover with plastic wrap until ready to use.

Set a wire rack over a piece of wax or parchment paper. Place the cooled cookies on the wire rack and pour the remaining white

These are great big, flat cookies, just waiting to be extravagantly swirled and drizzled with color. Each one is a whole party on a cookie.

To be perfectly honest, these are really about the icing rather than the cookie: Letters, messages, monograms, and patterns are just the beginning of what you can do. For kids' parties, showers, any casual celebration, choose your colors and then go crazy. Consider the possibilities: red, white, and blue for July Fourth; red and green for Christmas; blue, silver, and white for Hanukkah; pink, green, and yellow for Easter. We made them for our son's first birthday party; his name is short enough (Gio!) that we could fit his whole name on each cookie.

While you're in a colorful mood, pour tall glasses of pink lemonade, with enough tartness to cut through the sugar of the cookies.

icing onto them. Using a metal icing (offset) spatula, cover the cookies completely with an even layer of white icing. Before the icing sets, use forks or squeeze bottles to drizzle the other 4 colors of icing over the cookies to make spidery lines (we like to criss-cross the different colors back and forth across the cookies). Let harden 1 hour. Store in an airtight container.

MAKES 10 LARGE COOKIES

honey bunches

Imagine a great cookie version of trail mix, or the best granola ever. Honey Bunches date from Gale's early days as a chef—the 1970s, when for a time honey, oats, and yogurt completely replaced sugar, flour, and cream. Fortunately we've all come to our senses now, and realized that each style of cooking has its time and place, but these still taste great. Honey Bunches highlight the unique flavor of honey, with soft coconut and oats plus a walnut crunch built in. They keep very well in a cookie jar for about a week and also travel well in a knap-sack, whether to school or up a mountain trail.

8 tablespoons (1 stick) unsalted butter
1½ cups quick-cooking rolled oats
½ cup flaked sweetened coconut
½ cup coarsely chopped walnuts
¼ cup all-purpose flour
⅔ cup honey
24 walnut halves

Heat the oven to 350 degrees. Butter 2 mini muffin tins (or use 1 tin and bake in 2 batches).

Melt the butter over low heat in a small saucepan. Meanwhile, combine the oats, coconut, walnuts, and flour and mix. Stir the honey into the melted butter and bring to a boil, stirring often. Pour the butter mixture over the dry ingredients and mix well.

Press 1 heaping tablespoon of the mixture into each mini muffin cup. Bake until just beginning to brown, 15 to 20 minutes. Remove from the oven and immediately press a walnut half on top of each honey bunch. Let cool 10 minutes in the pan, then transfer to a wire rack and cool completely. Store in an airtight container.

MAKES 24 COOKIES

➢ *Cold milk makes a perfect, creamy contrast to these warm, chunky cookies.*

"Peace goes into the making of a poet
as flour goes into the making of bread."
Pablo Neruda

indian cornmeal dough nuts

raspberry-stuffed french toast

"real good" banana–whole wheat bread

currant-buttermilk oat muffins

cinnamon-chocolate scones

quick pecan sour cream coffee cake

double blueberry muffins

chocolate chip pancakes

big apple pancake

oatmeal waffles

brown sugar wheat scones

cinnamon apple bumpy bread

featherlight corn muffins

sharon's stickier buns

personality profile: Of all the ingredients, flour is the most down-to-earth, and the whole world relies on her for sustenance. Strong but soft, flour is supportive and self-effacing, like a hardworking but loving mother.

Without flour, there simply is no baking. Compared to flour, things like butter, sugar, and eggs are frills and luxuries: Flour is what makes it baking. From the earliest times, one of mankind's great quests has been a steady supply of flour for the "daily bread" that sustains us—whether it is corn, rye, wheat, rice, or a host of other flours used in virtually all cuisines, around the world. Now that we are lucky enough to have any number of different flours available to us, as well as the miraculous (but taken-for-granted) all-purpose flour, we love to experiment.

Morning is the time when sugar takes a back seat in flavor and lets flour shine through—we're thinking of muffins, quick breads, pancakes, waffles, and scones—so here you will find recipes such as Currant-Buttermilk Oat Muffins and Oatmeal Waffles, where rolled oats act as the flour, and "Real Good" Banana–Whole Wheat Bread, which takes its substance from nutty whole wheat flour. We're great believers in cutting heavy, bran-rich flours with lighter all-purpose flour, so that the flavor and texture can shine without overpowering. That principle governs our formulas for Brown Sugar Wheat Scones and also Featherlight Corn Muffins, in which we cut the heaviness of cornmeal with all-purpose flour.

Though we don't often consider the soft, heavy bags of all-purpose flour at the supermarket to be a miracle, they have certainly changed the lives of American bakers in the century since they were introduced. Home baking used to be a decidedly iffy process, with different kinds and crops of wheat producing different, unpredictable, often unpleasant results. Any given field of wheat is profoundly affected by the climate in which it grows—by the soil, temperature, humidity, growing season, and other factors. These conditions determine the level of protein in the wheat, which will in turn determine how much gluten the flour can develop.

What happens in breadmaking is this: Dry yeast wakes up when you mix it with water or milk. Like most of us, the yeast wakes up hungry. When you add the flour (usually wheat flour, which contains more protein than any other), the yeast first eats the natural sugar in the milk, then moves on to the protein in the flour. As yeast chews on the protein molecules, they are converted into gluten. Gluten is the elastic strands that make dough look all cobwebby when you stretch it between your fingers. Mixing, stirring, and kneading all encourage the gluten to "develop."

With no added yeast, as in most of the recipes in this book, flour develops little gluten. It can be leavened with baking powder or soda (yeast is much stronger than either) and can stretch to absorb some liquid. The role of the baking process, in fact, is to allow the flour to absorb liquid—a reaction that is possible only at certain temperatures, starting at around 300 degrees.

Some notes on different flours: All-purpose flour is just that. Different wheat strains are blended by the manufacturer to a balance of gluten, starch, and protein. We always use unbleached all-purpose flour. Bread flour is "harder" than all-purpose flour (that is, it contains more protein and less starch). Bread flour also contains some malt, a naturally sweet substance that gives the yeast something to eat right away. We use bread flour for Sharon's Stickier Buns and some other lightly sweetened yeast doughs. Cake flour is "softer," with less protein; we use it only when a very light crumb is needed, such as in angel food cakes.

Morning baking is usually family time and is often children's first cooking experience. Pancakes, French toast, and waffles are fascinating even to tiny children; older ones, of course, love to fill muffin tins and cut out scones. Have a good morning!

indian cornmeal dough nuts

½ **cup milk**
⅔ **cup yellow cornmeal**
1 **cup all-purpose flour**
½ **cup granulated sugar**
1 **teaspoon baking powder**
½ **teaspoon ground cinnamon**
⅛ **teaspoon ground nutmeg**
¼ **teaspoon salt**
⅓ **cup (5⅓ tablespoons) unsalted butter, melted**
1 **egg, beaten**
Oil for deep-frying
Confectioners' sugar

Unlike most doughnuts, these really are "nuts" of dough: hot nuggets of golden cornmeal that are fun to make and eat. It's like having hush puppies for brunch or dessert, with crunch outside from the crust and inside from the cornmeal. The flavors remind us of Indian pudding, a dense Early American dessert made from then-plentiful corn and molasses. Indian pudding has mostly gone the way of hoecakes and Waldorf salad—for one reason or another, we don't eat it much anymore—but we love this version. (For another time-travel recipe, see our Dessert Waldorf Salad with Roquefort, page 224.) Cinnamon and nutmeg stand in here for the dark, spicy sweetness of molasses.

Dough nuts, thanks to their small size, are much easier to make than doughnuts. The recipe can be easily doubled. These are great with a scoop of vanilla ice cream.

Heat the milk in a saucepan over medium heat just until it comes to a boil. Immediately turn off the heat.

Place the cornmeal in a large bowl. Add the hot milk and mix lightly.

Sift together the flour, sugar, baking powder, cinnamon, nutmeg, and salt.

Stir the melted butter and the egg into the cornmeal mixture. Stir the flour mixture into the cornmeal mixture and mix well. If the dough does not hold together, add more flour 1 tablespoon at a time. The dough should be firm enough to handle, but keep it soft by using as little flour as possible.

Place the dough in a bowl, cover, and refrigerate 30 minutes. Flour your hands and turn the dough out onto a lightly floured surface. Pull off handfuls of dough and roll into logs 1 inch in diameter. Using a sharp knife, cut into 1½-inch lengths.

Meanwhile, heat the oil in a deep fryer (or at least 2 inches of oil in a deep, heavy pot) to 350 degrees. Do not overheat, or the dough nuts will burn before they cook through. Working in batches to avoid crowding the pot, fry the dough nuts, turning occasionally, until golden brown, 4 to 5 minutes. Drain on paper towels, sprinkle lightly with confectioners' sugar, and serve immediately.

MAKES 4 TO 6 SERVINGS

These flavors say autumn to us; hot apple cider with cinnamon sticks is a natural here.

raspberry-stuffed french toast

1 medium loaf (about 8 ounces, or 12 medium-thick slices) Brioche
   (page 86), or store-bought brioche, challah, or other egg bread
4 eggs
2 cups milk
⅔ cup heavy cream
Pinch of salt
½ teaspoon pure vanilla extract
½ cup granulated sugar
8 ounces very cold cream cheese, in one block
Unsalted butter
1 cup fresh raspberries (or thawed frozen)
Confectioners' sugar

Cut the bread into 12 slices. Put 6 plates in the oven to warm at
200 degrees.

Whisk the eggs until foamy. Add the milk, cream, salt, vanilla,
and granulated sugar and whisk to blend. Pour into a sheet pan
(with sides). Arrange the bread slices in the pan in a single layer
and let soak.

Meanwhile, using a sharp knife, slice the cream cheese into 12
thin slices.

Heat a large skillet or griddle over medium-high heat. Add about
a tablespoon of butter and heat until melted and foamy. Working
in two batches if necessary, arrange half the soaked bread slices
in the skillet. Cook until golden brown, 3 to 5 minutes. Lay 2 slices
of cream cheese on top, then place ⅙ of the raspberries on top of
the cheese. Cover each with another slice of soaked bread and
press firmly with the back of a spatula. Turn the "sandwich" over
and brown on the other side, about 3 minutes more.

Transfer to the warmed plates, sprinkle lightly with confectioners' sugar, and serve.

MAKES 6 SERVINGS

Coffee from East African regions (Kenya, for example) is famous for
its fruity, berry flavors and is perfect here.

Even the most timid Sunday cook can
master basic French toast—a couple
of eggs, some milk, a few slices of
bread—and from there it's a short hop
to this outrageously lush dish. It oper-
ates on a similar principle to a grilled
cheese sandwich, but with cream
cheese and sweet raspberries melting
into a fruity-creamy filling. Invite
friends over to share them, and you'll
soon have regulars for Sunday brunch.

Raspberries are truly a cook's best
friend. They are absolutely beautiful,
utterly delicious, and unbelievably easy
to cook with: no peeling, pitting,
hulling, trimming, stemming, or any
other pesky task.

Photograph on page 151.

8 ounces (2 sticks) unsalted butter, melted
½ cup dark brown sugar, packed
½ cup honey
2 eggs
3 very ripe bananas, mashed
2 cups whole wheat flour
1½ teaspoons baking soda
½ teaspoon salt
½ cup sour cream or yogurt (not fat-free)
½ cup coarsely chopped walnuts

Tinkering with recipes that you already know, adjusting them to suit your personal taste and cooking style, is the first sign of a smart and confident cook. This banana bread was the very first recipe that Gale "created," at the tender age of nineteen. Everyone was making banana bread then; this moist one, with its batter of whole wheat flour infused with tangy sour cream and chunked up with walnuts, has stuck with us.

In our minds, banana bread screams "seventies" as much as smiley-face buttons and spinach-and-bacon salad, but the fact is we still love to eat it. This is terrific toasted and spread with cream cheese.

Heat the oven to 325 degrees. Line a 6-cup loaf pan with parchment or wax paper.

Mix the butter, sugar, and honey together in a large bowl. Add the eggs and bananas, mixing until almost smooth.

Mix the flour, baking soda, and salt together. Working in batches, add the flour mixture to the banana mixture, alternating with dollops of sour cream. Mix in the walnuts. Pour into the pan.

Bake until firm on top and a toothpick inserted into the center comes out dry and clean (a few crumbs are okay), about 70 minutes.

Turn out onto a wire rack and let cool. Serve at room temperature.

MAKES 1 LOAF

For a really sublime and substantial breakfast or snack, eat this with a blended smoothie of raspberries, yogurt, lime juice, orange juice, and honey.

currant-buttermilk oat muffins

2 cups rolled oats (not quick-cooking)
2 cups buttermilk
1½ cups all-purpose flour
1½ teaspoons baking powder
1½ teaspoons baking soda
1 teaspoon salt
1 teaspoon ground cinnamon
2 large eggs
¾ cup light brown sugar, packed
12 tablespoons (1½ sticks) unsalted butter, melted
⅔ cup dried currants or raisins

Combine the oats and buttermilk in a large bowl and let sit at room temperature for 30 minutes, stirring occasionally.

Heat the oven to 375 degrees. Butter 12 muffin cups or line them with paper liners. Butter the top of the muffin tin to prevent the muffin tops from sticking.

Sift the flour, baking powder, baking soda, salt, and cinnamon together.

Add the eggs to the oat-milk mixture and combine. Add the sugar and mix. Add the butter and mix. Gradually add the flour mixture and mix. The batter will be a bit lumpy. Fold in the currants. *(The batter can be made up to this point and refrigerated overnight.)*

Use a large spoon or an ice-cream scoop to fill the muffin cups three quarters full. Bake until the muffins are risen and golden brown and a toothpick inserted in the center comes out clean (a few crumbs are okay), 20 to 25 minutes.

MAKES ABOUT 12 MUFFINS

When you have a complete breakfast like this in one hand, use the other to drink a steaming, milky caffè latte.

It's magic: Here's a creamy, nutty bowl of oatmeal—with plenty of brown sugar, milk, and currants swirled in—in the shape of a muffin. It's like a whole breakfast in your hand.

Buttermilk contains neither butter nor milk; it's what's left of cream **after** butter has been churned. But we think of it as more than a mere by-product; buttermilk is tangy and rich-tasting, but very low in fat. It adds an old-fashioned flavor in baking that we love.

cinnamon-chocolate scones

3¾ cups all-purpose flour
¼ teaspoon salt
¼ cup sugar
3 tablespoons baking powder
1 teaspoon ground cinnamon
8 tablespoons (1 stick) cold unsalted butter, cut into pieces
1¼ cups milk
1½ cups semisweet chocolate chunks or morsels

Do you like **pain au chocolat**? You'll love these scones. Lofty and flaky, scones contain lots of baking powder to make them rise. They hold their shape beautifully, but sadly they do not age well; the airy interior dries quickly. Eat them the same day they are made.

In Britain, where scones come from, they come in only two flavors: plain and currant. The British kind are great at teatime with jam and cream, but these are real eye openers in the morning, especially with an all-American cup of joe. Coffee, cinnamon, and chocolate are a wonderful flavor combination.

Heat the oven to 375 degrees.

Mix the flour, salt, sugar, baking powder, and cinnamon in a mixer fitted with a paddle attachment (or using a hand mixer) at low speed. With the mixer running, add the butter and mix until coarse and sandy. You should still be able to see small lumps of butter.

Add the milk and mix until almost combined, then add the chocolate chunks and mix just to distribute them evenly through the dough. Do not overmix; there may still be some flour not mixed in. That's fine.

Turn the dough out onto a lightly floured surface. Knead the dough 10 times to bring it together and smooth it out.

Flour a rolling pin and roll out the dough 1 inch thick. Using a biscuit or cookie cutter or a clean empty can, cut out circles about 2½ inches in diameter. Transfer to an ungreased sheet pan.

Lightly knead the scraps together just until combined, then roll out again and continue cutting out circles until all the dough is used.

Bake until light golden brown, about 15 minutes.

MAKES ABOUT 12 SCONES

⌁ *To echo the flavors of the scone, drink a strong coffee with chocolate overtones like Arabian Mocha Sanani.*

quick pecan sour cream coffee cake

FOR THE CAKE

8 tablespoons (1 stick) unsalted butter, slightly softened

1 cup granulated sugar

3 eggs

2 cups sifted all-purpose flour

1 teaspoon baking soda

1 teaspoon baking powder

¼ teaspoon salt

1 cup sour cream

½ cup golden raisins

FOR THE TOPPING

¾ cup light brown sugar, packed

1 tablespoon all-purpose flour

1 teaspoon ground cinnamon

2 tablespoons cold unsalted butter, cut into pieces

1 cup chopped pecans

We can't imagine a bakery without coffee cake, so when we opened the Vanilla Bean Bakery, this simple one went right on the daily menu. It's just what you want in a coffee cake: bumpy and lumpy on the top, bright yellow cake underneath, and completely homey throughout. The batter and topping can be mixed separately the night before and the cake baked in the morning.

Heat the oven to 350 degrees. Butter an 8- or 9-inch square cake pan.

MAKE THE CAKE

Cream the butter in a mixer fitted with a paddle attachment (or using a hand mixer) until smooth. With the mixer running, slowly add the sugar and mix. Add the eggs and mix until the mixture is light and fluffy.

Sift the sifted flour, baking soda, baking powder, and salt together. Working in batches, add them to the butter-sugar mixture, alternating with dollops of sour cream. Mix in the raisins. Pour the batter into the prepared pan.

MAKE THE TOPPING

Combine the brown sugar, flour, and cinnamon in a medium bowl. Add the butter and, using your fingertips, pinch the ingredients together into a sandy, crumbly mixture. Add the pecans and mix. Sprinkle the mixture over the cake.

Bake until the cake is risen and browned, about 30 minutes. Let cool 10 minutes in the pan. Serve in squares.

MAKES 1 CAKE

Real coffee cake calls for real coffee—maybe with a drop of real cream.

double blueberry muffins

8 tablespoons (1 stick) unsalted butter, slightly softened
1 cup plus 2 tablespoons sugar
2 eggs
1 teaspoon pure vanilla extract
2 teaspoons baking powder
¼ teaspoon salt
2½ cups fresh blueberries (or thawed frozen)
2 cups all-purpose flour
½ cup milk
¼ teaspoon ground cinnamon

Here's a mighty challenger to the ever-popular blueberry muffin. An extra shot of blueberries makes for a juicy, fruity, and psychedelically swirly muffin that brightens even the stormiest morning mood. A simple, lightly crunchy topping of cinnamon sugar also raises the ante on those plain old blueberry muffins.

Professional bakers use ice-cream scoops to fill their muffin tins; the kind with the sweeping blade helps you fill the cups evenly, without wasting batter.

Heat the oven to 375 degrees. Butter 12 muffin cups or line them with paper liners. Butter the top of the muffin tin to prevent the muffin tops from sticking.

Cream the butter in a mixer fitted with a paddle attachment (or using a hand mixer) until smooth. Add 1 cup of the sugar and mix. Add the eggs, vanilla, baking powder, and salt and mix.

In a shallow bowl, mash ¾ cup of the blueberries with the back of a fork. Add to the batter and mix. With the mixer running at low speed, add half of the flour, then half of the milk, and mix. Repeat with the remaining flour and milk. Fold in the whole blueberries by hand until well mixed. In a separate small bowl, mix the remaining 2 tablespoons of sugar with the cinnamon.

Use an ice-cream scoop or large spoon to fill the muffin cups three quarters full. Sprinkle the cinnamon sugar over the muffins and bake until golden brown and risen, 25 to 30 minutes. Let cool in the pan at least 30 minutes before turning out.

MAKES ABOUT 12 MUFFINS

For even more tangy-fresh fruit flavor, squeeze tangerines, oranges, or a combination and serve the juice over ice alongside a basket of warm muffins. Wow!

chocolate chip pancakes

4 tablespoons (½ stick) unsalted butter
1 cup milk
1¼ cups all-purpose flour
1 tablespoon sugar
4 teaspoons baking powder
¾ teaspoon salt
2 eggs
6 ounces semisweet chocolate chips, or less to taste
Butter

Combine the butter and milk in a small saucepan and heat over low heat just until warm and the butter is melted. Let cool slightly. Mix the flour, sugar, baking powder, and salt together.

Whisk the eggs with a fork in a large bowl. Whisk in the milk mixture. Add the dry ingredients and mix just until barely blended. Do not overmix. Stir in the chocolate chips.

Heat a griddle or large skillet over medium heat. Add about a teaspoon of butter and heat until melted and bubbly. Ladle 3 tablespoons of batter for each pancake onto the hot surface and cook until bubbly on the top and golden brown on the bottom. Turn and cook until golden brown on the other side, about 30 seconds more. Repeat until all the batter is used up. Serve hot.

MAKES ABOUT 24 PANCAKES

With a hot, sweet, chocolaty pancake, cold milk or malted milk is the only way to go.

We may be chefs, but we're also parents; so even at our house, kids' tastes often determine the menu. This recipe combines two favorite kid foods— chocolate chips and pancakes—but we've yet to find a grown-up who didn't like them, too.

When we moved to Europe to cook for three years, we were amazed to discover that chocolate chips were almost unknown there, an exotic foodstuff found only in strange, crumbly versions of "American" cookies. We were glad to come home.

big apple pancake

There's a popular tradition in Chicago, where Gale grew up, of going to the wonderful Walker Brothers' Pancake House for Sunday breakfast. Of course, there is also a parallel tradition of driving to Walker Brothers', exclaiming "Oh no, look at that line!" and driving home again. Fortunately, Gale's mom was resourceful enough to create her own recipe for Walker Brothers' wonderful apple pancake long ago.

Today, this recipe is an artifact, because the pancakes at Walker Brothers' have evolved into a richer and sweeter version; we still stick to the light apple character of the old version. The apples are lightly sautéed, then the batter is poured over and the mixture is puffed in the oven, rather like a breakfast version of French **tarte Tatin** (though this also makes a fine dessert). For maximum drama, take the hot pan straight from the oven to the table and squeeze the lemon over it there. The sizzle is most impressive!

3 tablespoons unsalted butter
2 large firm apples, peeled, cored, and sliced ¼ inch thick
¼ cup light brown sugar, packed
3 eggs
1 teaspoon granulated sugar
Pinch of salt
½ cup milk
½ cup all-purpose flour
¼ teaspoon ground cinnamon
2 lemon wedges

Heat the oven to 450 degrees.

Over medium heat, melt 2 tablespoons of the butter in a large ovenproof skillet (preferably with curved sides). Add the apple slices and cook, stirring, until tender, about 10 minutes. Add 2 tablespoons of the brown sugar and stir to combine.

Whisk the eggs, granulated sugar, salt, milk, and flour together. Pour this batter over the apples in the skillet, transfer to the oven, and bake until puffy, about 10 minutes.

Meanwhile, mix the cinnamon and the remaining 2 tablespoons of brown sugar together. Cut the remaining tablespoon of butter into pieces. When the pancake puffs, remove from the oven, dot with butter, sprinkle with cinnamon sugar, and return to the oven to bake until browned, about 10 minutes more. As the pancake comes out of the oven, squeeze the lemon wedges over the top. Serve the pancake in wedges right out of the pan.

MAKES 4 SERVINGS

> *For authentic old time Chicago luxury, serve this with strong coffee topped with whipped cream.*

oatmeal waffles

2 cups buttermilk
¼ cup orange juice
⅔ cup rolled oats (see sidenote)
1 egg
2 tablespoons light brown sugar, packed
½ cup all-purpose flour
½ cup whole wheat flour
1½ teaspoons baking soda
½ teaspoon salt
2 tablespoons melted butter or vegetable oil
Butter for cooking

The night before you plan to serve the waffles, combine the buttermilk, orange juice, and oats in a medium bowl. Mix well, cover, and refrigerate overnight.

The next morning, whisk the egg in a large bowl. Add the sugar and mix. Add the remaining ingredients and the oat mixture and mix well. The batter may be slightly lumpy.

Heat and lightly butter a waffle iron. Spoon a generous ½ cup of batter onto the hot iron and close the lid. Cook until no more steam escapes from the iron and the waffle is golden on both sides, about 5 minutes. Serve immediately.

MAKES 4 SERVINGS

With the orange and oat flavors of the waffles, plus melting butter and maple syrup...what could be better than cold, fresh apple cider?

It hadn't occurred to us until our little son Gio started eating real breakfasts that a waffle iron is a magical item. You pour cold, lumpy batter into a mysterious machine, leave it alone for a while, and open it to find hot, nut-brown waffles inside! He just loves them.

When Gio wakes up, he is ready to begin his day; we are still bleary from a night in the restaurant. He demands to "MIX NOW," but the last thing we want to do is cook. So we devised a waffle recipe that is improved by being started the night before. Use quick-cooking oats for a tender waffle, plain if you prefer a more substantial, chewy waffle. The light tang of orange juice and buttermilk adds a wonderful flavor. Serve with butter and Allspiced Apple Butter (page 247) or maple syrup.

brown sugar wheat scones

2 cups all-purpose flour
1¾ cups whole wheat flour
¼ teaspoon salt
¼ cup plus 2 tablespoons light brown sugar, packed
3 tablespoons baking powder
8 tablespoons (1 stick) cold unsalted butter, cut into pieces
1¼ cups milk
1 cup raisins or dried currants
2 tablespoons heavy cream

Heat the oven to 375 degrees.

Mix the flours, salt, ¼ cup of the brown sugar, and the baking powder in a mixer fitted with a paddle attachment (or using a hand mixer) at low speed. With the mixer running, add the butter and mix until coarse and sandy.

Add the milk and mix until almost combined, then add the raisins and mix just to distribute them evenly through the dough. Do not overmix; there may still be some flour not mixed in. That's fine.

Turn the dough out onto a lightly floured surface. Knead the dough 10 times.

Flour a rolling pin and roll out the dough 1 inch thick. With a biscuit or cookie cutter or a clean empty can, cut out circles about 2½ inches in diameter. Transfer to an ungreased baking sheet.

Lightly knead the scraps together just until combined, then roll out again and continue cutting out circles until all the dough is used.

Brush the tops of the scones with cream and sprinkle with the remaining 2 tablespoons of brown sugar. Bake until light golden brown, about 15 minutes.

MAKES 8 TO 10 SCONES

Try an aromatic tea such as English Breakfast or Earl Grey, brewed not too strong.

If you've ever wondered why bran muffins often weigh as much as this book, you are going to like these scones. The key to baking with whole wheat flour—which, of course, includes the bran and germ of the wheat—is to cut it with other flours. Unless you are baking bread, whole wheat flour simply does not behave well on its own. Because these scones are light and airy, you can appreciate the grain's flavor in this recipe—without being weighted down by the bran. Chewy-sweet raisins are a welcome interruption.

cinnamon apple bumpy bread

FOR THE BREAD

½ cup plus 2 tablespoons lukewarm water

¾ teaspoon salt

3 tablespoons sugar

2 tablespoons unsalted butter, cut into pieces

1½ ounces fresh yeast or 3 ounces active dry yeast

3 cups bread flour

1 egg

FOR THE FILLING

2½ teaspoons ground cinnamon

1½ tablespoons sugar

¾ cup canned apple pie filling

1 egg yolk

FOR THE GLAZE

4 tablespoons (½ stick) unsalted butter, melted

¼ cup sugar

1 teaspoon ground cinnamon

Bet you've never made bread by chopping up dough with a big knife and squishing it together with your hands. But that's just what works best for this soft, sweet breakfast bread. When you fold in apples, sugar, and cinnamon beforehand, then brush the top with more cinnamon, you are rewarded with a knobbled loaf with rich ores of apple filling running through it.

The name of this loaf used to be "Apple Cinnamon" Bumpy Bread, but we then realized that the punch of toasty cinnamon beats out the sweetness of the apples here. For sheer homey atmosphere, you can't beat the smell of baking cinnamon.

Butter a 7-cup loaf pan and place it on a baking sheet. Butter a large bowl.

MAKE THE DOUGH

In a mixer fitted with a dough hook, mix the water, salt, sugar, butter, yeast, flour, and egg at low speed for 8 minutes. Remove the dough to the buttered bowl and cover with a damp cloth. Let rise in a warm place for 1 hour.

Turn the dough out onto a lightly floured work surface and roll out into a large circle, about 14 inches in diameter and ⅛ inch thick.

ADD THE FILLING

Place the cinnamon, sugar, apple pie filling, and egg yolk in the center of the dough. Fold one side of the dough over the filling, then the other, as though you are folding a letter. With a large knife, chop the dough into 1-inch pieces. Using your hands, lightly toss the dough pieces together, turning them over. Push the pieces of dough back together into a loose loaf and transfer to the pan.

Cover with a damp towel and let rise in a warm place until the dough is 1 inch above the pan rim, 1 to 1½ hours.

Heat the oven to 350 degrees. Bake the loaf until golden brown,

30 to 40 minutes. Let cool in the pan for 15 minutes, then turn out onto a wire rack.

MAKE THE GLAZE

While the bread is still warm, set the wire rack and bread on a sheet pan. Thickly brush the bread on all sides (including the bottom) with melted butter. Mix the sugar and cinnamon in a large shallow dish and roll the loaf in the cinnamon sugar. Return the bread to the rack and let cool completely.

MAKES 1 LARGE LOAF

This heavenly-smelling bread calls for an aromatic Latin American coffee such as Costa Rican, roasted dark and brewed strong.

featherlight corn muffins

A good corn muffin is morning music: light, cheerful, and gentle on the spirit and stomach. These practically float off the plate and hover over the newspaper.

Frankly, we're amazed by some of the crumbly yellow boulders that pass for corn muffins these days. Our diagnosis: too much cornmeal. You'd think that using more cornmeal would yield more corn flavor, but it doesn't seem to work that way. Cornmeal must be cut with other flours or it can turn bitter and soapy. Like many foods in the Gand household when Gale was growing up, corn muffins were interpreted as vehicles for a thick schmear of butter. These muffins have the butter already in them.

Great with milk or coffee. Or, for a Southern combination, brew up some strong, sweet tea and serve it over ice.

1 cup all-purpose flour
½ cup yellow cornmeal
¼ cup sugar
1½ teaspoons baking powder
¼ teaspoon salt
2 eggs
¼ cup milk
8 tablespoons (1 stick) unsalted butter, melted

Heat the oven to 350 degrees. Butter and flour 8 muffin cups or line them with paper liners.

Sift the dry ingredients together.

Whisk the eggs and milk together in a large bowl. Add a third of the dry ingredients to the egg mixture, then a third of the melted butter, and stir gently just until incorporated. Repeat with the remaining dry ingredients and melted butter, being careful not to overmix; there may be a little flour not mixed in at the end. That's fine.

Use an ice-cream scoop or large spoon to fill the muffin cups half full. Bake until risen, light golden brown, and firm to the touch, about 15 minutes. Let cool at least 15 minutes in the pan.

MAKES 8 MUFFINS

sharon's stickier buns

FOR THE DOUGH

1 cup water

3 cups bread flour

5 tablespoons unsalted butter, cut into pieces

¼ cup powdered milk

5 teaspoons sugar

1 ounce fresh yeast or 2 ounces active dry yeast

1¾ teaspoons salt

FOR THE HONEY SCHMEAR

¾ cup light brown sugar, packed

4 tablespoons unsalted butter, slightly softened

2 tablespoons honey

2 tablespoons light corn syrup

1 tablespoon water

TO FINISH THE BUNS

1¼ cups pecan halves

½ cup sugar

1½ teaspoons ground cinnamon

4 tablespoons unsalted butter, melted

MAKE THE DOUGH

Combine all the ingredients for the dough in a mixer fitted with a dough hook. Mix at low speed for 2 minutes, then increase the speed to medium and mix for another 6 minutes. To test if the dough is ready, stretch a small piece of dough into a thin sheet and hold it up to the light. If you see a web-like pattern, the dough is developed; the webs are the strands of gluten. If you don't see them, mix the dough at medium speed 2 minutes more, then test again. Transfer the dough to a clean bowl, cover with a slightly damp cloth, and refrigerate at least 2 hours or overnight.

When we were contemplating a sticky bun for the Vanilla Bean Bakery, we knew we first would have to answer the question, "What's the absolutely stickiest thing you can think of?" Anyone who has tried to keep a jar of honey clean, or has read a Winnie-the-Pooh book, knows that honey is about as sticky as it gets. Our sous-chef Suzette immediately volunteered her mother Sharon's excellent honey schmear for the purpose. It has the perfect effect, since you want your sticky buns to look almost wet and shiny; a dry-looking sticky bun is no good at all. With melted butter and pecans, plus cinnamon sugar inside, don't be surprised if Winnie-the-Pooh himself shows up on your doorstep. The honey-sweet aroma is ravishing—and neighborhood-filling.

Photograph on pages 158–159.

MAKE THE HONEY SCHMEAR

Mix the brown sugar, butter, honey, and corn syrup in a mixer until smooth. Add the water and mix until smooth, adding more water as needed to make the mixture spreadable.

FINISH THE BUNS

Butter 10 cups of a large muffin tin. Spoon 2 tablespoons of the honey schmear into the bottom of each cup. Sprinkle 2 tablespoons of pecans on the schmear.

Mix the sugar and cinnamon together. On a lightly floured surface, roll the chilled dough into a 10-inch square about ¼ inch
thick. Brush with the melted butter and sprinkle with the cinnamon sugar. Firmly roll up the dough like a jelly roll, making sure
the roll has about the same diameter as the muffin cups. Transfer
to a sheet pan and refrigerate 30 minutes. Using a sharp knife or a
taut length of dental floss, cut the dough into 10 slices, each about
1 inch thick. Place one slice flat (cut side down) in each muffin
cup. Cover with a damp cloth and let rise in a warm place until
they reach the rim of the pan, about 1 to 1½ hours. *(Or, cover and
let rise in the refrigerator overnight.)*

Heat the oven to 350 degrees.

Bake until golden brown, 25 to 30 minutes. Meanwhile, line a
sheet pan with parchment paper. Let the buns cool in the pan for
2 minutes, then flip the pan over onto the sheet pan. Carefully lift
off the muffin pan, leaving the buns and toppings on the sheet
pan. Let cool.

MAKES 10 LARGE BUNS

☞ *You'll want plenty of hot coffee to cut through the wonderful richness and melt the schmear.*

eggs

"An egg is always an adventure."
Oscar Wilde

pumpkin crème brûlée

apricot rice pudding

hungarian crêpes with peanut butter and jam

mango flan on chocolate

paris-brest custard cake

coconut cream pie with chocolate-painted crust

creamy cranberry bread pudding

lemon custard–filled sugar brioche

grilled pain perdu with buttermilk

pavlova

vanilla soufflé with satin chocolate sauce

personality profile: There's a wholesomeness and a wholeness about a fresh egg that makes it especially lovable. Nourishing and maternal, an egg can be breakfast, lunch, dinner, and dessert. But it's never bland or dull; an egg also has a powerful magic side and a changeable temperament. Sugar, flour, and butter are smooth and consistent; an egg holds a dual personality, chemistry, and power inside that innocent-looking shell.

Ask any pastry chef: What is the single most miraculous ingredient in dessert making? You'll get one answer: the egg. That beautifully smooth oval is filled with both fat (the yolk) and water (the white), chemical opposites that coexist in nature only within the confines of an eggshell. Depending on just how an egg is cooked, it may be as dense as a hard-boiled egg, as light and airy as a soufflé, as brittle as a meringue, as rich and creamy as custard. Although eggs are essential in so many desserts, the recipes in this chapter—for custards, cream pie, crème brûlée, and meringue—highlight the flavor, texture, and abilities of the egg.

Together, the yolks and whites of an egg provide protein, fat, moisture, and substance; separately, they work culinary alchemy by binding, lightening, coloring, and flavoring other ingredients. A rich golden egg yolk is a marvelous carrier for flavors like lemon, chocolate, mango, and coconut; a stiffly whipped white gives the solid but melting quality that makes mousses, cream pies, and meringues sublime. The "mouth feel" of an egg, whether separated or combined, is another gift to bakers: Nothing else can make custards so smooth and flavorful, French toast so tender, bread pudding so light but rich to the bite.

Both egg yolks and egg whites (unlike butter, sugar, and flour, say) can be whipped with air to make them lighter in color and texture, and greater in volume. The resulting air pockets throughout the dessert heat up during baking, ensuring even cooking and smooth texture.

In most custard desserts, the yolks are whipped with sugar and blended with cream, gelatin, or starch, then cooked down into a sweet, thick mass. Whether it's called *crema*, flan, *pots de crème*, custard, or pudding, the process and principles are essentially the same.

Soufflés and meringues rely on egg whites whipped with sugar, then gently cooked until dry, leaving a stiff but fragile dessert that dissolves on the tongue.

A few practical notes: All the eggs in this chapter, and this book, are grade large. Brown or white makes no nevermind; they're all the same inside. Eggs taste best when used as soon after laying as possible, but the shell, which is porous, allows the contents to breathe and protects them from deterioration for quite a while in your refrigerator. None of the recipes in this chapter calls for raw eggs.

Although whites and yolks cohabitate quite happily in the shell, they often need to be separated in baking. Technically speaking, the fat molecules in the yolk prevent the protein molecules in the white from bonding with air molecules—which is why even a speck of yolk can prevent a whole bowl of whites from whipping stiff. Eggs are most easily separated at refrigerator temperature, but the whites whip best at room temperature. Separate them right out of the refrigerator, then set the whites aside to warm up. Keep the yolks refrigerated until you use them. And when you're ready to bake, turn to page 14 for notes on how to whip egg whites.

Like butter, sugar, and flour, eggs are an everyday ingredient with magical possibilities. After making some of these recipes, you'll understand them better than ever before.

pumpkin crème brûlée

1½ cups heavy cream
½ cup whole milk
⅛ teaspoon ground cinnamon
2 pinches of ground nutmeg
1 pinch of ground ginger
1 pinch of ground cloves
4 egg yolks
½ cup granulated sugar
¼ cup canned pumpkin puree
⅓ cup coarse or raw sugar

Crème brûlée, though extremely fashionable, is really nothing new. It was frequently served at the White House during the Jefferson administration. A shameless Francophile, Thomas Jefferson established the tradition of installing a French chef in the Presidential kitchens (and also introduced vanilla to American cooks).

The modern era in crème brûlée began at New York's superfabulous Le Cirque restaurant in the late 1970s, but it's hard to get excited about the lukewarm, thin-skinned versions now served in many restaurants. The appeal of crème brûlée should come from the contrast of the cold, creamy custard and the brittle, crackling-hot sugar on top (after all, the name means "burnt cream"). Some scoff at the flavored crème brûlée trend, but we find that the flavorings aren't usually the problem—it's the method. Here's how to achieve the true effect in a home kitchen. Don't be afraid to almost burn the sugar—that's the whole point!

Heat the oven to 300 degrees.

In a medium saucepan, heat the cream, milk, cinnamon, nutmeg, ginger, and cloves over medium heat, stirring occasionally, just until it comes to a boil. Immediately turn off the heat and set aside to infuse at least 15 minutes.

Whisk the egg yolks with the granulated sugar in a large bowl. Whisking constantly, gradually pour in the hot cream mixture. Whisk in the pumpkin puree.

Pour the mixture into 4 ovenproof ramekins and arrange in a hot-water bath (page 15). Bake in the center of the oven until almost set but still a bit soft in the center, 30 to 40 minutes. The custard should "shimmy" a bit when you shake the pan; it will firm up more as it cools.

Remove from the water bath and let cool 15 minutes. Tightly cover each ramekin with plastic wrap, making sure the plastic does not touch the surface of the custard. Refrigerate at least 2 hours. *(Or refrigerate until ready to serve, up to 48 hours.)*

Heat a broiler to very hot (or fire up your kitchen torch). Uncover the chilled custards. Coat the top of each custard completely with an even layer of coarse sugar.

Place the ramekins on a baking sheet or in a roasting pan and broil until the sugar is melted and well browned, 1 to 2 minutes. Let cool 1 minute before serving.

MAKES 4 SERVINGS

This custardy, lightly spiced dessert demands a strong drink to cut through its richness. Espresso will do the trick; so will the power of a good French Cognac.

apricot rice pudding

1 cup raw short-grain rice (such as Arborio), rinsed in a colander until the water runs clear

4½ cups milk

¼ cup diced dried apricots

¼ vanilla bean, split lengthwise and soft insides scraped out and reserved

½ teaspoon freshly grated lemon zest

4 egg yolks

½ cup sugar

Bring the rice, milk, apricots, vanilla scrapings, and lemon zest to a simmer in a covered heavy saucepan over medium heat. Immediately reduce the heat to as low as possible, cover tightly, and simmer gently, stirring occasionally, until the rice is very tender, 20 to 25 minutes. Turn off the heat.

Stir the egg yolks into the cooked rice mixture and stir just until thickened, 1 to 2 minutes. Stir in the sugar.

Spoon the rice pudding into ramekins or dessert cups and let cool. Cover tightly with plastic wrap and refrigerate at least 2 hours. *(Or refrigerate until ready to serve, up to 24 hours.)*

MAKES 6 TO 8 SERVINGS

Cool rice pudding and a cup of strong hot cocoa make a great combination, especially after a spicy meal or a long session of ice skating. For a more mellow mood, try a tea that complements the apricots, such as camomile or jasmine, or a fruity dessert wine like Muscat de Beaumes de Venise.

Gale has a soft spot for what she calls "Grandma stuff." She swoons for old-fashioned flowers like hollyhocks and sweet peas, old-fashioned rituals like afternoon tea, and old-fashioned desserts like bread pudding, mince pie, and strawberry shortcake—all the desserts girls used to learn at their mothers' knees. This is that kind of dessert, partly because you barely need a recipe for it: It's simply rice cooked in milk rather than water, seasoned with sugar instead of salt. Having made rice pudding once, you've mastered the method.

Vary it endlessly with raisins, dried cranberries, fresh cherries, different flavorings (try rose water or orange-blossom water instead of lemon zest), and last-minute toppings of chopped pistachios or pecans. We use short-grain rice such as Arborio, Asian sticky rice, or paella rice, since it is starchier and makes a creamier, more luscious pudding, but long-grain rice will work, too.

Photograph on page 139.

hungarian crêpes
with peanut butter and jam (PALACSINTA)

2 eggs
½ cup milk
½ teaspoon salt
1 teaspoon granulated sugar
½ cup all-purpose flour
Unsalted butter
Peanut butter (smooth or chunky)
Jam (such as strawberry, raspberry, apricot, peach, plum, blackberry)
Confectioners' sugar

Gale's mother, Myrna, always had a terrific knack for pastry. Instead of a green thumb for gardening, she used to say that she and Gale had a white thumb, for baking.

Many of Myrna's specialties have their roots in Hungary, where her family came from, and where fine baking has a long, long tradition. Crêpes are popular all over Eastern Europe, usually spread with the region's famous fruit compotes and jams. Adding peanut butter (Myrna's own innovation) makes them all-American and kid-friendly. Gale's brother Gary, as a resolute 6-year-old vegetarian, practically lived on them.

Photograph on page 153.

Whisk the eggs and milk together in a medium bowl. Whisk in the salt, granulated sugar, and flour. Set aside for 30 minutes.

Heat the oven to 200 degrees and put a platter in the oven to heat.

Melt about ½ teaspoon butter in a nonstick 8- to 10-inch skillet over medium heat. When it foams, pour or ladle in about 2 tablespoons batter. Lift and swirl the pan so the batter coats the bottom. Replace the pan on the burner and cook just until set and the underside is lightly browned. Using a spatula or your fingers, flip and cook until the other side is lightly browned. Transfer to the warmed platter. Repeat until the batter is used up.

Remove the crêpes from the oven. One by one, spread each crêpe with a thin layer of peanut butter and jam and roll up like a cigar. Place 2 rolled crêpes on each of 4 serving plates. Sprinkle with confectioners' sugar and serve.

MAKES 4 SERVINGS

Whenever you have peanut butter and jelly—in any form—a tall glass of ice-cold milk belongs right alongside.

mango flan on chocolate

FOR THE FLAN

3 cups sugar

½ cup water

4 cups milk (not skim)

½ vanilla bean, split lengthwise

7 eggs

2 egg yolks

½ cup fresh mango puree (1 small mango, peeled, pitted, and pureed in a food processor)

FOR THE OPTIONAL CHOCOLATE BROWNIE BASE

¾ cup all-purpose flour

½ cup cocoa powder

¼ teaspoon baking powder

¼ teaspoon salt

6 tablespoons unsalted butter, slightly softened

1 cup sugar

2 eggs

1 teaspoon pure vanilla extract

½ cup semisweet chocolate chips

MAKE THE FLAN

Pour 2 cups of the sugar into the center of a deep saucepan. Carefully pour the water around the sugar, trying not to splash any sugar onto the sides of the pan. Do not stir; gently draw your finger through the center of the sugar twice, making a cross, to moisten it. Over medium-high heat, bring to a boil without stirring. Reduce the heat to a fast simmer and cook without stirring until amber-caramel in color, 10 to 20 minutes. Immediately remove from the heat.

Meanwhile, set six 1-cup ramekins or shallow coffee cups nearby. When the caramel is cooked, quickly pour about ¼ cup caramel into each ramekin and swirl to coat the sides. Set aside to cool.

Heat the oven to 300 degrees.

Bring the milk and vanilla bean to a boil in a saucepan over medium heat. Immediately turn off the heat and set aside to infuse. Meanwhile, whisk together the eggs, additional egg yolks, and the remaining 1 cup of sugar in a large bowl. Whisk about ½ cup of the hot milk into the egg mixture. Whisk the remaining hot milk into the egg mixture. Whisk in the mango puree until

How to describe the taste of a mango? It's like burying your nose in the sweetest honeysuckle, slurping on the juiciest peach, and diving into a tropical sea, all at the same time. But instead of dealing with an actual sticky, hard-to-peel mango at dessert time, think ahead and use the sun-warmed flesh to infuse a delicate flan. **Flan** is the Latin American term for **crème caramel,** or **crema catalana,** depending on whether you're speaking to a Frenchman or a Spaniard.

If you have time to make rounds of dark chocolate brownie to rest the creamy flans on, you'll adore the effect—but it's certainly not required for a great dessert.

smooth. Strain the mixture into a pitcher to smooth it, removing the vanilla bean and mango fibers.

Pour the mixture into the caramel-lined ramekins and arrange in a hot-water bath (page 15). Bake in the center of the oven until dry and set in the center, 30 to 35 minutes.

Remove from the water bath and let cool. Tightly cover each ramekin with plastic wrap. Refrigerate at least 2 hours. *(Or refrigerate until ready to serve, up to 24 hours.)*

MEANWHILE, MAKE THE CHOCOLATE BROWNIE BASE
Heat the oven to 350 degrees. Grease a 9×13-inch baking pan and line it with parchment or wax paper, pressing into the corners. Sift together the flour, cocoa powder, baking powder, and salt.

Cream the butter in a mixer fitted with a paddle attachment (or using a hand mixer) until fluffy. Mix in the sugar. Mix in the eggs and vanilla and mix until light and fluffy.

Add the dry ingredients to the butter mixture and mix just until combined. Mix in the chocolate chips.

Pour into the pan, smooth the top, and bake until the cake is firm in the center and the surface is dry and shiny, 55 to 60 minutes. Let cool in the pan. Run a knife around the edges of the pan and turn out the whole cake onto a work surface. Peel off the parchment paper. Using a ramekin as a guide, use a sharp knife to cut out 6 brownie circles the same size as the ramekins.

To serve, place a brownie circle on each serving plate. Turn a flan out on top of the cake (you may need to dip the bottom of each ramekin in hot water to loosen the caramel, and/or run a knife around the edge of the ramekin). The caramel will pour out and serve as the sauce, and will also soak into the brownie.

MAKES 6 SERVINGS

Mexican hot chocolate, with its cinnamon notes and toasty flavor, goes wonderfully with both the brownie and the flan—as well as being geographically correct with these tropical flavors!

paris-brest custard cake

FOR THE PASTRY

1 cup water

8 tablespoons (1 stick) unsalted butter

½ teaspoon salt

1½ teaspoons granulated sugar

1 cup all-purpose flour

3 or 4 eggs, plus 1 egg for an egg wash

½ cup sliced blanched almonds

FOR THE FILLING

2 cups whole, 2% fat, or 1% fat milk

½ vanilla bean, split lengthwise

6 egg yolks

⅔ cup granulated sugar

¼ cup cornstarch

1 tablespoon unsalted butter

2 cups chilled heavy cream

2 tablespoons light brown sugar, packed

Confectioners' sugar

MAKE THE PASTRY BASE

Heat the oven to 425 degrees.

Trace a circle 10 inches in diameter on a piece of parchment paper. Use the parchment paper to line a baking sheet, pencil side down (you should still be able to see the circle).

Bring the water, butter, salt, and granulated sugar to a rolling boil over medium-high heat. When it boils, immediately take the pan off the heat. Add all the flour at once and stir hard with a wooden spoon until all the flour is incorporated, 30 to 60 seconds. Return the pan to the heat and cook, stirring, 30 seconds to evaporate some of the moisture.

Scrape the mixture into a mixer fitted with a paddle attachment (or use a hand mixer). With the mixer running at medium speed, and working 1 egg at a time, add 3 of the eggs, stopping after each addition to scrape down the sides of the bowl. Mix until the dough is smooth and glossy and the eggs are completely incorporated. The dough should be thick, but should fall slowly and steadily from the beaters when you lift them out of the bowl. If the dough is still clinging to the beaters, add the remaining egg and mix until incorporated.

There's no one more creative than a fun-loving pastry chef with an event to commemorate. When our son, Gio, turned one, we decided that his birthday party would be a celebration of his Italian-American heritage. Gale immediately visualized a cake topped with "spaghetti and meatballs." She made it with white frosting pushed through a ricer for the spaghetti, chocolate truffles (page 106) for the meatballs, and strawberry puree for the tomato sauce. Believe it or not, it was delicious.

In the same spirit, a pâtissier (his name is lost to history) on the outskirts of Paris came up with this dessert to celebrate a new athletic event in the early years of the twentieth century: the annual bicycle race from Paris to the city of Brest, in Brittany. You'll see what inspired him when you make the dessert: The ring of pastry distinctly resembles an old-fashioned bicycle wheel. It's much easier to make than it looks.

Note that you may need 3 **or** 4 eggs for this recipe, depending on your dough—which itself depends on the weather, the age of the flour, and a host of other factors. Add 3 eggs at first, then check the consistency as directed in the recipe.

Using a pastry bag fitted with a large plain tip, pipe the dough onto the penciled circle on the baking sheet, making a circle of dough. Pipe a second circle *around* the first one, hugging it so that the two rings touch closely all the way around. Pipe a third circle, using up all the remaining dough, *on top of* the first two, into the crack between them so that all three rings touch closely, forming one big ring with three parts.

Whisk the remaining egg with 1½ teaspoons water. Brush the surface of the dough with the egg wash (do not use all the egg wash). Sprinkle the almonds over the surface. Bake 15 minutes, then reduce the heat to 375 degrees and bake until puffed up and golden brown all over, including the crevices, about 25 minutes more. If you undercook the pastry, it may deflate. Try not to open the oven door too often during the baking. Let cool on the baking sheet. *(The recipe can be made up to this point up to 24 hours in advance. Hold at room temperature, lightly covered with aluminum foil.)*

MAKE THE FILLING

Bring the milk and vanilla bean to a boil in a medium saucepan over medium heat. Immediately turn off the heat and set aside to infuse for 10 to 15 minutes.

Whisk the egg yolks and granulated sugar until light and fluffy. Add the cornstarch and whisk vigorously until no lumps remain. Whisk in ¼ cup of the hot milk mixture until incorporated. Whisk in the remaining hot milk mixture. Pour the mixture through a strainer back into the saucepan. Cook over medium-high heat, whisking constantly, until thickened and slowly boiling. Remove from the heat and stir in the butter. Let cool slightly. Cover with plastic wrap, lightly pressing the plastic against the surface to prevent a skin from forming. Chill at least 2 hours or until ready to serve. *(The custard can be made up to 24 hours in advance. Refrigerate until 1 hour before using.)*

When ready to serve, whip the cream and brown sugar until stiff.

Using a long serrated knife, cut the pastry ring horizontally in half. Set the top half aside. Using a clean pastry bag, pipe the custard filling onto the bottom half. Pipe the whipped cream on top of the custard. Place the top half of the pastry lightly on the top, dust with confectioners' sugar, and serve, cut into sections.

MAKES 10 TO 12 SERVINGS

The festive sound of popping Champagne corks marks almost any French occasion you can think of, including the end of a bicycle race. We recommend a not-too-dry sparkling wine here, such as a demi-sec *Champagne, to cut through the richness of the custard but still provide some sweetness.*

coconut cream pie
with chocolate-painted crust

3 ounces semisweet chocolate
One 9-inch Plain and Perfect Pie Crust (page 30), prebaked and cooled
3½ cups milk (not skim)
½ cup canned cream of coconut, such as Coco Lopez
1 vanilla bean, split lengthwise
8 egg yolks
1⅓ cups sugar
½ cup cornstarch
2 tablespoons cold unsalted butter, cut into pieces
⅜ cup chilled heavy cream
¾ cup flaked or shredded coconut

Stir the chocolate until melted in the top half of a double boiler set over barely simmering water. Brush the baked pie shell up to the rim with the melted chocolate (see photograph). Set aside to cool and harden at room temperature or, uncovered, in the refrigerator.

Bring the milk, cream of coconut, and vanilla bean to a simmer in a large saucepan over medium heat. Immediately turn off the heat and set aside to infuse for 15 minutes. Do not remove the vanilla bean.

Meanwhile, whip the egg yolks and sugar together in a mixer fitted with a whisk attachment (or using a hand mixer) until pale yellow and fluffy. With the mixer running at low speed, mix in the cornstarch, then gradually pour in the hot milk mixture.

Strain the mixture back into the saucepan to smooth it. Whisking constantly, cook over medium-high heat until thick and just boiling. When the mixture thickens, the whisk will leave trail marks on the bottom of the pot and the mixture will have a few large bubbles boiling up to the top. Pour the mixture into a bowl and stir in the butter.

Half-fill a large bowl with ice water. Rest the bowl containing the custard in the ice water and let cool, stirring frequently to cool the mixture. When the custard is cool, whip the cream until stiff. Fold the whipped cream and coconut into the custard.

Pour the mixture into the chocolate-coated pie shell and smooth the top. Refrigerate uncovered at least 2 hours. (*Or refrigerate until ready to serve, up to 24 hours.*) Serve cold.

MAKES 1 PIE

Since he was a kid, Rick has demanded a coconut cream pie as his birthday "cake" every single year. Coconut was still an exotic flavor when he was growing up, bringing a whiff of the tropics to snowy Rochester, New York, and a Caribbean glamour to his mother Gloria's Italian-American kitchen. When he and Gale met, she knew she had to reinvent that coconut cream pie to make him her own—and it worked!

It's the thin layer of dark chocolate painted onto the crust that makes it so memorable. The brittle semisweet chocolate makes a great contrast to the soft creaminess of the coconut and vanilla filling. In our opinion, this coconut cream pie is just about as good as a pie can get.

Cream of coconut is most commonly used for making piña coladas, which explains why you will find it in the drinks and snacks aisle of your supermarket, near the sour mix.

Photograph on page 152.

Icy cold chocolate milk echoes the creamy-chocolaty coolness of the pie; if you feel like using your blender, a slushy chocolate malted would be even better.

creamy cranberry bread pudding

Gale is quite used to receiving impromptu marriage proposals from men who taste her desserts. In fact, she's so blasé that she keeps track of precisely which dishes inspire the most passion in her customers. Drum roll, please...this one is the winner!

Classic bread pudding is a spectacularly easy dessert that can be served warm or cool, with no adornment beyond a dusting of powdered sugar—yet people will still let out screams of pleasure when you bring it to the table. Starting with lightly toasted bread cubes adds yet another flavor dimension. Tangy cranberries are one of our favorite fruits for baking; their slightly sour bite adds a great flavor and texture element to the creamy sweetness of this bread pudding.

Dried cranberries may seem new and trendy, but they were among the foods a homesick Benjamin Franklin begged his daughter to send him when he was posted to London in 1768. The cranberry industry on Cape Cod is one of America's oldest agricultural projects, and the harvest is still worth seeing. When the scrubby bushes are overwhelmed by a rush of water, millions upon millions of shiny berries float to the surface, creating a landscape seemingly paved with rubies.

◯

The simplicity of this creamy dessert means that you can spice it up with a mug of mulled cider, mulled wine, or cinnamon tea.

½ recipe Brioche (page 86) or ½ large bakery challah (about 8 ounces bread)
2 cups half-and-half
2 cups heavy cream
Pinch of salt
1 vanilla bean, split lengthwise
6 eggs
1 cup granulated sugar
½ cup orange juice
1 cup dried cranberries
Confectioners' sugar

Heat the oven to 350 degrees.

Cut the crusts off the bread and cut into 1-inch cubes. You should have about 3½ cups of cubes. Arrange on a baking sheet and toast in the oven until light golden brown, about 10 minutes. Set aside to cool. Leave the oven on.

Heat the half-and-half, cream, salt, and vanilla bean in a saucepan over medium heat, stirring occasionally. When the cream mixture reaches a fast simmer (do not let it boil), turn off the heat. Set aside to infuse 10 to 15 minutes.

Whisk the eggs and sugar together in a large mixing bowl. Whisking constantly, gradually add the hot cream mixture. Strain into a large bowl to smooth the mixture and remove the vanilla bean. Add the bread cubes, toss well, and let soak until absorbed. Fold the mixture occasionally to ensure even soaking.

Bring the orange juice to a simmer in a small saucepan. Add the cranberries and simmer until plumped and softened, about 5 minutes. Drain and set aside.

Divide the cranberries among 6 ramekins, custard cups, or dessert cups (or use a deep baking dish), reserving enough to sprinkle on the top of each pudding. Divide the soaked bread among the dishes, then pour any remaining custard over the bread. Dot with the remaining cranberries. Arrange the puddings in a hot-water bath (page 15). Bake until set and golden brown on top, about 30 minutes for individual puddings and 40 to 45 minutes for one big pudding. Serve warm or chilled, dusted with confectioners' sugar.

MAKES 6 SERVINGS

lemon custard–filled sugar brioche

FOR THE BRIOCHE

1½ cups all-purpose flour

1¼ cups plus 2 tablespoons bread flour

1 teaspoon salt

¼ cup sugar

1 ounce fresh yeast or 2 ounces active dry yeast

2 tablespoons warm water

4 eggs

8 ounces (2 sticks) cold unsalted butter, cut into pieces

FOR THE LEMON CUSTARD

4 eggs

1 cup sugar

⅔ cup fresh lemon juice (from 3 to 4 lemons)

Freshly grated zest of 1 lemon

4 tablespoons (½ stick) unsalted butter, softened

1 cup chilled heavy cream

MAKE THE BRIOCHE

The day before you plan to make the dessert, combine the flours, salt, and 2 tablespoons of the sugar in a mixer fitted with a dough hook and mix. Dissolve the yeast in the water. With the mixer running at low speed, add the yeast mixture to the flour mixture. Add the eggs and mix well. Add the butter and mix at medium speed until smooth, about 10 minutes. Do not skimp on the mixing time; this is how the dough gets kneaded. Transfer to a clean bowl, cover tightly with plastic wrap, and refrigerate overnight.

The next day, turn the dough out onto a floured work surface. Cut into 12 equal pieces. Flour your hands and shape the dough into balls. Butter a sheet pan and arrange the balls on it. Loosely drape plastic wrap over the pan and let rise in a warm place until doubled in bulk, 2 to 3 hours.

MEANWHILE, MAKE THE LEMON CUSTARD

Bring about an inch of water to a simmer in a large saucepan. Whisk the eggs and sugar in a mixer fitted with a whisk attachment (or using a hand mixer) until very light yellow and fluffy. Whisk in the lemon juice and lemon zest. Rest the mixing bowl in the saucepan, with the bowl's base above the simmering water (pour out some of the water if necessary). Cook, whisking occa-

There's something Victorian about this delicate and elegant, but rich and indulgent, concoction. The puffy, sugar-sprinkled brioche rolls, slathered with a lemon curd lightened with whipped cream, are really very luxurious. Gale says this is what she would make for a lady who fainted from wearing tight corsets. Translation: It's comforting, fortifying, and filling, probably too much so for a mere dessert. Try it for a brunch or afternoon tea party, or when you're planning a light dinner for later in the day.

For a smaller party, you might make a half batch of custard, and use only half the dough for the rolls, shaping the remaining dough into a single loaf. Place in a buttered 6-cup loaf pan, bake with the rolls, and use it to make Creamy Cranberry Bread Pudding (page 85) or Grilled Pain Perdu with Buttermilk (page 88). You can also simply make a half recipe of brioche, halving all the ingredients **except** the yeast. If you have fresh yeast left over from the recipe, it can be stored in the freezer until you need it again.

sionally, until the mixture is thickened and custardy, about 10 minutes. Remove the bowl from the hot water and whisk in the butter until melted.

Half-fill a large bowl with ice water. Rest the bowl with the custard inside the ice water and let cool, folding the mixture occasionally.

Whip the cream until stiff in a clean bowl. Fold into the cooled lemon custard. Cover and refrigerate until ready to serve. (*The custard can be made up to this point up to 24 hours in advance and refrigerated until ready to serve.*)

Heat the oven to 350 degrees. Remove the plastic wrap from the brioche rolls and sprinkle them with the remaining 2 tablespoons of sugar. Bake until golden brown, 20 to 25 minutes. After 15 minutes, rotate the pan to ensure even cooking. When baked, immediately remove to a wire rack and let cool to room temperature.

Cut the top third off each roll and set aside. Make a hollow in the center of each roll, and pipe or spoon on a generous dollop of custard. Replace the tops and serve, passing any remaining custard at the table.

MAKES 12 SERVINGS

Tea brewed in the pot has a strong, balanced character that will stand up to the lemon custard. Try Darjeeling, Earl Grey, or another powerfully flavored tea in the English tradition, adding a bit of milk to each cup (lemon slices would fight with the lemon custard).

grilled pain perdu with buttermilk

2 ripe peaches, preferably white, pitted and sliced
1 pint raspberries
2 tablespoons light brown sugar, packed
3 eggs
Pinch of salt
½ cup granulated sugar
½ teaspoon pure vanilla extract
1 cup half-and-half
1 cup buttermilk
8 thick slices Brioche (use half of the recipe on page 86), bakery challah,
  or another soft white bread
Ice cream, preferably almond or vanilla (optional)

Clean your grill well and heat it to very hot.

Meanwhile, toss together the peaches, raspberries, and brown sugar and set aside to macerate.

Whisk the eggs in a medium bowl. Whisk in the salt, sugar, and vanilla. Gradually whisk in the half-and-half and the buttermilk. Pour the mixture into a shallow baking dish. Working in batches if necessary, place the bread in the dish and let soak, then turn and soak on the other side.

Grill the soaked bread until golden brown, then turn and repeat on the other side. Serve right off the grill, garnishing each serving with a scoop of ice cream and a spoonful of peaches and raspberries with their syrup.

MAKES 4 TO 6 SERVINGS

We wouldn't dream of tampering with the combination of French toast and good old American coffee; but why not make it French roast?

Pain perdu was probably invented as a thrifty way to make dessert from pieces of stale bread, but it feels luxurious enough for royalty—as most people already know from eating it for brunch, under the name of French toast.

In France, **pain perdu** (which means "lost bread") is served only as a dessert. We like to make it on the grill, which gives it a lovely campfire taste, but you could certainly brown it in butter over high heat if you prefer. Gale switched to grilling her pain perdu when invited to participate in a grilling event—always a challenge for a pastry chef. She was sure there must be more to grilled desserts than the usual fruit kebabs!

With ice cream and ripe fruit macerated in sugar, plus the creamy tang of vanilla and buttermilk, this easy but impressive dessert is complete. White peaches have a delicate, floral flavor that we first encountered, unforgettably, at the outdoor fruit market in Nice. Today we are happy to bring them in from growers in Washington State, and they are just as wonderful.

pavlova

Easy, pretty, light, and summery, Pavlova has become the national dessert of both Australia and New Zealand (the kiwi fruit on top is the giveaway). Traveling and cooking there, we encountered it on the dessert menu of every elegant restaurant we entered; it's Down Under's equivalent of crème brûlée. And it's equally irresistible: a fluffy pillow of meringue topped with a layer of snowy whipped cream. As you bite, the crisp exterior of the meringue quickly melts into the soft interior, helped along by tangy-sweet mouthfuls of ripe fruit. Pavlova looks quite impressive, but it's **very** easy to do.

A bit of vinegar in the meringue helps the egg whites whip stiff. (Technically speaking, the acid in the vinegar loosens the bonds between the egg white molecules, freeing them up to bond with air and sugar molecules instead.) Using raspberry vinegar will add a subtle, almost ghostly raspberry flavor to the meringue, but is not necessary. If you don't care for kiwi fruit, ripe peach or nectarine would stand in nicely.

Photograph on page 129.

⌒

This summery dessert calls for a tall glass of iced peach or passionfruit tea, garnished with a crisp sprig of mint. For a party, put out the fixings for Pimm's Cup; see the Drinks chapter for a recipe.

½ cup egg whites, at room temperature (from about 4 eggs)
⅛ teaspoon cream of tartar
⅛ teaspoon salt
1 cup granulated sugar
1½ teaspoons cornstarch
1 tablespoon raspberry or red wine vinegar
½ teaspoon pure vanilla extract
1¼ cups heavy cream
2 tablespoons light brown sugar, packed
2 kiwi fruits, peeled and thinly sliced, or 1 cup of another ripe fruit, such as peaches or nectarines
10 strawberries, green parts trimmed off, thinly sliced, or other berries, such as raspberries or blackberries

Heat the oven to 350 degrees.

Whip the egg whites, cream of tartar, and salt in a mixer fitted with a whisk attachment (or using a hand mixer) until foamy. Add the granulated sugar, cornstarch, vinegar, and vanilla and continue whipping until stiff, smooth, and glossy, about 8 minutes more.

Draw or trace a circle 9 inches in diameter with a pencil on a sheet of parchment paper. Line a sheet pan with the parchment paper, pencil side down (you should still be able to see the circle). Spoon the egg whites into the circle, using the back of the spoon to smooth the top and sides of the disk.

Bake in the center of the oven for 10 minutes, then reduce the heat to 300 degrees and bake until the meringue has puffed up and cracked on the top and the surface is lightly browned to the color of *café au lait*, about 45 minutes more. Turn off the oven, prop the oven door open, and let the pavlova cool in the oven at least 30 minutes, to room temperature. This ensures a gradual cooling, which protects the delicate meringue.

Whip the cream and brown sugar together until stiff. Spoon it in the center of the cooled pavlova and spread out to within ½ inch of the edge. Arrange the slices of kiwi around the edge. Arrange the strawberry slices in the middle. To serve, slice into wedges with a serrated knife.

MAKES 8 TO 10 SERVINGS

vanilla soufflé
with satin chocolate sauce

FOR COATING THE DISH
2 tablespoons unsalted butter, melted
¼ cup granulated sugar
FOR THE SOUFFLÉ
1 cup milk (not skim)
1 vanilla bean, split lengthwise
⅓ cup plus 1½ tablespoons granulated sugar
⅓ cup all-purpose flour
1½ tablespoons unsalted butter, softened
4 large eggs, separated
Confectioners' sugar
FOR THE SATIN CHOCOLATE SAUCE
2 ounces unsweetened chocolate
4½ ounces semisweet chocolate
¼ cup light corn syrup
⅓ cup hot water

Heat the oven to 350 degrees.

Brush 4 to 6 individual soufflé dishes (or one 7-cup soufflé dish) well with melted butter. Put the sugar inside one dish and toss to coat, then tip the excess sugar into the next dish and repeat. Place the dishes in the refrigerator to chill.

MAKE THE SOUFFLÉS
Reserve 3 tablespoons of the milk and place the remainder in a large saucepan. Add the vanilla bean and heat just to a boil, then turn off the heat and set aside to let the vanilla bean infuse.

Meanwhile, whisk the ⅓ cup granulated sugar, the flour, and the remaining reserved milk in a medium bowl. Add a little of the hot milk and whisk to combine, then add the flour mixture to the hot milk mixture in the saucepan. Bring to a simmer over medium heat, whisking occasionally. Simmer just until thickened, about 1 minute. Turn off the heat. Add the butter, stir, cover, and set aside for 15 minutes. Remove the vanilla bean and whisk in the egg yolks.

Whip the egg whites in a mixer fitted with a whisk attachment (or using a hand mixer) until soft peaks form. Add the remaining 1½ tablespoons sugar and continue whipping until stiff and glossy. Fold into the milk mixture.

Time was, you couldn't call yourself a cook if you didn't have a soufflé in your repertoire, usually orange or chocolate. In her many cookbooks, our beloved Julia Child devotes more words to the subtleties of the soufflé than to almost any other subject, and we know that many home cooks today are daunted by "fear of falling" when it comes to this lofty dessert. But a basic soufflé isn't really any more difficult than an angel food cake or a pie, and oh, is it worth it. This cloudlike dessert is a wonderful venue for the creamy-sweet flavor of pure vanilla. We like a hot, dark chocolate sauce for contrast, but a simple raspberry puree or no sauce at all is also wonderful.

Pour the mixture into the soufflé dishes, filling them three quarters full. Run your thumb around the inside rim of each dish, making a shallow "moat" around the edge of the batter. This will help the soufflés rise straight up. Dust the surfaces with confectioners' sugar. *(The soufflés can stand at this point for up to 30 minutes.)*

Bake in the center of the oven until puffed and light golden brown, 20 to 30 minutes. Do not open the oven door unless absolutely necessary.

MAKE THE SAUCE

Combine the two chocolates in the top half of a double boiler set over barely simmering water. Stir constantly until melted, then whisk in the syrup and water without removing the double boiler from the heat. Whisk until smooth and shiny. *(The sauce can be made up to 24 hours in advance and refrigerated. To rewarm, stir over low heat or heat in a microwave.)*

At the table, serve the hot soufflés by poking a hole in each one and pouring chocolate sauce into the hole, then drizzling sauce over the tops. For a large soufflé, spoon onto dessert plates and drizzle sauce on each serving.

MAKES 4 TO 6 SERVINGS

The creamy flavor of the vanilla bean calls for a delicate drink, and so does the texture of the soufflé. Champagne or another sparkling wine is the answer, lightly sweetened with a drop of raspberry or blackcurrant liqueur.

chocolate

"The ladies of the New World, it seems, love chocolate madly, and make considerable use of it."

Dumas père

rich chocolate fudge pie

black-and-whites

dark german chocolate cake with
 toasted almond-coconut goo

karen's chocolate sour cream layer cake

chocolate panini

lana's chocolate chip mandelbrot

harriet's chewy chocolate pavé

gale's famous truffles

chocolate-sprinkled crème brûlée

moist chocolate polenta cake

milk chocolate–orange mousse

brooklyn blackout cake

steamed chocolate pudding cake

chocolate-banana napoleon

chocolate éclairs

white chocolate mint semifreddo

crunchy chocolate hazelnut bars

personality profile: Suave and seductive in its refined state, chocolate always retains a hint of its dark and bitter past. Chocolate is strong, with a brutish streak—but smooth and sensual, like a powerful man in a soft Armani suit. Everyone adores chocolate, so he can be spoiled and oversweet; but when teased and gently treated, he can be most malleable. He is addictive, of course: No one is more intense, or knows more about giving pleasure. One warning: Chocolate tends to dominate any gathering you invite him to.

It's funny: No one ever confesses to a midnight obsession with vanilla, or begs us to put a fourth dessert flavored with orange on our menu. People love all our desserts, but only chocolate seems to inspire true passion—with all its attendant cravings, joys, needs, and demands. Humans seem to be meant to eat chocolate. Can it really be just a coincidence that cocoa butter's melting point is 98.6 degrees?

Hot chocolate whipped with vanilla and honey was a sacred and nourishing drink of the Maya and Aztecs. This was at a time when most Europeans were still drinking cold barley beer for breakfast! Both chocolate and vanilla were "discovered" by European explorers in the Americas in the fifteenth century.

As soon as European explorers took the precious stuff back to the Old World (Cortés kept a huge mug at hand when aboard ship), its smoky-nutty-sweet flavor became an object of fascination. Once the Spanish nuns in Central American missions devised a way to blend chocolate and vanilla with sugar and cream, the stage was set for the chocolate craze of the seventeenth century. Cocoa beans were expensive and heavily taxed (even more so than coffee beans), but royals and noblewomen could not resist their addiction to hot chocolate; in the court of Louis XIV, it was known as "the Queen's one passion," perhaps not even excluding the king.

Chocolate gradually made the switch from the breakfast table to the dessert kitchen, thanks to the ingenuity of Swiss confectioners, who created a method for separating a cocoa bean into its component parts, cocoa butter and chocolate liquor, and then recombining them into what we know as chocolate. Cocoa butter is where the smooth melting texture comes from; chocolate liquor is the thick brown paste where the flavor resides. The art of making chocolate is in the refining and rebalancing of the texture and flavor elements. Different brands of chocolate have strongly different characters, based on the roasting, sweetening, blending, and a host of other processes.

For example, at the Valrhona plant in France, where some of the finest chocolate in the world is made, eighteen kinds of beans from four continents are gathered. They are roasted separately, to the careful specifications of the Valrhona experts, who crush the beans in their hands to smell and taste each batch as it roasts; the butter and liquor are then separated by a progression of enormous machines. And then the blending, the work of the masters, begins.

As far as most of us are concerned, the story begins *after* the chocolate is blended, whether into dark, unsweetened, milk, bittersweet, semisweet, or white chocolate, depending on its proportions of cocoa butter, chocolate liquor, cream, and sugar. Dark chocolate is an intense, adult taste, a flavor for after dinner rather than daytime (though we know that some succumb to temptation early in the day with a Cinnamon-Chocolate Scone [page 61] or *pain au chocolat*). In choosing a chocolate dessert to make, keep in mind who you are cooking for: Children tend to prefer the lighter flavor of milk chocolate. (It is, of course, the chocolate of choice for candy bars.) White chocolate is cocoa butter flavored with milk and vanilla rather than with chocolate liquor; it has a strong following, despite its lack of real chocolate flavor.

In the following chapter, there is something for everyone: a pure chocolate hit in Rich Chocolate Fudge Pie, Gale's Famous Truffles, and the mighty Brooklyn Blackout Cake; and comforting chocolate classics like Steamed Chocolate Pudding Cake and voluptuous Chocolate Éclairs. Chocolate's affinity for other flavors and textures shines in Milk Chocolate–Orange Mousse and Harriet's Chewy Chocolate Pavé. Even you white chocolate renegades have a chilled White Chocolate Mint Semifreddo—though we couldn't leave out a hot dark-chocolate sauce for the top!

These recipes were tested with freshly bought supermarket chocolate. If the chocolate you buy looks cloudy when you unwrap it at home, that doesn't mean it is bad or old. This "bloom" is caused by the shifting of cocoa butter in the chocolate; it tends to rise to the surface at warm temperatures, but the chocolate isn't affected. In a home kitchen, chocolate will last nine months to a year at most. Gale tends to use Callebaut chocolate in her professional baking, and it will work well in these recipes, too. However, other professional and European chocolate brands may be too intense in flavor, or higher in cocoa butter. See page 14 for instructions on the best way to melt chocolate.

Cocoa powder is made from cocoa beans, dried, roasted, and pounded to a fine powder. Its chocolate flavor quotient is high, but it can also be mildly acidic, look for "Dutch-process" or "European-style" cocoa, which has been alkalized for better flavor and stability. Don't ever substitute sweetened instant cocoa mix for cocoa powder; it's not the same thing at all!

Chocolate is one of the most highly refined products we use in cooking—compare it to an apple, or an egg—and yet it has a primitive power. Don't forget that the mouth-filling, voluptuous quality of a great chocolate dessert is the surest way to seduce anyone—whether you are baking for your kid's birthday party, your wife's new boss, your ex-boyfriend, in-laws, or even an elusive lover. Use it wisely.

rich chocolate fudge pie

6 ounces bittersweet chocolate
18 tablespoons (2¼ sticks) unsalted butter
9 eggs
1½ cups sugar
1 teaspoon pure vanilla extract
¼ teaspoon salt
One 9-inch Plain and Perfect Pie Crust, prebaked (page 30)

Heat the oven to 250 degrees.

Melt the chocolate and butter together in the top of a double boiler set over barely simmering water, stirring frequently. When melted, transfer to a large bowl and whisk in the eggs, sugar, vanilla, and salt.

Pour the mixture into the prebaked pie crust and smooth the top. Bake in the center of the oven until almost set but still a bit soft in the center, 40 to 45 minutes. It should "shimmy" a bit when you shake the pan; it will firm up more as it cools.

Let cool at room temperature. For a fudgier pie, serve at room temperature; for a firm pie, refrigerate uncovered at least 2 hours or, lightly covered, overnight. Remove from the refrigerator 1 hour before serving.

MAKES 1 PIE

To cut through and accentuate the richness of the fudge, serve strong espresso coffee. But skip the usual lemon peel, which would fight with the chocolate flavor.

This pie is the result of an entire week dedicated to fudge-making, when Gale experimented with restaurateur Rich Melman's idea for an after-dinner fudge cart at Oprah Winfrey's restaurant, The Eccentric. The cart never materialized, but this pie sure did. Serve it with cold, not-too-stiff unsweetened whipped cream for maximum effect.

black-and-whites

8 tablespoons (1 stick) unsalted butter

1 cup granulated sugar

2 eggs

½ cup milk

¼ teaspoon pure vanilla extract

⅛ teaspoon pure lemon extract

1¼ cups cake flour

1¼ cups all-purpose flour

½ teaspoon baking powder

¼ teaspoon salt

FOR THE ICING

4 cups confectioners' sugar

6 tablespoons milk

1 teaspoon pure vanilla extract

2 tablespoons cocoa powder

Julia, who grew up in New York City, sent us a dozen of these when we opened the Vanilla Bean Bakery. We thought it was just a thoughtful gift, until she called and informed us that we were required to come up with a recipe for them! We loved them immediately—combining chocolate and vanilla in a single dessert always sounds good to us—and they went right onto the menu. Black-and-whites are a classic New York bakery confection, but they are getting harder and harder to find. Here's our attempt at preservation.

⌒

A good black-and-white is sweet and a bit cakey; with iced coffee and a dash of milk, you have the ideal cold contrast.

Heat the oven to 350 degrees. Line 2 baking sheets with wax or parchment paper.

Cream the butter in a mixer fitted with a paddle attachment (or using a hand mixer) until smooth. Add the granulated sugar and beat until fluffy. Add the eggs, milk, and extracts and mix to combine. Combine the flours, baking powder, and salt and mix well. Add the dry ingredients to the sugar-egg mixture and mix to blend.

Using an ice-cream scoop, scoop the dough onto the pans. With the back of a spatula, press and spread each cookie into a circle about 5 inches in diameter and ⅜ inch thick.

Bake for about 20 minutes, until golden. Let cool on wire racks.

MAKE THE ICING

Stir the confectioners' sugar, milk, and vanilla together until smooth. Transfer half of the icing to another bowl and stir in the cocoa until smooth.

Turn the cooled cookies over, so that the flat bottoms face up. Spread white icing on half of each flat surface, then spread the other half with chocolate icing. Let set at room temperature for 30 minutes.

MAKES 12 LARGE COOKIES

dark german chocolate cake
with toasted almond-coconut goo

1¼ cups flaked or shredded coconut

1¼ cups sliced almonds

FOR THE CAKE

3 cups sugar

2¾ cups all-purpose flour

1 cup plus 2 tablespoons cocoa powder, preferably Dutch-process

2¼ teaspoons baking powder

2¼ teaspoons baking soda

1½ teaspoons salt

3 eggs

1½ cups milk

¾ cup vegetable oil

1 tablespoon pure vanilla extract

1½ cups very hot water

FOR THE CARAMEL

2½ cups sugar

½ cup water

1 cup heavy cream

This combination of velvety dark chocolate cake and creamy coconut is one of the most popular cakes at Brasserie T. The elements of the recipe are traditional, but instead of making the usual layer cake, we like to combine them at the last minute; the delectable contrast between the cake and the topping is more noticeable. Rewarming the coconut "goo" just before serving is another twist on the luscious experience. Pecans are more traditional than almonds, and can be substituted if you like.

While we're talking about tradition, did you know that German chocolate cake has nothing at all to do with Germany? German's was a brand of sweet baking chocolate, popular for a time in the Midwest. You could have knocked us over with a feather when we found out.

Note that the cake is baked in a sheet pan, not a cake pan: You're looking to create a thin layer of cake.

Photograph on page 135.

Heat the oven to 350 degrees.

Spread the coconut and almonds on separate sheet pans and toast, stirring occasionally, just until golden brown, 10 to 15 minutes. Set aside to cool.

MAKE THE CAKE

Line the bottom and sides of a 14×17-inch sheet pan (with sides) with parchment or wax paper.

Sift together the 3 cups sugar, flour, cocoa, baking powder, baking soda, and salt. Transfer to a mixer fitted with a whisk attachment (or use a hand mixer) and blend briefly.

Whisk together the eggs, milk, oil, and vanilla extract. Add to the dry ingredients and mix at low speed for 5 minutes. Gradually add the hot water, mixing at low speed just until combined. The batter will be quite thin.

Pour the batter into the pan and bake until a tester inserted in the center of the cake comes out clean (a few crumbs are okay), 25 to 30 minutes. Let cool in the pan.

MEANWHILE, MAKE THE CARAMEL

Pour the 2½ cups sugar into the center of a deep saucepan.
Carefully pour the water around the sugar, trying not to splash
any sugar onto the sides of the pan. Do not stir; gently draw
your finger through the center of the sugar to moisten it. Bring to
a boil over medium-high heat without stirring. Reduce the heat
to a fast simmer and cook without stirring until amber-caramel in
color, 10 to 20 minutes. Immediately remove from the heat. Using
a wooden spoon, slowly and carefully stir in the cream (it will
bubble up and may splatter). Stir in the toasted coconut and
almonds. Set aside.

When ready to serve, cut the cake in the pan into 6 even strips,
each about 3 inches wide. Using diagonal strokes of the knife, cut
each strip into 4 triangles (see photograph on page 131). If the
sauce has stiffened, rewarm it over low heat (or in a microwave)
until softened. Place a triangle on each plate, drizzle with sauce,
and rest another triangle on top at a different angle. Drizzle with
more sauce and serve.

MAKES 12 SERVINGS

*Pour hot, not-too-strong coffee into tall, heavy glasses; at the last
minute, add scoops of vanilla ice cream, mix, and drink up.*

karen's chocolate sour cream layer cake

FOR THE CAKE

8 ounces (2 sticks) unsalted butter, softened

3 cups light brown sugar, packed

4 eggs

2 teaspoons pure vanilla extract

¾ cup cocoa powder, preferably Dutch-process

1 tablespoon baking soda

½ teaspoon salt

3 cups sifted cake flour

1⅓ cups sour cream

1½ cups hot coffee

FOR THE FROSTING

4 tablespoons (½ stick) unsalted butter, slightly softened

8 ounces cream cheese

4 ounces unsweetened chocolate, melted (page 14)

¼ cup cooled coffee

2 teaspoons pure vanilla extract

3 cups confectioners' sugar

Here's a dessert that really justifies the name "layer cake." It's high and lofty, going up and up in delicious layers like a chocolate skyscraper. The striped effect of the dark brown cake and pale brown frosting is elegant and dramatic.

Like good chocolate, sour cream has bitter, sweet, and creamy elements; maybe that's why they go together so well. The cake here has toasty notes of caramel and coffee; the frosting is chocolate and coffee fluff smoothed with cream cheese. The finished product is so very light and moist that it is best eaten chilled, to keep the crumbs from floating away from your fork.

Heat the oven to 350 degrees. Butter and flour three 9-inch round cake pans. Cut 3 circles of wax paper or parchment paper to fit the bottoms of the pans, then press them in.

MAKE THE CAKE

Cream the butter in a mixer fitted with a whisk attachment (or using a hand mixer) until smooth. Add the sugar and eggs and mix until fluffy, about 3 minutes. Add the vanilla, cocoa, baking soda, and salt and mix. Add half of the flour, then half of the sour cream, and mix. Repeat with the remaining flour and sour cream. Drizzle in the hot coffee and mix until smooth. The batter will be thin.

Pour into the pans and bake until the tops are firm to the touch and a toothpick inserted into the center comes out clean (a few crumbs are okay), about 35 minutes. Halfway through the baking, quickly rotate the pans in the oven to ensure even baking, but otherwise try not to open the oven.

Let cool in the pans 10 minutes. Turn out onto wire racks and let cool completely before frosting.

MAKE THE FROSTING

Cream the butter and cream cheese together until smooth. Drizzle in the melted chocolate and mix. Add the coffee and vanilla and mix. Add the confectioners' sugar one cup at a time, mixing well after each addition. Mix until well blended and fluffy.

To frost the cake, use a spatula to cover two of the cake layers with frosting. Stack them together. Flip the third cake layer over and rest it on the top to create a very flat top for the cake. Frost on the sides and top. Cover and refrigerate until ready to serve.

MAKES 10 TO 12 SERVINGS

We've all had chocolate milk, but this mocha-flavored dessert cries out for coffee milk — that is, coffee syrup or cooled sweet espresso mixed with frosty milk.

chocolate panini

When you think you have no dessert in the house, think again! The end of a sourdough bread and that baking chocolate you always have in the pantry can be instantly transformed into a crisp, voluptuously melting chocolate treat. Kids love the idea (and the reality) of a chocolate sandwich; this is the ultimate after-school snack. But it's fun for grown-ups, too, eaten with the fingers as a satisfying finale to a light meal. Like a grilled cheese sandwich, these panini are buttered on the outside. You can even make them in the toaster oven while the table is being cleared.

Eight ½-inch-thick slices of sourdough bread or peasant bread, buttered on one side

3 ounces semisweet chocolate, chopped with a heavy knife

Heat the oven to 450 degrees.

Lay four slices of the bread, buttered side down, on an ungreased sheet pan. Sprinkle evenly with the chopped chocolate, covering the bread to within ¼ inch of the crust. Cover each with a second slice of bread, buttered side up. Press closed.

Bake until the bread is golden and the chocolate begins to melt, 5 to 7 minutes. Using a spatula, carefully turn each sandwich over and bake 5 to 7 minutes more.

Let cool slightly before serving, to keep the chocolate from burning your mouth.

MAKES 4 SERVINGS

With piping hot dark chocolate, what could possibly taste better than cold milk?

lana's chocolate chip mandelbrot

8 tablespoons (1 stick) unsalted butter, softened
1¼ cups sugar
2 tablespoons vegetable oil
4 eggs
½ cup fresh lemon juice
1 teaspoon pure vanilla extract
5¼ cups all-purpose flour
½ teaspoon baking soda
2 teaspoons baking powder
½ teaspoon salt
2 cups semisweet chocolate chips
1 cup coarsely chopped pecans or almonds

Heat the oven to 350 degrees.

Cream the butter in a mixer fitted with a paddle attachment (or using a hand mixer) until fluffy. Add the sugar and mix until smooth. Add the oil and mix. With the mixer running, add the eggs one at a time. Add the lemon juice and vanilla extract and mix.

Combine the flour, baking soda, baking powder, and salt. Working in batches, and mixing after each addition, add the dry ingredients to the butter mixture and mix well. Add the chocolate chips and pecans and mix just until incorporated.

Turn the dough onto a work surface and divide into 5 equal pieces. Shape into 5 logs, about 1¼ inches in diameter. (If the dough is sticky, oil your hands lightly.) Butter a large sheet pan and place the logs on it, leaving some space between them. Bake until light golden brown, 25 to 30 minutes. Let cool 20 minutes, then use a heavy serrated knife (such as a bread knife) to cut the logs into ¾-inch-thick cookies. Spread out to cool to room temperature. Store in an airtight container.

MAKES ABOUT 4 DOZEN COOKIES

Instead of soda, Gale's mom, Myrna, grew up drinking chocolate phosphates—chocolate syrup with seltzer squirted in. Try it, or add whole milk to turn it into an egg cream.

Playing the elegant against the down-home is our favorite strategy for coming up with new desserts, but a great example has been under our nose for years: our friend Lana's chocolate chip mandelbrot. Lana is one of our son Gio's favorite people in the world, and one of ours, too. (No, it's not because of the cookies.)

Mandelbrot are like a brilliant synthesis of chocolate chip cookies and biscotti. They are a traditional German-Jewish cookie (the name means "almond bread," though we prefer the richer flavor of pecans here); the chocolate chips are Lana's clever addition. The lemon juice flavors the dough very lightly, giving the cookies a sweet-and-sour effect. They freeze beautifully after baking, so we made this an extra-large recipe. Of course, we sometimes have trouble waiting for them to thaw, so we happen to know that they're great frozen, too.

harriet's chewy chocolate pavé

2 tablespoons unsalted butter, melted

1 tablespoon Armagnac, Cognac, or boiling water

1 cup pitted prunes, quartered

12 ounces semisweet chocolate

8 tablespoons (1 stick) unsalted butter

5 eggs, separated

2½ tablespoons granulated sugar

1 cup chilled heavy cream

2 tablespoons light brown sugar, packed

If you look forward to going to the movies alone because it means you get a whole box of Raisinets all to yourself, this is the dessert of your dreams.

We'll come clean right away: There are prunes in this dessert. Yes, that's right: prunes and chocolate together. And we're proud of it. Our friend Harriet loves the combination, and this dessert persuaded us to love it, too. Chocolate can take on many different textures—hard, soft, powdery, melting, pourable—but one thing it isn't is chewy. That is, until you combine it with dried fruit. The chewiness is just wonderful, and we'd bet you wouldn't be able to put your finger on the prunes if we didn't tip you off.

The classic French flavor combination of prunes and Armagnac provides the background for a dark, satisfying concoction that is definitely a chocolate dessert first. In French, a **pavé** is a brick or a cobblestone, but also a "brick" of cake or terrine that is sliced for serving.

Brush a 6-cup loaf pan with melted butter. Let cool. Line the pan with wax paper or parchment paper and set aside. Combine the Armagnac and prunes and set aside to soften.

Melt the chocolate and butter together in the top of a large double boiler set over simmering water, stirring often. Turn off the heat and let cool slightly. Whisk in the cold egg yolks, then set the mixture aside in the double boiler. Do not turn on the heat. The mixture will stay warm over the hot water.

Whip the cold egg whites in a mixer fitted with a whisk attachment (or using a hand mixer) until they form soft droopy peaks. With the mixer running, slowly add the granulated sugar and whip until stiff and glossy, about 30 seconds. Fold the egg whites into the warm chocolate mixture until barely blended. Fold in the prunes (with any liquid that has collected in the bowl) until no streaks of egg white remain.

Pour into the pan and cover tightly with plastic wrap. Chill at least 2 hours or overnight.

When ready to serve, whip the cream and brown sugar together until soft peaks form. Unmold the *pavé* onto a serving platter and peel off the paper. Serve in slices, topped with whipped cream.

MAKES 10 SERVINGS

The brandy in the recipe calls for an echo in your glass. Drink Armagnac, Cognac, or an aged, raisiny port.

gale's famous truffles

1½ cups crème fraîche or sour cream
2 tablespoons finely ground espresso-roast coffee beans
12 ounces best-quality bittersweet chocolate, chopped (page 14)
1½ pounds semisweet chocolate
1½ cups Dutch-process cocoa powder

Combine the crème fraîche and coffee in a saucepan and bring to a boil over medium heat. As soon as it boils, turn off the heat.

Meanwhile, put the chopped bittersweet chocolate in a medium bowl. Strain the hot crème fraîche mixture into the bowl. Whisk until the chocolate is melted and the mixture is smooth. Cover and let rest in a cool place overnight—do not refrigerate. The mixture will become firm but not hard.

The next day, using a pastry bag fitted with a large plain tip, pipe bite-size "kisses" (shaped like Hershey's Kisses) of the mixture onto baking sheets lined with parchment paper. Refrigerate briefly just until set, about 30 minutes. Use your palm to gently press down the point that sticks up on each truffle. Transfer to the freezer and freeze until hard, 2 to 3 hours or overnight.

Melt the semisweet chocolate in the top of a double boiler set over barely simmering water. It should be liquid, but not so hot that you can't touch it; if it is too hot for you, wear disposable surgical gloves. Spread the cocoa powder out on a sheet pan with sides.

Working in two batches to avoid crowding the pan of cocoa, dip the frozen truffle centers one at a time into the melted chocolate, shake off any excess, and set them down in the cocoa. When the truffle centers are dipped and the chocolate has started to set, gently but thoroughly shake the sheet pan to roll the truffles around in the cocoa until coated. Carefully remove to another sheet pan and refrigerate, uncovered, 30 minutes. (You can sift the unused cocoa and use it for another purpose.)

Transfer to an airtight container and keep chilled until almost ready to serve. Bring to room temperature before serving.

MAKES 50 TO 60 TRUFFLES

Truffles are so festive that they demand a sparkling drink; wine mavens may squawk, but Gale likes rosé champagne with truffles on her birthday. Or try a spritzer of raspberry syrup and carbonated water.

We've noticed some interesting behavior among people who are lucky enough to eat these cocoa-covered treasures often: our regulars at Brasserie T. Just the word **truffles** is enough to make these chocolate lovers' nostrils twitch with excitement, like a truffle hound on the scent.

These are undoubtedly the best truffles we've ever had, only excepting those of the masters at the Bernachon pastry shop in Lyon, France, who created the mixture of chocolate and crème fraîche on which they are based. When Gale was apprenticing at the Bernachon bakery, she used to eat these at night in her hotel room, one after another, trying to figure out how the Bernachons made them so wonderful. Making truffles is simple and fun, especially when you're dipping them in chocolate and nestling them in cocoa powder—but don't forget to start the process a few days ahead.

Photograph on page 142.

chocolate-sprinkled crème brûlée

2⅓ cups heavy cream

⅓ cup half-and-half

½ vanilla bean, split lengthwise

8 egg yolks

½ cup granulated sugar

4 teaspoons shaved bittersweet or semisweet chocolate (see sidenote)

½ cup coarse, raw, or Demerara sugar

Chocolate vs. vanilla is one of the first oppositions kids learn: red vs. blue, dog vs. cat, and math vs. English are other important ones. You either like one or the other, but not both. Fortunately, as you get older, you learn that combinations, like getting two pets, ordering swirl ice cream cones, and making a dessert like this one, are more rewarding in the end.

In this dessert, we capitalize on the basic structure of a crème brûlée by slipping a fine layer of chocolate between the cool vanilla custard and the hot, crisp sugar. The shavings of chocolate melt darkly into the vanilla background, creating the effect of a tiled mosaic seen through a stained glass covering of melted sugar. You can use either bittersweet or semisweet chocolate here; shave it into curls with a sturdy vegetable peeler, and don't worry if they break up into shards.

Heat the oven to 300 degrees.

Heat the cream, half-and-half, and vanilla bean in a saucepan over medium heat just until it comes to a boil. Immediately turn off the heat. Set aside to infuse for 10 minutes.

Whisk the egg yolks with the granulated sugar in a large bowl just until combined. Whisking constantly, gradually pour in the hot cream mixture. Strain the mixture into a pitcher to smooth it and to remove the vanilla bean.

Pour the mixture into 4 to 6 ovenproof ramekins and arrange in a hot-water bath (page 15). Sprinkle the custards with the chocolate shavings. Bake in the center of the oven until almost set but still jiggly in the center, 30 to 40 minutes. (The custard will finish cooking as it cools.) Remove from the water bath and let cool 15 minutes. Tightly cover each ramekin with plastic wrap, making sure the plastic does not touch the surface of the custard. Refrigerate at least 2 hours or until ready to serve.

When ready to serve, preheat a broiler to very hot (or fire up your kitchen torch). Uncover the custards. Coat the top of each custard completely with an even layer of coarse sugar.

Place the ramekins on a baking sheet and broil until the sugar is melted and well browned, about 2 minutes. Let cool 1 minute before serving.

MAKES 4 TO 6 SERVINGS

The sweetly burnt sugar topping is wonderful with a similarly flavored dark-roast coffee such as Italian roast.

moist chocolate polenta cake

16 ounces semisweet chocolate

8 ounces (2 sticks) unsalted butter

11 eggs, separated

¾ cup granulated sugar

2 tablespoons brandy or liqueur, such as Cognac, Grand Marnier, Amaretto,
   or Sambuca

½ cup imported polenta or domestic cornmeal (not quick-cooking)

Confectioners' sugar

Heat the oven to 300 degrees. Butter a 9×13-inch cake pan and line it with parchment or wax paper.

Melt the chocolate and butter together in the top of a double boiler set over barely simmering water. Stir well and set aside to cool slightly.

Meanwhile, in a mixer fitted with a whisk attachment (or using a hand mixer), whip the egg yolks and ½ cup of the granulated sugar until very light yellow and fluffy.

In a clean, dry bowl, whip the egg whites until soft peaks form. Add the remaining ¼ cup of sugar and continue whipping just until stiff and glossy, about 30 seconds more.

Fold the egg yolks into the hot chocolate mixture until barely blended. Fold in the whites until barely blended. Sprinkle the brandy and polenta evenly over the surface of the batter and fold in. Pour into the prepared pan and bake until the center is firm and a tester inserted into the center comes out clean (a few crumbs are okay), 1 to 1¼ hours.

Let cool in the pan. Cut into squares, dust with confectioners' sugar, and serve.

MAKES 1 CAKE

This oh-so-Italian dessert demands espresso or strong coffee fired up with a shot of grappa—or, for an elegant touch, the liqueur you used to flavor the cake.

We were formally introduced to this cake of dazzling simplicity, texture, and flavor at one of our favorite food shops in the world, Peck in Milan. But it turns out that we've known it for years.

After we perfected our own polenta cake and put it on the menu at the elegant Italian restaurant where we then cooked, we thought we'd impress Rick's parents, both proud Italian cooks, with our creativity. We were sure it was truly a cutting-edge dessert. As soon as Rick's father tasted it, he gasped. "Your grandmother used to make this!" he exclaimed. So much for the cutting edge; but we love it when our food brings back memories. It's one of the best reasons to cook for people, whether you're bringing back old memories or creating new ones.

Photograph on page 144.

milk chocolate–orange mousse

5 ounces milk chocolate

3 ounces semisweet chocolate

2 cups chilled heavy cream

⅔ cup egg whites (from about 5 eggs)

⅓ cup sugar

1 teaspoon freshly grated orange zest

1 tablespoon thawed frozen orange juice concentrate or Grand Marnier liqueur

Even our most chocolate-addicted friends do occasionally grow tired of pure chocolate desserts; that's when we feed them this. Rick loves the combination of orange and chocolate, so that's where we started when we decided it was time to expand our chocolate repertoire. The chocolate hit is subdued by using part milk chocolate; the milk chocolate in turn is sparked with orange flavor to keep it from being **too** smooth. The result is aromatic and magical; it looks like a chocolate dessert, but the flavor is quite orangey.

For the milk chocolate, try to use bar chocolate rather than chips, which don't melt very well. If you must use chips, don't be concerned if they don't melt all the way; your mousse will be chocolate chip instead! You can also serve this mousse frozen.

Melt the chocolates together in the top of a large double boiler set over barely simmering water. Stir well and set aside to cool slightly.

Whip the cream in a mixer fitted with a whisk attachment (or using a hand mixer) until stiff. Refrigerate it.

In a clean, dry bowl, whip the egg whites until soft peaks form. Add the sugar and continue whipping just until stiff and glossy, about 30 seconds more.

Whisking hard, whisk about a third of the egg whites into the chocolate until well blended. Fold in the next third of the egg whites. Fold in the remaining egg whites just until barely combined (the mixture will be streaky). Add the orange zest, orange juice concentrate, and whipped cream and fold until smooth.

Use a pastry bag fitted with a large plain or star tip to pipe the mousse into serving dishes, or simply spoon it into a large serving bowl. Cover lightly and refrigerate at least 1 hour or until ready to serve.

MAKES ABOUT 8 SERVINGS

Chilled elegant mousse and hot earthy coffee are a sensual combination; choose a syrupy Sumatra.

brooklyn blackout cake

FOR THE CAKE

8 tablespoons (1 stick) unsalted butter, softened

¼ cup vegetable shortening

2 cups sugar

3 eggs

2 teaspoons pure vanilla extract

¾ cup cocoa powder, preferably Dutch-process

1 teaspoon baking powder

1 teaspoon baking soda

½ teaspoon salt

2¼ cups cake flour

1 cup milk

FOR THE CUSTARD

3 cups water

2½ cups sugar

1 tablespoon corn syrup

1½ cups cocoa powder, preferably Dutch-process

Scant ⅔ cup cornstarch

6 tablespoons unsalted butter, cut into pieces

½ teaspoon pure vanilla extract

Heat the oven to 375 degrees. Butter and flour two 9-inch round cake pans. Cut 2 circles of parchment paper or wax paper to fit the bottoms of the pans, then press them in.

MAKE THE CAKE

Cream the butter and shortening together in a mixer fitted with a whisk attachment (or using a hand mixer). Add the sugar and mix until light and fluffy. Add the eggs one at a time, mixing after each addition. With the mixer running at low speed, add the vanilla, cocoa, baking powder, baking soda, and salt and mix. With the mixer running at low speed, add about a third of the cake flour, then about a third of the milk, and mix. Repeat with the remaining cake flour and milk and mix.

Pour into the pans and bake until dry and springy to the touch and a tester inserted into the center comes out clean (a few crumbs are okay), 30 to 35 minutes. Let cool in the pans for 15 minutes, then turn out onto wire racks and let cool completely, to room temperature.

New Yorkers are famously argumentative and there's nothing they like better than an argument about something that doesn't exist—that way, no tiresome facts can interfere with the fun of arguing. One of Brooklyn's longest-running arguments (after "Who makes the best pizza, Patsy's or Totonno's?" and "Can you make a real egg cream without Fox's U-bet chocolate syrup?") is about Ebinger's Blackout Cake. Can mere mortals make Blackout Cake, especially without the signature blue box?

Ebinger's was a chain of bakeries in Brooklyn renowned for the purity of its ingredients, the sparkling cleanliness of its stores, and the deep chocolatiness of this cake. Even though the last Ebinger's finally closed in 1972, some devotees kept Blackout Cakes in their freezers for years afterward. Even though we didn't have access to one of these "fossils" from another era, this recipe has been extensively tested on Ebinger's fans, especially our friends Karen and Jeff, who grew up in Brooklyn. They're a tough crowd, but they tell us we've finally got it right. The custard filling is finally the perfect deep, velvety, very, very dark brown.

You can tell this is a commercial baking recipe by the vegetable shortening, which is often combined with butter to keep costs down and quality high. It's not the same as real butter, but it belongs in this recipe for the light crumb it creates. Blackout Cake is best made all in one shot, and served the same day it is made.

Photograph on page 142.

Using a long serrated knife, cut the cake layers horizontally in half. Reserve 3 halves for the finished cake and put the remaining half in a food processor, breaking it up with your hands. Pulse into fine crumbs.

MEANWHILE, MAKE THE CUSTARD

Pour 2½ cups of the water, the sugar, corn syrup, and cocoa powder into a large saucepan and bring to a boil over medium-high heat, whisking occasionally. Dissolve the cornstarch in ½ cup of water. Whisk into the cocoa mixture in the saucepan and return the mixture to a boil, whisking constantly. Cook, whisking constantly, until very thick, 3 to 4 minutes. Remove from the heat and stir in the butter and vanilla. Pour into a bowl. Cover with plastic wrap, lightly pressing the plastic against the surface to prevent a skin from forming. Chill until firm, about 45 minutes.

To finish the cake, place a cake layer on a cake plate or serving platter (reserving the most even layer for the top) and spread with cooled custard. Top with another layer of cake, then custard, then one more layer of cake. Cover the top and sides of the cake with the remaining custard. Coat the cake with the cake crumbs. Chill until ready to serve, at least 2 hours. Serve the same day.

MAKES 8 TO 10 SERVINGS

This is an easy call. Make a classic Brooklyn egg cream: chocolate syrup and milk stirred with seltzer.

steamed chocolate pudding cake

2 eggs
1 cup sugar
1 cup milk
2 tablespoons unsalted butter, melted
½ teaspoon pure vanilla extract
1½ ounces unsweetened chocolate, melted (page 14)
1½ cups all-purpose flour
¼ teaspoon salt
1½ teaspoons baking powder

Heat the oven to 350 degrees. Thickly butter 8 ovenproof ramekins, coffee cups, or custard cups.

Whip the eggs in a mixer fitted with a whisk attachment (or using a hand mixer) until light and fluffy. Add the sugar and mix until combined. Add the milk, butter, vanilla, and chocolate and mix until combined.

Sift the flour with the salt and baking powder twice. Add to the egg mixture and mix until combined. Pour the batter into the ramekins, filling each about two thirds full. Cover each cup with foil. Arrange the cups in a hot-water bath (page 15) and bake until firm on top, 30 to 40 minutes.

Remove the cups from the water and remove the foil. Serve warm.

MAKES 8 SERVINGS

Bring out the cocoa with marshmallows, for a warming double-chocolate hit on a wintry day.

Doesn't the very word "pudding" make your toes curl with pleasure? Us too. When we first moved to England, Gale couldn't understand why people kept referring to her as a "pudding chef." Sure, she was reasonably famous for her bread puddings and rice puddings (find out why on pages 185 and 178), but that was hardly the limit of her repertoire. But she smiled and nodded and eventually figured out that the English call any dessert a "pudding."

This is a classic pudding cake, separating during the baking into a moist chocolate cake on top and a rich chocolate pudding layer underneath. It seems like magic, and it is, but it's easy, too. Serve warm, with whipped cream.

chocolate-banana napoleon

1½ cups heavy cream

6 ounces semisweet chocolate, coarsely chopped, or 1 cup semisweet chocolate morsels

1 sheet frozen puff pastry

¼ teaspoon ground cinnamon

3 tablespoons sugar

3 ripe bananas

1 recipe hot Satin Chocolate Sauce (pages 90–91)

French pastry cooks certainly know which side their bread is buttered on (so to speak). As Napoleon began his rise to power late in the eighteenth century, countless dishes named for him cropped up all over the Empire. The eventual victor was the familiar stack of puff pastry interleaved with creamy filling or fillings.

This is a simplified version of a napoleon: Much of it can be done ahead, and using fresh bananas and frozen puff pastry, a great blessing to home cooks, makes it super easy. It's fun to press your fork through the layers of crisp pastry, cloud-like chocolate, and soft banana, and even more fun to press your teeth through them. The haunting note of cinnamon really pulls the chocolate and banana flavors together.

The day before you plan to serve the dessert, heat the cream in a saucepan over medium heat just until it boils. Immediately turn off the heat. Meanwhile, put the chocolate in a medium bowl. Pour the hot cream over the chocolate and whisk until melted and smooth. Cover and refrigerate overnight (or up to 2 days). Also the day before, remove the frozen puff pastry from the freezer and thaw in the refrigerator, loosely wrapped, overnight.

The next day, heat the oven to 375 degrees. Butter a sheet pan.

Combine the cinnamon and sugar. Unfold the puff pastry sheet onto a lightly floured work surface and sprinkle liberally with cinnamon sugar. Roll the dough with a rolling pin to make it slightly thinner and to press the cinnamon sugar into the surface. Cut into 12 rectangles, making 4 rows of 3 rectangles, and transfer them to the pan. Bake until golden brown and puffed, 10 to 15 minutes. Let cool on a wire rack.

Remove the chocolate mixture from the refrigerator and, using a mixer fitted with a whisk attachment or a paddle attachment, whip it until stiff and fluffed. (*This can be done up to 2 hours in advance. Keep refrigerated.*)

When ready to serve, slice the bananas into ¼-inch-thick coins. Place a rectangle of puff pastry on each of 6 dessert plates. Top each rectangle with a generous dollop of the whipped chocolate, smoothing it to cover the pastry. Divide the banana slices on top, in overlapping rows, then top with another rectangle of puff pastry. Pour warm chocolate sauce over each napoleon, letting it drip down the sides, and serve immediately.

MAKES 6 SERVINGS

A Napoleonic choice: French-roast coffee or Cognac.

chocolate éclairs

FOR THE FILLING

2 cups milk

½ vanilla bean, split lengthwise

6 egg yolks

⅔ cup sugar

¼ cup cornstarch

1 tablespoon cold unsalted butter

FOR THE PASTRY

1 cup water

8 tablespoons (1 stick) unsalted butter

½ teaspoon salt

1½ teaspoons sugar

1 cup all-purpose flour

3 or 4 eggs

FOR THE EGG WASH

1 egg

1½ teaspoons water

FOR THE CHOCOLATE GLAZE

½ cup heavy cream

4 ounces semisweet chocolate, coarsely chopped

MAKE THE FILLING

Bring the milk and vanilla bean to a boil in a saucepan over medium heat. Immediately turn off the heat and set aside to infuse for 15 minutes.

Whisk the egg yolks and sugar until light and fluffy. Add the cornstarch and whisk vigorously until no lumps remain. Whisk in ¼ cup of the hot milk mixture. Whisk in the remaining hot milk mixture, then pour the mixture through a strainer back into the saucepan. Cook over medium-high heat, whisking constantly, until thickened and slowly boiling. Remove from the heat and stir in the butter. Let cool slightly. Cover with plastic wrap, lightly pressing the plastic against the surface to prevent a skin from forming. Chill at least 2 hours or until ready to serve.

Heat the oven to 425 degrees. Line a sheet pan with parchment.

MAKE THE PASTRY

Bring the water, butter, salt, and sugar to a rolling boil in a large saucepan over medium-high heat. When it boils, immediately take the pan off the heat. Add all the flour at once and stir hard

In French, an **éclair** is a flash of lightning, a bright idea, or an instant of time, and that's about how long it will take before your homemade chocolate éclairs will disappear.

Don't fret if your work with the pastry bag comes out a bit lumpy or untidy—just concentrate on getting the elements (light pastry, smooth custard, dark chocolate) right and they'll taste great. The key to the pastry (called **pâte à choux** in French) is to stir very hard when adding the flour, so that it quickly reaches the temperature at which it can absorb the water and begin to develop stretchy gluten fibers. Heating the dough also evaporates some of the moisture, so that the dough can absorb the eggs better. We told you baking was a series of chemistry experiments! When choux pastry is baked, it puffs and stretches into the texture we also love in profiteroles and cream puffs.

In French salons de thé, *or tearooms, they make their coffee with the "French press" method; the coffee comes out thick and fragrant, perfect with a creamy éclair.*

with a wooden spoon until all the flour is incorporated, 30 to 60 seconds. Return to the heat and cook, stirring, 30 seconds, to dry the mixture out slightly.

Scrape the mixture into a mixer fitted with a paddle attachment (or use a hand mixer). With the mixer running at medium speed, working 1 egg at a time, add 3 of the eggs. Stop mixing after each addition to scrape down the sides of the bowl. Mix until the dough is smooth and glossy and the eggs are completely incorporated. The dough should be thick, but should fall slowly and steadily from the beaters when you lift them out of the bowl. If the dough is still clinging to the beaters, add the remaining egg and mix until incorporated.

Using a pastry bag fitted with a large plain tip, pipe fat lengths of dough (about the size and shape of a jumbo hot dog) onto the lined baking sheet, leaving 2 inches between them. You should have 8 to 10 éclairs.

MAKE THE EGG WASH

Whisk the egg and water together. Brush the surface of each éclair with the egg wash. Use your fingers to smooth out any bumps or points of dough that remain on the surface.

Bake 15 minutes, then reduce the heat to 375 degrees and bake until puffed up and light golden brown, about 25 minutes more. Try not to open the oven door too often during the baking. Let cool on the baking sheet.

Fit a medium-size plain pastry tip over your index finger and use it to make a hole in the end of each éclair (or just use your fingertip). Using a pastry bag fitted with a medium-size plain tip, gently pipe the custard into the éclairs, using only just enough to fill the inside (don't stuff them full).

MAKE THE GLAZE

Bring the cream to a boil in a small saucepan over medium heat. Immediately turn off the heat. Put the chocolate in a medium bowl. Pour the hot cream over the chocolate and whisk until melted and smooth. Set aside and keep warm. *(The glaze can be made up to 48 hours in advance. Cover and refrigerate until ready to use, and rewarm in a microwave or over hot water when ready to use.)*

Dip the tops of the éclairs in the warm chocolate glaze and set on a sheet pan. Chill, uncovered, at least 1 hour to set the glaze. Serve chilled.

MAKES 8 TO 10 SERVINGS

white chocolate mint semifreddo

1½ cups heavy cream
5 ounces white chocolate, coarsely chopped
½ cup egg whites (from about 4 eggs)
2 tablespoons sugar
¼ teaspoon pure mint extract

Two days before you plan to serve the dessert, heat the cream over medium heat in a small saucepan just until it boils. Immediately turn off the heat. Place the chocolate in a medium bowl. Pour the hot cream over the chocolate and whisk until melted and smooth. Strain into another bowl, cover, and refrigerate overnight.

The next day, remove the mixture from the refrigerator and, using a mixer fitted with a whisk attachment or a hand mixer, whip it into fluffy, soft peaks. Return it to the refrigerator.

Make collars for the ramekins: Cut 6 strips of wax paper 8 inches long and 3 inches wide. Wrap them around the tops of the ramekins, so that each ramekin has a 1½-inch collar above the top. Tape closed.

Whip the egg whites in a clean dry bowl until soft peaks form, then add the sugar and mint extract and continue whipping until glossy and stiff, about 30 seconds more. Fold into the white chocolate mixture, then spoon the mixture (or pipe through a pastry bag) into the collared ramekins. Smooth the tops. Freeze at least 4 hours or overnight. Remove the collars and serve frozen.

MAKES 6 SERVINGS

➤ *For contrast to the cool mint, brew up sweet, hot espresso and serve it with lemon peel.*

Ganache is a word that we've been seeing on more and more dessert menus. It has a rich, fancy, very French sound, but ganache is just a combination of chocolate and cream. Depending on the proportions, the mixture can be used in a variety of ways: as a glaze, a filling, or a candy center, to name just the ways we use it in this book. With enough cream added, it becomes whip-able, and that's the foundation of this white-chocolate dessert. White chocolate is devastatingly popular, but it's also not exactly chocolate. It's mostly cocoa butter enhanced with sugar and vanilla. White chocolate is not the same thing as the "confectionery coating" or "white coating" you see in the market; real white chocolate contains cocoa butter.

A **semifreddo** ("half-cold," in Italian) is simply a chilled dessert that never quite freezes hard; the texture is smooth, rich, and melting in the mouth. You could also make this with milk or dark chocolate instead of white, or serve it with Satin Chocolate Sauce (you'll find the recipe on pages 90–91).

Note that you'll need two days (though less than an hour of work time) and six 1-cup ramekins or dessert cups for making this dessert. The paper "collars" help the mixture rise above the edges of the ramekins, which makes for a fetching presentation.

crunchy chocolate hazelnut bars

12 ounces semisweet chocolate
½ cup Nutella, available at large supermarkets
6 tablespoons heavy cream, heated to lukewarm
1½ cups crushed (not powdered) Pepperidge Farm Bordeaux cookies
2 tablespoons cocoa powder
¾ cup crème fraîche or sour cream
3 tablespoons Amaretto or another almond liqueur
¾ cup heavy cream, chilled
Confectioners' sugar for dusting
Whipped cream, for serving (optional)

Gianduja gelato, Baci chocolate kisses, and Nutella paste are popular European sweets that combine chocolate and hazelnuts, but the combination has never hit the big time here. Now we've sneaked it into a homey-sounding cake that is actually remarkably elegant.

The idea is to reconstruct the combination of chocolate and crisp that makes the Kit Kat® candy bar so addictive. There are two layers of mousse, one with bits of crisp cookie mixed in. Both are of very soft chocolate that quickly melts on the tongue; complementary flavors like hazelnut, crème fraîche, and almond are added with a light hand.

The bubbles in demi-sec *Champagne echo the crisp layers here;* demi-sec, *meaning half-dry, has a bit of natural sweetness that helps it stand up to the chocolate.*

Butter an 8-inch square baking pan and line it with wax or parchment paper, pressing into the corners.

Melt 6 ounces of the chocolate in the top of a double boiler set over barely simmering water, stirring occasionally. Whisk in the Nutella, the warmed cream, and the crushed cookies. Pour into the pan and, working quickly with the back of a spatula, spread the mixture out to cover the bottom of the pan. Refrigerate 15 minutes, then dust with 1 tablespoon of the cocoa and return to the refrigerator while you make the top chocolate layer.

Melt the remaining 6 ounces of chocolate in the top of a double boiler set over barely simmering water, stirring occasionally. Stir in the crème fraîche and Amaretto and let cool to room temperature.

Meanwhile, whip the heavy cream until stiff. Fold into the chocolate mixture. Pour over the chilled chocolate layer and spread evenly.

If you want the top to look more decorative, rough it up with a spatula, bringing up peaks and points on the surface. Chill until hard, about 2 hours.

To serve, use the tip of a sharp knife to cut sixteen ½×4-inch bars. Dust the surface with the remaining tablespoon of cocoa and a sprinkling of confectioners' sugar. On each of 8 serving plates, place 2 bars, crisscrossed. If possible, let rest at room temperature for 20 minutes to warm up slightly. If desired, serve with a dollop of whipped cream.

MAKES 8 SERVINGS

citrus

"Oranges . . . the taste equivalent of gold."
Alice Walker

perfected lemon tart

tangerine-soaked tea cake

pink grapefruit sorbet

not-your-usual lemon meringue pie

elsie's lemon poppyseed cake

oranges simmered in red wine

brown derby grapefruit cake with
  grapefruit–cream cheese frosting

cathy's lemon buttercups

chocolate-dipped pink grapefruit rind

orange sandwich cookies

four-citrus granita

lemon-buttermilk ice cream with
  strawberry-rhubarb preserves

double-stuffed lime-ooo bars

personality profile: Citrus is the brightest of all the ingredients, a breath of warmth and light that is perky enough to spark any gathering. Her tongue can be sharp, but her sweet nature makes it all worth-while. Dressed in sunny, bright colors and wearing an irresistible perfume, citrus is never tiresome and always feels fresh and bright, waking up tired palates with a squeeze.

BUTTER SUGAR FLOUR EGGS

You citrus lovers know who you are. You're the ones who find yourselves ordering lemon tart night after night, who look forward to winter because it means that the tangerines are coming, who are content to nibble on a chocolate chip cookie now and then but would walk over hot coals for the perfect lemon square. Others say that chocolate breeds obsession, but you happen to be addicted to the aromatic combination of puckery tartness and bracing sweetness only citrus can provide.

We have to confess that we sometimes belong in this group of dessert radicals. For anyone who loves to eat as much as we do (and we hope that means you), lemons and limes, oranges, and grapefruits are a godsend. After a wonderful meal (or ten or twenty if we're on a research trip in Paris or New York) sometimes we simply don't have the appetite for an intense chocolate or substantial fruity dessert. But citrus, with its bright flavors, sun-soaked colors, and light perfumes, always has a magically enticing appeal.

Citrus has been weaving its spell at least since the year 4000 B.C., when citrons, the ancestors of lemons, limes, and oranges, were already being cultivated in India. As citrus fruits scattered all around the globe, hugging the warmth of the equator, geography and interbreeding gave rise to a vast and colorful family that includes grapefruits and mandarins, clementines and bergamots, blood oranges and kumquats, tangelos and honeybells. The orange family, with its lovely blossoms and natural sweetness, is probably the most universally beloved. The Romans grew thousands of acres of oranges in North Africa and Spain (to produce the orange-blossom essence they sprinkled on desserts), but after invaders tore up the orchards it took almost another thousand years for oranges and lemons to make their way back up and into Europe. Crusaders carried lemons back to France from far-off Palestine.

Nineteenth-century American children looked forward all year to the one or two oranges they might see in their stockings at Christmastime, and ate them slowly to make them last, like candy. Today orange juice is such a standard feature of daily life in America that we barely notice its extraordinary flavor, but when you make our Tangerine-Soaked Tea Cake or Perfected Lemon Tart, you'll gain a new appreciation of the whole citrus family.

Throughout this chapter, we use the juice, flesh, and the incredible scented peel of the fruits to lend flavor and, just as important, aroma, to our desserts. We always use fresh juice or, if we're cooking in bulk, frozen unsweetened concentrates. Fresh-squeezed orange and grapefruit juices are easy to get and also to make for recipes. Fresh lemon and lime juices require a bit more elbow grease, but there is no real substitute. You can get frozen lemon juice at the supermarket, but those lime and lemon juices bottled in plastic are thin, sour, and have lost their all-important fragrance. Roll the whole fruits on a hard surface or microwave them for 30 seconds beforehand to get the most juice out of them.

To zest a whole fruit, you can use a vegetable peeler, being careful to pick up only the thin top layer of zest and leaving the white pith behind. If you just need a few teaspoons, use a hand-held paddle grater or, if you can find one, an efficient zester.

The key to great citrus desserts lies in capturing and celebrating the fruit's tartness, and then toning it down. We do this with flavor hits of sweetness (as in Chocolate-Dipped Pink Grapefruit Rind) and creaminess (as in Lemon-Buttermilk Ice Cream and Brown Derby Grapefruit Cake with Grapefruit–Cream Cheese Frosting). Then we get out of the way, letting the flavors speak for themselves and letting these everyday fruits shine like the sun.

perfected lemon tart

After a filling, savory meal, what could be better than the tartness of lemon, smoothed with sweet and creamy additions and poured into a crumbly crust? We realized the power of a good lemon tart after eating our way through a glorious multicourse meal at the London restaurant Chez Nico that ended with the best lemon tart we had ever had. After finishing it, we magically felt hungry again—for more lemon tart! All eight people at the table had another piece. This easy, classic version has a delicately nutty walnut crust.

⬯

This lemon tart has such a perfect balance of sweet and tart that it can dance with a whole range of hot brews, from dark-roast coffee at one end of the flavor spectrum to camomile tea at the other.

FOR THE CRUST

10 tablespoons (1¼ sticks) unsalted butter, slightly softened

¾ cup confectioners' sugar

1 egg

1⅝ cups all-purpose flour

¼ cup finely ground walnuts (page 14)

FOR THE FILLING

5 eggs

1½ cups granulated sugar

1 scant cup fresh lemon juice (from about 6 lemons)

¾ cup heavy cream

Freshly grated zest of 1½ lemons

MAKE THE CRUST

Cream the butter in a mixer fitted with a paddle attachment (or using a hand mixer) until fluffy. Add the confectioners' sugar and mix well. Add the egg and mix well. Add the flour and mix just until incorporated. Add the walnuts and mix well, but do not work the dough more than necessary.

Shape the dough into a thick disk, wrap it in wax paper, and refrigerate 1 to 2 hours. Roll out for a 10-inch tart pan with a removable bottom, following the directions on page 31. Press the rolled-out crust lightly against the edges of the tart pan, leaving a thick edge sticking up a bit over the top edge of the pan. Prebake the crust as for a single-crust pie crust, following the directions on page 31.

MAKE THE FILLING

Once the crust is baked and cooled, heat the oven to 325 degrees. Whisk the eggs, then whisk in the sugar until blended. Whisk in the lemon juice, cream, and lemon zest. Pour into the baked tart shell and bake in the center of the oven until almost set but still soft in the center, 35 to 40 minutes. (The filling will finish cooking as it cools.) Let cool at room temperature. Remove the sides of the pan, cover, and refrigerate at least 2 hours. *(Or refrigerate until ready to serve, up to 24 hours.)* Serve cold.

MAKES 1 TART

tangerine-soaked tea cake

FOR THE CAKE

¼ cup plain dry bread crumbs

Freshly grated zest of 3 tangerines or oranges

3 tablespoons fresh tangerine or orange juice (see sidenote)

1 tablespoon fresh lemon juice

3 cups sifted all-purpose flour

½ teaspoon baking soda

½ teaspoon salt

8 ounces (2 sticks) unsalted butter, slightly softened

2 cups sugar

3 eggs

1 cup buttermilk

FOR THE GLAZE

½ cup fresh tangerine juice

1 tablespoon fresh lemon juice

⅓ cup sugar

MAKE THE CAKE

Heat the oven to 350 degrees. Butter a 6-cup loaf pan. Line the bottom with parchment or wax paper, pressing it in firmly. Pour the bread crumbs into the pan and shake to coat the sides, then tip out any extra crumbs.

Stir the tangerine zest, tangerine juice, and lemon juice together and set aside.

Sift the pre-sifted flour, baking soda, and salt together.

Cream the butter in a mixer fitted with a paddle attachment (or using a hand mixer) until fluffy. Add the sugar and mix well. Add the eggs one at a time, mixing after each addition. With the mixer running at low speed, and mixing after each addition, add the dry ingredients and the buttermilk in alternating batches until the batter is just mixed. Add the fruit juice and zest and mix.

Pour into the pan and set on a sheet pan. Bake on the sheet pan until the cake is firm in the center and a tester inserted into the center comes out dry and clean (a few crumbs are okay), 1 to 1¼ hours.

MEANWHILE, MAKE THE GLAZE

In a bowl, stir the juices and sugar together until the sugar is dissolved.

The sweet, perfumey tangerine is a member of the Mandarin family, as are clementines, satsumas, and other loose-skinned oranges that are easy to peel and exceptionally flavorful. We love their fragrance, taste, and even their name: the very word **tangerine** has a satisfying juiciness to it. Their season runs from early winter to late spring; at other times, feel free to use fresh oranges instead, or good-quality juice from the market. One year, we wanted to serve slices of this to all of our customers as Brasserie T's birthday cake, which falls on Bastille Day, July Fourteenth. The party's theme was "Let Them Eat Cake!" With no tangerines at hand, we used Tropicana® tangerine-orange juice in all 46 cakes we made, and they were terrific.

Cooking with Julia Child at home when Gale filmed her BAKING WITH JULIA episodes was both a delight and an honor. As she watched Julia cheerfully dress a salad using her turkey baster, Gale came up with the idea for "basting" this cake with its citrusy glaze. A pastry brush will work, too, but may rough up the surface of the cake.

When the cake is done, let cool in the pan 15 minutes (it will still be warm). Run a knife around the sides of the pan. Set a wire rack on a sheet pan with sides (to catch the glaze) and turn the cake out onto the rack. Peel off the wax paper. Using a turkey baster or pastry brush, spread the glaze all over the top and sides of the cake and let soak in. Use all the glaze, including any glaze that drips through onto the sheet pan.

Let cool at room temperature. Wrap in plastic wrap and refrigerator. *(Well wrapped, the cake will last up to a week.)* Serve at room temperature, in thin slices.

MAKES 1 CAKE

This juicy cake's sweetness is especially good when cut with unsweetened iced tea—cooled with refreshing mint ice cubes.

pink grapefruit sorbet

When our friend Bob Payton brought us to England to reinvent the cuisine at his luxurious country-house hotel, Stapleford Park, he was determined to show the English that American cooking could be brilliant. To that end, he asked us to create perfect recipes for homey American treats like chocolate-chip cookies and pecan pie, as well as for more elegant fare.

This was one of Bob's favorites. In fact, he loved it so much that he would go around the dining room insisting that each customer try it. Fortunately, they loved it, too. It makes a simple, light dessert or "intermezzo" between courses that looks beautiful in a glass or white bowl. If you don't have a sorbet maker, you can make it into a granita by using the method for Four-Citrus Granita on page 167.

1¾ cups fresh pink grapefruit juice
¼ cup fresh lemon juice
2 cups water
1½ cups sugar

Combine the fruit juices in a bowl.

Bring the water and sugar to a boil in a medium saucepan over medium heat. Skim off any scum that rises to the top. Stir into the fruit juices, let cool slightly, and taste for sweetness.

Freeze in an ice-cream maker according to the manufacturer's instructions. Serve in frosted glasses.

MAKES 4 SERVINGS

Sorbet is so light, cool, and refreshing that it practically is a drink! We wouldn't add a thing.

not-your-usual lemon meringue pie

FOR THE LEMON CURD

4 large eggs

1 cup sugar

⅔ cup fresh lemon juice

Freshly grated zest of 1 lemon

4 tablespoons (½ stick) cold unsalted butter, cut into pieces

FOR THE PHYLLO TRIANGLES

6 sheets thawed phyllo dough (see sidenote)

8 tablespoons (1 stick) unsalted butter, melted

6 tablespoons sugar

FOR THE MERINGUE

1 cup egg whites (from about 8 eggs), at room temperature

¾ cup light brown sugar, packed

FOR THE GARNISH

8 mint sprigs

Confectioners' sugar

½ cup pureed fresh or frozen raspberries (optional)

THE DAY BEFORE YOU PLAN TO SERVE THE DESSERT,
MAKE THE LEMON CURD

Bring about an inch of water to a simmer in a large saucepan.
Whisk the eggs and sugar together in a mixer fitted with a whisk
attachment (or using a hand mixer) until very light yellow and
fluffy. Whisk in the lemon juice and lemon zest. Rest the mixing
bowl in the saucepan, with the bowl's base above the simmering
water (pour out some of the water if necessary). Cook, whisking
occasionally, until the mixture is thickened and custardy, about 15
minutes. Remove the bowl from the heat and stir in the butter. Let
cool, cover, and refrigerate overnight.

MAKE THE PHYLLO TRIANGLES

Heat the oven to 350 degrees. Line 2 large sheet pans with parchment paper. Place 1 sheet of phyllo on one pan and brush generously with melted butter. Sprinkle evenly with 1 tablespoon of
sugar, then place another sheet of phyllo on top. Brush with
melted butter, sprinkle with 1 tablespoon sugar, and lay another
sheet of phyllo on top. Brush the top with melted butter and sprinkle with 1 tablespoon sugar.

Any fresh lemon meringue pie is a
wonderful thing, but this one is a reve-
lation. All the key elements are there:
homemade lemon curd stacked with an
easy meringue and crisp triangles cut
from store-bought phyllo makes for a
pretty (and pretty tall) dessert that
lies somewhere between a pie and a
napoleon.

Working with store-bought phyllo
dough is much easier than you'd think.
Keep the box of phyllo refrigerated; or,
if you buy it frozen, thaw it overnight
in the refrigerator. When ready to use,
unroll the pastry onto a work surface
and keep it covered with a towel. You
can lightly mist the towel with water if
you have a spray bottle handy, but
don't dampen it under the tap: Too
much moisture causes the sheets to
stick together. We'd definitely recommend making the phyllo triangles in
advance; they keep beautifully when
stored in an airtight container.

The meringue can be made up to two
hours in advance and whipped up again
just before assembling the dessert; it
can also be browned under a hot
broiler if you don't have a blowtorch.
(But note that blowtorches are easy to
find at hardware stores, and you can
even order a miniature one from the
Williams-Sonoma catalogue.)

Photograph on page 130.

Repeat on the other pan with the remaining 3 sheets phyllo, butter, and sugar. You will have 2 stacks of phyllo dough, each 3 sheets thick. You may not use all the melted butter.

With the tip of a sharp knife, cut each stack into 3 strips and cut each strip into 4 triangles, as shown on page 131. Cover both stacks with parchment paper. Place one of the pans on top of the other to weight it down. Then place another, empty sheet pan on the very top. (This is to keep the phyllo from buckling during baking.) Bake 10 to 12 minutes, until the phyllo is golden brown. Let cool without unstacking the pans.

MAKE THE MERINGUE

Whip the egg whites in a clean, dry bowl until soft peaks form. Add the brown sugar and continue whipping until stiff and glossy, about 30 seconds more. Gently spoon the meringue into a pastry bag fitted with a large plain tip.

ASSEMBLE THE DESSERT

Squeeze a dab of meringue on each of 8 plates and press one phyllo triangle down on it. Spoon on a heaping tablespoon of lemon curd in the center, then pipe on some meringue. Brown the meringue with a blowtorch (or under a broiler). Place another phyllo triangle on top and repeat, topping off with a final phyllo triangle. Garnish with a mint sprig, a dusting of confectioners' sugar, and raspberry puree, if desired (see photograph on page 131).

MAKES 8 SERVINGS; CAN BE HALVED

Lemon meringue pie, even a fancy one like this, always takes us back to our favorite diner, the Golden Bear in Deerfield, Illinois — and its "endless cup o' coffee." For real diner flavor, add half-and-half.

elsie's lemon poppyseed cake

⅓ cup (2½ ounces) poppyseeds

1 tablespoon freshly grated lemon zest

1 cup milk

2 eggs

1½ cups sugar

2 cups all-purpose flour

2½ teaspoons baking powder

½ teaspoon ground cinnamon

¼ teaspoon ground nutmeg

¾ cup vegetable oil

1 teaspoon pure vanilla extract

1 teaspoon almond extract

Mix the poppyseeds, lemon zest, and milk together. Set aside to soak for at least 1 hour or overnight. If soaking overnight, keep refrigerated.

Heat the oven to 350 degrees. Line a 6-cup loaf pan with wax paper.

Whip the eggs and sugar in a mixer fitted with a whisk attachment (or using a hand mixer) until light and fluffy.

Sift the dry ingredients together. With the mixer running, drizzle the oil, vanilla extract, and almond extract into the egg mixture. With the mixer running, add alternating batches of dry ingredients and poppyseed-milk mixture to the egg mixture. The batter will be somewhat thin. Pour into the pan.

Bake 1 to 1¼ hours, until the center is raised and cracked and the whole cake is firm and dry on the top. Try not to open the oven during the baking. Do not underbake, as this cake falls easily.

Let cool in the pan for 5 minutes, then turn out onto a wire rack and let cool before serving.

MAKES 1 CAKE

↦ *As you know from drinking espresso, lemon and sweet black coffee are a great combination; sweet spice tea is also terrific with this delicate cake.*

Poppyseeds always make Gale, and anyone who's heard Gale's stories, think of her Grandma Elsie Grossman. She was a baking fiend, and cookies were a specialty. In fact, she made so many cookies that she had to keep them in a separate freezer in the basement. On family visits, after the eight-hour drive to Grandma Elsie's in Cleveland, Gale and her brother Gary shot out of the car like cannonballs aimed for the freezer. They didn't even wait for the cookies to thaw.

Grandma Elsie's basement also contained stacks of illicit Fiestaware, covered with a bright orange glaze that Grandpa George (thus our son's name Giorgio), a chemist, had invented. The dishes were recalled because it turned out that the orange glaze took its brightness from uranium, but she still couldn't bear to part with them. Additional hazards in the obstacle course were bottles of fermenting homemade root beer, which often exploded, and an ironing board that tended to fall out from the wall. But it was all worth it for the cookies.

Grandma Elsie put poppyseeds in lots of her cookies, and they pop up often in Gale's baking, too. Soaking poppyseeds in milk is a great way to tease out their elusive flavor. This cake tastes best the day **after** it is made.

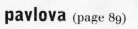

pavlova (page 89)

not-your-usual lemon meringue pie (page 126)

Follow this guide for cutting the phyllo or slicing the Dark German Chocolate Cake (page 100).

cathy's lemon buttercups (page 164)

**honeycomb and honey-lavender ice cream
with warm strawberry salad** (page 46)

warm taffy apples with cinnamon pastry twists

(page 180)

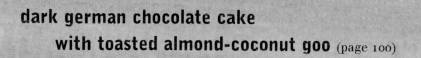

**dark german chocolate cake
with toasted almond-coconut goo** (page 100)

sugar-crusted breton butter cake (page 26)

apricot rice pudding (page 78)

gale's famous truffles (page 106)

three-color poached pears (page 179)

144

moist chocolate polenta cake (page 108)

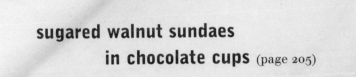

sugared walnut sundaes in chocolate cups (page 205)

new year's eve venetian mask cookies (page 276)

*You can also
use the grating
disk of the
food processor
when making
this shortbread.*

lydia's austrian
raspberry shortbread (page 23)

brooklyn blackout cake (page 110)

**fresh mozzarella with sweet strawberries
and mint drizzle** (page 228)

raspberry-stuffed french toast (page 58)

152

coconut cream pie
with chocolate-painted crust (page 84)

**hungarian crépes
with peanut butter and jam** (page 79)

halloween boo!scotti (page 266)

holiday cookie projects (page 272)

sharon's stickier buns (page 70)

brown butter tuiles (page 29)

oranges simmered in red wine

4 seedless oranges

1 bottle (750 ml) light-bodied red wine, such as Beaujolais or a young
   Chianti

2 cups brewed cinnamon or other spiced tea

2 cinnamon sticks

4 whole cloves

2 star anise pods

6 black peppercorns

¼ cup honey

¼ cup light brown sugar, packed

4 fresh mint leaves, julienned

Anyone who savors the cold, fruity snap of a glass of sangría will adore this concoction. Fruit poached in wine is, to us, the essence of simple European style—and one of our favorite light desserts. Oranges aren't a traditional choice for poaching (see our version of poached pears, page 179), but we love the jewel-like colors of this dish: The slices stay bright orange in the center, picking up the purply-garnet hues of the red wine around the edges. This would make a wonderful no-fat dessert with Thanksgiving Cranberry Angel Food Cake (page 265). Serve chilled, with ice cream.

Photograph on page 140.

Cut a slice off the top and bottom of each orange to expose the flesh. Cutting from top to bottom and following the contours of the orange, completely remove the peel and white pith. Discard the peel and set the oranges aside.

Combine all of the remaining ingredients except the mint leaves in a saucepan. Heat to a simmer. Add the whole peeled oranges and simmer, uncovered, 10 minutes, turning the oranges every 2 minutes. Remove from the heat and set aside to cool to room temperature in the liquid. Turn occasionally. Chill.

To serve, cut each orange crosswise into ½-inch-thick slices. Spread the slices, overlapping them, on small serving plates. (The outsides of the oranges will be redder than the insides.) Drizzle a little liquid over each plate and sprinkle with mint.

MAKES 4 SERVINGS

A delicate floral tea like jasmine can balance the tartness of the dessert and pick up on its spicy notes

brown derby grapefruit cake with grapefruit–cream cheese frosting

FOR THE CAKE

3 eggs, separated, at room temperature

¼ cup vegetable oil

¼ cup fresh grapefruit juice

3 tablespoons freshly grated grapefruit zest

½ teaspoon freshly grated lemon zest

1½ cups sifted cake flour

¾ cup sugar

1½ teaspoons baking powder

½ teaspoon salt

FOR THE FROSTING

2 grapefruits

12 ounces cream cheese, slightly softened

2 teaspoons fresh lemon juice

1 teaspoon freshly grated lemon zest

¾ cup confectioners' sugar

This legendary layer cake made its debut at Hollywood's Brown Derby restaurant. According to THE BROWN DERBY RESTAURANT BOOK, owner Robert Cobb (as in Cobb salad) created it after gossip doyenne Louella Parsons demanded more "diet" food on the menu.

Any diet that includes cream cheese frosting sounds good to us. This is a very beautiful, tangy, and fragrant cake; the unexpected tang of grapefruit makes it very popular. Using pink grapefruit for the top is a pretty touch.

Photograph on pages 136–137.

Heat the oven to 350 degrees. Butter and flour a 9-inch cake pan. Cut a circle of parchment paper or wax paper to fit the bottom of the pan and press it in.

MAKE THE CAKE

Whisk the egg yolks in a mixer fitted with a whisk attachment (or using a hand mixer). With the mixer running, drizzle in the oil. Drizzle in the grapefruit juice. Add the grapefruit and lemon zests and mix.

Sift the sifted flour, sugar, baking powder, and salt together. Add to the egg yolk mixture and mix.

Whip the egg whites in a clean, dry bowl until stiff but not dry. Fold into the cake batter. Pour the batter into the pan. Bake until dry and springy in the center, 25 to 30 minutes. Let cool in the pan 15 minutes. Run a spatula around the edge of the cake, turn out onto a wire rack, peel the paper off the top, and set aside to finish cooling.

MAKE THE FROSTING

Using a small, sharp knife, cut a slice off the top and bottom of each grapefruit to expose the flesh. Cutting from top to bottom and following the contours of the fruit, remove the peel and white pith completely. Using a small sharp knife, cut the grapefruit sections free of the membrane and set aside to drain on paper towels, turning occasionally.

Beat the cream cheese in a mixer fitted with a paddle attachment (or using a hand mixer) until smooth and fluffy. Add the lemon juice and zest and mix. Gradually add the sugar and mix until smooth. Chop 1 or 2 grapefruit sections to measure 2 teaspoons, add to the frosting, and mix.

With a long serrated knife, cut the cake in half horizontally. Lift off the top layer and transfer the bottom layer to a serving plate. Frost the cut side and arrange half the remaining grapefruit sections on top. Replace the top layer of cake. Frost the top and sides and arrange the remaining grapefruit sections on top.

MAKES 1 CAKE

A glass of super-chilled milk is great with the soft and lofty layers of this cake, and with its sweet-and-sour flavors. Or take it to a tea party.

cathy's lemon buttercups

2 cups all-purpose flour
¼ teaspoon salt
8 ounces (2 sticks) cold unsalted butter, cut into pieces
½ cup sour cream
2 egg yolks
8 ounces cream cheese, at room temperature
½ cup confectioners' sugar
1 teaspoon pure vanilla extract
1 teaspoon freshly grated lemon zest
Confectioners' sugar

Combine the flour and salt in a large bowl. Add the butter and, using your fingertips, pinch the ingredients together into a sandy, crumbly mixture.

In a mixer fitted with a paddle attachment (or using a hand mixer), mix the sour cream and 1 egg yolk until very smooth. Add the flour mixture and mix until the dough comes together. The dough may feel a little dry. Form into a disk, wrap it in plastic wrap, and chill at least 4 hours or overnight.

In a mixer fitted with a paddle attachment, mix the cream cheese, remaining egg yolk, the ½ cup confectioners' sugar, vanilla, and lemon zest until smooth.

On a work surface thickly dusted with confectioners' sugar, roll out the pastry to a squarish or rectangular shape, ⅛ inch thick. Using the tip of a sharp knife or a pizza cutter, cut into 3×3-inch squares. Place a teaspoon of filling in the center of each square.

Gently gather the corners of a square together with your fingers (but don't pinch them together). Rest in a mini muffin cup, but don't push the cookie down into the cup. Repeat with the remaining squares and refrigerate 30 minutes.

Heat the oven to 375 degrees. Bake until light golden brown, 25 to 30 minutes. The cookies will settle down into the cup and the "petals" will open outward slightly. Let cool in the pan on a wire rack.

MAKES ABOUT 24 COOKIES

The delicious filling has the flavor and texture of a fresh cheese danish; it always makes us want a cup of morning coffee, such as French roast.

Rick grew up in snowy Rochester, New York, and his family keeps winter at bay by baking Christmas cookies that bring color and cheer. The baking begins in October. All the women in Rick's large family seem to bake a lot, but Aunt Cathy is the queen of the cookie sheets. She dazzles us every year with her four Christmas trees and seemingly endless variety of Christmas cookies. The trays she puts out for visitors hold hundreds of cookies, and we always eat at least fifteen, one of each variety. These are our perennial favorite.

Pale yellow lemon buttercups are an outrageously cute, delicate, and buttery cookie, filled with a dab of cheese filling that reminds us of a classic cheese danish. The flowery shape is achieved by pushing the sides of a "cup" of cookie dough inward, so that the corners form four blooming petals.

Photograph on page 132.

chocolate-dipped pink grapefruit rind

1 large pink grapefruit
2 cups sugar
2 cups water
6 ounces semisweet chocolate

There aren't many items we would crave from a thirteenth-century dessert menu. Consider baked pears stuffed with lentils, cream-and-mustard pudding with honey, and figs simmered in beef broth. But candied fruit, a familiar sight at medieval banquets, is still a wonderful thing. Just as olives, fish, and capers were (and are) preserved with salt, fruit was simmered in sugar syrup to preserve its color, taste, and texture.

Here, we use the technique on something we used to throw away: the rind of a thick-skinned grapefruit (or orange). The white pith, often dismissed as "bitter," acts as a sponge for the syrup and reveals its own delicate flavor and softly chewy texture. Whenever we make Brown Derby Grapefruit Cake (page 162), we save the rind for making these pretty and toothsome "comfits," as Chaucer might have called them. The chocolate is a very modern, and very optional, addition. If you prefer, roll the finished candies in granulated sugar instead, for a bit of crunch.

Cut a slice off the top and bottom of the grapefruit to expose the flesh. Cutting from top to bottom and following the contours of the fruit, cut off the rind and white pith in 1-inch-wide strips. Scrape off any grapefruit pulp adhering to the strips, but leave the pith intact.

You now have several 1-inch-wide strips of grapefruit rind and pith. Cut each one into strips, each about ¼ inch wide by 3 inches long.

Meanwhile, boil a kettle full of water. Pour about a quart of the boiling water into a saucepan, return to a boil, add all the grapefruit rind, and boil 30 seconds. Drain in a strainer and rinse under cold running water. Repeat the boiling and rinsing process 2 times more, using fresh boiling water from the kettle each time.

Combine the sugar and 4 cups water in a saucepan and bring to a boil. Add the blanched rind and reduce the heat to a simmer. Simmer until tender, about 1 hour. Drain in a strainer and let cool 15 minutes until cool enough to handle. Using your fingers, arrange the strips on a wire rack so that they do not touch each other. Let cool.

Melt the chocolate in the top of a double boiler set over barely simmering water. Line a baking sheet with parchment or wax paper. Using your fingers, dip the strips into the chocolate, coating about two thirds of each strip. Let excess chocolate drip back into the pot. Place the coated strips on the baking sheets. Let cool at room temperature. Store, refrigerated, in an airtight container.

MAKES ABOUT 50 PIECES

Nibble on these intense, sweet morsels when the time comes for heady after-dinner drinks like Cognac.

orange sandwich cookies

FOR THE COOKIES
10 tablespoons (1¼ sticks) unsalted butter, slightly softened
Freshly grated zest of 2 medium oranges
⅔ cup sifted confectioners' sugar
¾ teaspoon pure vanilla extract
⅛ teaspoon salt
1½ cups sifted flour
Confectioners' sugar
FOR THE FILLING
½ cup sifted Dutch-process cocoa powder
⅔ cup granulated sugar
3 tablespoons unsalted butter
⅓ cup heavy cream

Heat the oven to 325 degrees.

MAKE THE COOKIES
Mix the butter, orange zest, and ⅔ cup confectioners' sugar in a mixer fitted with a paddle attachment (or using a hand mixer) until light and fluffy. Add the vanilla and salt and mix. Add the sifted flour and mix until smooth. Refrigerate 30 minutes.

On ungreased cookie sheets, and working in batches if necessary, drop level teaspoons of the chilled dough 2½ inches apart. One by one, pick up the dough balls, roll into a smooth ball, and replace on the cookie sheet. Spread about 3 tablespoons of confectioners' sugar on a plate. Dip the bottom of a drinking glass into the sugar and use it to press the dough balls flat, into 1¼-inch circles. Dip the glass into the sugar as needed to keep the bottom dry and coated.

Bake until golden brown around the edges, 12 to 15 minutes. Let cool on the cookie sheets for 2 minutes. Transfer to wire racks and let cool completely.

MEANWHILE, MAKE THE FILLING
Mix the cocoa and sugar together. Melt the butter in a saucepan over low heat. Add the cocoa mixture and the cream and cook, stirring, until thickened, about 3 minutes. Set aside to cool; the mixture will continue to thicken as it cools.

To assemble the cookies, liberally spread half of the orange cookies with cocoa filling, keeping the filling a little bit away from

Like an Oreo in reverse, with blond cookies encasing a dark brown filling, these buttery little sandwiches are marvelously "pop-able." We make them small, so that you can just pop them in your mouth one after another. In fact, these cookies resemble an elegant French petit four as much as a homey American Oreo cookie. The orange and chocolate flavors are wonderful together.

the edges. Cover with a plain cookie and press together gently to create a sandwich. Store in an airtight container.

MAKES ABOUT 30 SANDWICH COOKIES

Earl Grey tea, flavored with the oil of the citrus fruit called bergamot, echoes the orange but is strong enough to stand up to the chocolate in these cookies. Add milk to cut its acidity.

four-citrus granita

The four members of the citrus family we know well—parents grapefruit and orange, baby lemons and limes—are merely the American branch of a truly global clan. Citrus fruits have fanned out across the world from their ancient home in China, with pomelos, bergamots, citrons, satsumas, kumquats, and even the modest ugli fruit taking root wherever the air is warm and the sun strong.

For this granita—a chunky, crystallized, even more refreshing version of sorbet—any kind and number of citrus juices can be used, though the overall effect should not be too tart. There should be a chorus of fruit, with no dominant voice.

Our inspiration for this recipe was the best glass of juice we ever had, at breakfast at our friend Roxanne's house. It was a grand meal—hash browns, sautéed tomatoes with herbs, fried fresh eggs with black pepper, sourdough bread, salty white cheese, and pitchers of just-squeezed juice from a mixed bag of citrus fruits grown by Roxanne's friends—that reminded us that sometimes there's just nothing like home cooking. This granita takes us back to that meal. It is great at brunch.

1¼ cups fresh orange or tangerine juice
½ cup fresh grapefruit juice
3 tablespoons fresh lemon juice
1 tablespoon fresh lime juice
¾ cup water
¾ cup sugar

Mix the citrus juices together in a bowl.

Bring the water and sugar to a boil in a saucepan, stirring occasionally. Turn off the heat and skim off any scum that rises to the top. Pour 1 cup of the syrup into the citrus juices and stir to combine. (Reserve the remaining syrup in the refrigerator for another use, such as sweetening iced tea or lemonade.)

Pour into ice cube trays to a depth of no more than ½ inch. Freeze overnight. At the same time, freeze the metal blade for your food processor and glasses for serving.

When ready to serve, unmold the cubes into a food processor fitted with the metal blade. Process, pulsing, just until crushed. Serve immediately in frosted glasses.

MAKES 4 TO 6 SERVINGS

We like to pour Champagne over the granita at the table, transforming it into an aromatic, slurpable slush.

lemon-buttermilk ice cream
with strawberry-rhubarb preserves

FOR THE PRESERVES

1½ pounds rhubarb, leaves trimmed off (see sidenote) and stems trimmed
of any brown edges, cut into 1-inch lengths

1½ pounds strawberries, green parts trimmed off, cut in half

1 cup water

Sugar

1½ tablespoons fresh lemon juice

FOR THE ICE CREAM

2½ cups heavy cream

1½ cups buttermilk

½ vanilla bean, split lengthwise

Zest of 2 lemons, peeled off in strips with a vegetable peeler

9 egg yolks

¾ cup sugar

¼ cup fresh lemon juice

MAKE THE PRESERVES

Combine the rhubarb, strawberries, and water in a large, heavy,
nonreactive pot. Bring to a boil over high heat, reduce to a bare
simmer, cover, and cook 20 minutes.

Rest a colander over a large bowl. Pour the rhubarb mixture into
the colander and drain 15 minutes. Set the colander and fruit
aside and measure the liquid in the bowl. Measure out an equal
amount of sugar, measured by volume (in cups). This is the correct amount of sugar for the recipe.

Return the liquid to the pot and bring to a boil over medium-
high heat. Add 1 tablespoon of the lemon juice. Working in ½-cup
batches, add the sugar, allowing the mixture to return to a boil
between additions and reserving the final ½ cup sugar for the end
of the recipe.

When the liquid begins to boil, check the temperature with a
candy thermometer. Boil the liquid until its temperature rises 8
degrees more; this is the point at which it will jell. (The boiling
point varies according to elevation and climate, so there is no
fixed "boiling point.") It will take 5 to 10 minutes. Immediately
turn off the heat and stir in the rhubarb and strawberries. Let sit
15 minutes to absorb the liquid.

The old-fashioned flavors of this dessert really speak to us of summer on an American farm, back when the ice for freezing the cream was dug out of layers of sawdust in the icehouse and kids took turns turning the crank of the machine. Ice cream is much easier to come by these days, but fresh-made is still a rare and glorious treat, and so are homemade preserves. Heroic farm wives used to spend hot summer days hovering over boiling cauldrons of fruit, so that their fami-lies could have strawberries and peaches in the dead of winter. Fortunately, this process is now entirely optional—but still highly rewarding.

Gale's method of cooking the fruit with minimal added sugar gives it a clearer fruit taste than commercial preserves. Be sure to trim off all the rhubarb leaves; they can be mildly toxic. Farm wives called rhubarb "pie plant" because putting it in a pie was the only way they could get anyone to eat it; rhubarb needs lots of sugar to balance its tartness.

Return the mixture to a boil over medium-high heat. Stir in the remaining ½ tablespoon lemon juice and the remaining ½ cup sugar. Boil 10 minutes, stirring gently (to avoid breaking up the fruit) and frequently (to prevent burning on the bottom). When the temperature reaches 215 degrees, remove from the heat and transfer to a metal bowl to cool to room temperature. Serve at room temperature, or cover and refrigerate until ready to serve.

MAKE THE ICE CREAM

Heat the cream, buttermilk, vanilla bean, and lemon zest in a saucepan over medium heat, stirring occasionally to make sure the mixture doesn't scorch on the bottom. When the cream mixture reaches a fast simmer (do not let it boil), turn off the heat and set aside to infuse for 10 to 15 minutes.

In a medium bowl, whisk the egg yolks and sugar together.

Whisking constantly, slowly pour the still-hot cream mixture into the egg yolk mixture. Return the mixture to the saucepan and cook over medium heat, stirring constantly with a wooden spoon. At 160 degrees, the mixture will give off a puff of steam. When the mixture reaches 180 degrees it will be thickened and creamy, like eggnog. If you don't have a thermometer, test it by dipping a wooden spoon into the mixture. Run your finger down the back of the spoon. If the stripe remains clear, the mixture is ready; if the edges blur, the mixture is not quite thick enough yet. When it is ready, quickly remove it from the heat.

Meanwhile, half-fill a large bowl with ice water. Rest a smaller bowl in the ice water. Strain the mixture into the smaller bowl to smooth it and remove the vanilla bean and lemon zest. Stir in the lemon juice. Let cool, stirring often, then freeze according to the directions of your ice-cream maker.

To serve, scoop ice cream into dessert glasses and top with preserves.

MAKES 8 TO 10 SERVINGS, WITH PRESERVES LEFT OVER

An old-fashioned infusion like lemon verbena tea completes this time-warp dessert.

double-stuffed lime-ooo bars

FOR THE CRUST

8 tablespoons (1 stick) unsalted butter, slightly softened

¼ cup confectioners' sugar

1 teaspoon pure vanilla extract

1 cup all-purpose flour

FOR THE CREAM CHEESE FILLING

16 ounces cream cheese

2 cups granulated sugar

2 eggs

2 teaspoons lemon extract or lime extract

FOR THE LIME FILLING

4 egg yolks

1 tablespoon cornstarch

¾ cup granulated sugar

½ cup water

¼ teaspoon salt

½ cup fresh lime juice (from about 4 limes)

2 teaspoons freshly grated lime zest

2 tablespoons unsalted butter, slightly softened

We call these Lime-Ooo bars because our friend Mary, who loves them, always puckers her mouth and says "Ooo!" when she first bites into one. The wonderful tartness of the lime flavor gets her every time. If you like lemon squares, you can certainly imagine how tasty a lime square would be; the two fillings, one creamy, one tart, both resting on a crumbly crust, really make these sublime. If you don't say "Ooo," we'll eat our Brasserie T baseball caps!

MAKE THE CRUST

Cream the butter and confectioners' sugar in a mixer fitted with a paddle attachment (or using a hand mixer) until smooth. Add the vanilla and mix. With the mixer running at low speed, add the flour and mix. Press the dough into an 8-inch square baking pan. Refrigerate until firm, about 30 minutes.

Heat the oven to 325 degrees. Prick the dough all over with a fork and bake until golden brown, about 30 minutes. Let cool.

MAKE THE CREAM CHEESE FILLING

Cream the cream cheese and sugar in a mixer fitted with a paddle attachment (or using a hand mixer) until smooth. Add the eggs and extract and mix at medium speed until smooth. Cover and refrigerate until ready to use.

MAKE THE LIME FILLING

Whisk the egg yolks, cornstarch, and sugar together in a medium-size nonreactive saucepan. Whisk in the water, salt, and lime juice and bring to a simmer over medium-low heat. Whisking constantly, cook until the mixture is thick enough to coat the back of a spoon. Remove from the heat, add the zest and butter, and stir until smooth. Let cool 10 minutes.

Reheat the oven to 325 degrees. Spread the cream cheese filling evenly over the cooled crust. Spread the lime filling over the cream cheese filling. Bake until the edges are light golden brown, 30 to 40 minutes. Let cool in the pan, on a wire rack, to room temperature. Refrigerate at least 1 hour or overnight before cutting into 16 squares with a sharp knife. Serve chilled.

MAKES 16 SQUARES

A hot tea with low acidity, like Darjeeling, melts through the sweet richness and balances the tartness.

fruit

"When one has tasted watermelons,
one knows what angels eat."
Mark Twain

apple pie as it should be

nectarine beignets

three-color poached pears

warm taffy apples with cinnamon pastry twists

plum crisp

strawberry shortcake with brown sugar
 and sour cream

raspberry cream tart

chilled pear and pineapple soup

blueberry hazelnut frangipane tart

bob's blueberry swirl ice cream

marthe's rhubarb streusel pot pies

peach-blackberry cobbler

gingery cherry pie with hazelnut crust

banana strudel with ginger-molasses ice cream

apple-cranberry bolster

many-melon salad with yogurt sauce and lime

personality profile: Like an apple-cheeked American girl, fruit is wholesome, but highly sensual. Infused with sweetness and warmed by the sun, open to the world and the air, fruit is easy to love, generously giving her pleasures. But fruit can be sensitive and thin-skinned; you have to choose your moment carefully. And unfortunately, even the sweetest fruit can quickly become spoiled. Treat her lovingly.

Ripe fruit is the greatest challenge a pastry chef will ever face. Fruits are the source of limitless ideas, but also the ingredients that need you the least. How are you supposed to take a jewel-like raspberry, a melon dripping sweet juice, a perfectly perfumed ripe pear—and make them *better*? It can't be done. That's why our fruit desserts are our simplest and most traditional: There's a reason strawberry shortcake, peach cobbler, and apple pie are classics. But you can combine fruits in ways that nature never thought of, carefully complementing their amazing flavors and aromas with a few other ingredients. And that's how there comes to be a sprinkling of brown sugar on our shortcake, blackberries in our peach cobbler, and a bit of vanilla in our apple pie.

Sugar, flour, butter, and chocolate are wonderful in their own right, but though they are natural, they are also highly processed. Fruit presents a dazzling array of living ingredients, formed not through human ingenuity but through nature's boundless and bewildering creativity. Fruit takes its nature from the sun, the air, the water, and the soil, and the interaction of these influences gives us such stimulating variety as raspberries *and* blackberries, honeydew *and* cantaloupe, peaches *and* nectarines, similar but deliciously different.

Long before there were pastry chefs, of course, fruit *was* dessert. Melons, dates, raisins, and figs are all mentioned in the Old Testament; Eve's apple, whether it was an apricot, a pomegranate, or a fig, as different scholars claim, is a powerful testament to the sweet allure of a fruit-laden tree. The Romans preserved apples in honey and wine, ate raw pears, and knew that dried plums after a heavy meal were a good idea! As cooking has evolved, fruit cookery has always evolved with it, often reflecting the trends of its time. For medieval cooks, for whom sugar was a delightful new luxury, candied fruit was the height of ele-

gance. Later, fruit pies became a filling breakfast and supper staple. Fast-forward to the 1950s, and fruit was being suspended in Jell-O!

We try for a simpler, more seasonal approach. Unlike other ingredients in baking, fruits change with the seasons and help us to mark the progress of the year. Even in the most anonymous supermarkets, you know it's spring when the first cherries and rhubarb arrive, and as the berries, melons, peaches, plums, and pears plunge in price and rise in flavor, summer comes, goes, and turns into fall. Winter is the time to revel in the wonderful citrus fruits (so delicious and useful that they get their own chapter). And we are lucky enough to live with certain "seasonless" fruits: Good-quality apples, pineapples, and bananas are available all year round, and some fruits, like cranberries and pie cherries, maintain excellent quality when frozen.

Fruit and cream is one of our favorite combinations, and it takes many shapes here: strawberries and sour cream loosely held in a sandwich of lemony biscuit dough; raspberries lightly stroked with a vanilla cream; blueberries swirled into freshly made ice cream scented with orange. Soft ripe fruit with a sweet, crumbly crust is also terrific: hence Marthe's Rhubarb Streusel Pot Pies, Plum Crisp with pecan topping, and the fragrant hazelnut crust on our cherry pie.

One way to make baking a tradition in your house is to celebrate the seasons with fruit desserts, making the same dessert each year as the new crops come in.

For most fruit, choosing it is as simple as smelling it. Ripe fruit smells like itself. Of course, even ripe fruit can have squashy blemishes, so avoid those—but mostly you can trust your instincts.

Fruit desserts are comforting, homey, and easy to love. Use the recipes in this chapter to remind yourself of the simple pleasures that nature— with just a little help from farmers, pickers, and cooks—can provide.

apple pie as it should be

What with all the Dutch apple, sour cream walnut apple, and apple-raisin pies floating around out there, if you love a plain apple pie as much as we do, you had better learn to make it yourself. And to make apple pie just as it should be—fragrant, tender, buttery, spicy sweet (but not too sweet), and crisp all at once—there are no shortcuts. The good news: It's not difficult. There are few things you can make at home that are more impressive than an apple pie (and that includes homemade patio furniture and Christmas wreaths). People positively melt when this pie comes out of the kitchen, with its bumpy, golden-brown crust blanketed over fruit, spices, and the lightest possible binding.

A little bit of precision will go a long way. For example, Granny Smith apples have exactly the tartness and firmness you want for this recipe. The cream and sugar on top aren't just a frill; they give the crust exactly the right gloss and crunch. The ratio of cinnamon to nutmeg gives exactly the right balance of flavors. Our tester Mary Ann, who thinks nothing of whipping up a crème brûlée, was so alarmed by the idea of pie crust that she had never made a pie in her life. But she followed this recipe exactly and met with complete success on her very first try.

⟜

For a pie party, make it coffee à la mode, with a scoop of vanilla ice cream sprinkled with cinnamon sugar; when it's just you alone with the pie in the kitchen, pour a tall glass of cold milk.

1 recipe Plain and Perfect Pie Crust (page 30) rolled out for a 2-crust 10-inch pie; bottom crust placed in the pan, top crust placed on a sheet pan, both crusts refrigerated
5 Granny Smith apples, peeled, cored, and thickly sliced
½ cup plus 1 tablespoon sugar
⅛ teaspoon salt
1½ tablespoons cornstarch
¼ teaspoon ground cinnamon
⅛ teaspoon ground nutmeg
1 teaspoon pure vanilla extract
1½ tablespoons cold unsalted butter, cut into pieces
1 tablespoon heavy cream
1 tablespoon sugar

Heat the oven to 425 degrees. Remove the pie crusts from the refrigerator.

Toss the apple slices, the ½ cup sugar, the salt, cornstarch, cinnamon, nutmeg, and vanilla together. Transfer to the pie shell. Dot with the butter. Brush the overhanging edges of the dough with water. Carefully place the top crust on top and pinch the edges together, turning under all around to make a thick edge. To decorate the rim, just press it all around with the back of a fork. Or, for a slightly more advanced look, press the thumb and forefinger of one hand together. Use them to gently push the thick dough rim *inward*, while pushing *outward* with the forefinger of the other hand, so that they intersect in a "V" with the dough in between. Repeat all around the rim to make a zig-zag edge.

With the tip of a pair of scissors, snip 4 evenly spaced small vent holes in the top crust. Brush the top of the pie with the cream, then sprinkle evenly with the remaining tablespoon of sugar.

Place the pie on a sheet pan to catch any juices that boil over. Bake in the center of the oven for 10 minutes, then reduce the heat to 375 degrees and bake until the crust is golden brown and the juices are bubbling at the vents, 40 to 50 minutes more. Check the pie after 30 minutes; if the crust is browning too quickly, cover lightly with foil.

Let cool at least 30 minutes before serving. Serve warm or at room temperature.

MAKES 1 PIE

nectarine beignets

1¼ cups all-purpose flour
¾ cup fruity, light white wine, such as Pinot Blanc or Pinot Grigio
2 eggs, separated
1 tablespoon vegetable oil
⅛ teaspoon salt
4 nectarines
Vegetable oil for frying
2 tablespoons granulated sugar
Confectioners' sugar

Put the flour in a mixing bowl and make a well in the center. Pour the wine, egg yolks, 1 tablespoon of vegetable oil, and salt into the well and whisk the wet ingredients together. Gradually whisk the flour into the wet ingredients to make a batter. When smooth, set aside for 20 minutes.

With the tip of a sharp knife, cut the nectarines in half from top to bottom. Pit them by unscrewing the two halves, pulling away from the pit. Cut each half into 3 even wedges (there's no need to peel them) and set aside.

Heat the vegetable oil in a deep fryer (or 2 inches of oil in a deep, heavy pot) to 350 degrees.

Whip the egg whites in a mixer fitted with a whip attachment (or using a hand mixer) until soft peaks form. With the mixer running, drizzle in the sugar and continue whipping just until stiff and glossy. When you are ready to serve, fold the egg whites into the batter until completely blended.

Working in batches to avoid crowding the pot, spear a nectarine wedge on a fork and dip into the batter. Drop into the oil and fry until golden brown, turning once. Drain on paper towels, sprinkle with confectioners' sugar, and serve immediately.

MAKES 6 SERVINGS

> *For some real New Orleans flavor, brew up Creole coffee: roasted coffee and chicory together. Or for an elegant occasion, drink a peachy-flavored Muscat de Beaumes de Venise, very cold.*

Like taffy apples and root beer floats, we think of beignets (aka fried dough) as fairground food—which we always love. We couldn't resist making them into a dessert that brings that great taste home. The challenge is making it happen fast, since fried dough is a good example of immediate gratification. The key word here is **immediate:** Beignets are at their wonderful peak just moments after they come out of the oil. Have your guests cluster around as you make them, and feed them one by one, like baby birds in the nest.

Flash-frying is a wonderful way to give ripe fruit a crisp crust without cooking it through. The result: warm fruit at its peak of flavor, full of sugar and juice, surrounded by a tender casing of hot crust. If done correctly (that is, at a temperature high enough to quickly cook the batter without letting it absorb oil), fried fruit is actually less fatty than many other desserts. You could also make this with bananas, peaches, or other soft fruit. To really dress them up, serve them in a bowl, with crème fraîche spooned over.

12 cups water
3 cups sugar
2 cups white wine
½ vanilla bean, split lengthwise
¼ cup grenadine
Freshly grated zest of ½ lemon
Freshly squeezed juice of ½ lemon
3 cups fruity red wine
Freshly grated zest of ½ orange
Freshly squeezed juice of ½ orange
6 ripe Bartlett pears

Poached pears are so elegant, so simple to make, so light and lovely that we eat them all winter; they're ideal desserts after the piping-hot stews we love to spoon up in the cold months. They're very amenable to other flavors, such as vanilla, orange, spices, and wine, so they never get dull. This pear dessert, which is really a wine dessert in disguise, lets you experience a single dish in three different ways, all at once. Poaching the pears in three different brews—one white, one pink, one red—creates a spectrum of color and flavor that wakes up the eye and the palate. It looks very complex and elegant, and yet could hardly be any easier. Only the math (you're dividing 12 cups of liquid and 6 pears into 3 pans) is a challenge, and we've done that for you!

You'll probably wonder what the wax paper circles are for. They keep the pear halves moist on top so that they absorb color evenly from the liquid, and prevent them from turning brown during the cooking.

Photograph on page 143.

Arrange 3 saucepans on the stove. In one, combine 4 cups water, 1 cup of the sugar, the white wine, and the vanilla bean. In the next, combine 5 cups water, 1 cup of the sugar, the grenadine, lemon zest, and lemon juice. In the last, combine 3 cups water, the remaining 1 cup of sugar, the red wine, orange zest, and orange juice. Bring them all to a simmer over medium-low heat, stirring occasionally.

Meanwhile, peel the pears and cut them in half from top to bottom. Using a melon baller, scoop out the seed pocket. Using a small knife, cut a shallow V down the center of the pear's cut face to remove the stem, strings, and bud end.

Cut out 3 circles of wax paper the same size as the saucepans. Place 4 pear halves in each saucepan and rest a wax paper circle directly on top of the pears. Bring to a gentle simmer and simmer without stirring until tender, about 15 minutes. When the pears can be pierced easily with a fork, they are done. Turn off the heat and let cool in the liquid. Serve at room temperature. *(Or refrigerate in the liquid overnight to let the pears absorb even more color and flavor. Bring to room temperature before serving.)*

To serve, arrange one pear half of each color in a spoke pattern on a white plate. Drizzle a spoonful of the grenadine poaching liquid over the pears and serve.

MAKES 4 SERVINGS

Gewürz *means "spicy" in German, and a cold, sweet, late-harvest Gewürztraminer wine from Alsace would lend a beautiful spicy perfume to this dessert.*

warm taffy apples
with cinnamon pastry twists

FOR THE APPLES

6 Granny Smith apples

12 tablespoons (1½ sticks) unsalted butter

1½ cups sugar

3 tablespoons brandy

1 tablespoon fresh lemon juice

FOR THE PASTRY TWISTS

½ sheet frozen puff pastry, thawed

2 tablespoons unsalted butter, melted

¼ cup sugar

1 teaspoon ground cinnamon

FOR THE SAUCE

2½ cups sugar

½ cup water

1 cup heavy cream

¼ cup coarsely chopped peanuts

MAKE THE APPLES

Peel and core the apples, leaving them whole. Cut off the tops and bottoms to give the apples flat surfaces to rest on.

Melt the butter in a medium skillet, over medium heat. Stir in the sugar and cook over medium-high heat, stirring, until the mixture begins to turn golden brown and caramelized. Add the brandy and lemon juice and stir to blend. Adjust the heat so the mixture remains at a simmer.

Place the apples in a single layer in the liquid and simmer until the submerged portion is tender, basting occasionally, about 15 minutes. Turn the apples over and cook until tender all the way through, about 15 minutes more. Remove from the liquid and set aside to cool.

MAKE THE TWISTS

Heat the oven to 400 degrees. Line a sheet pan with parchment or buttered wax paper.

Unroll the puff pastry on a work surface. Brush the pastry with melted butter. Toss the sugar and cinnamon together and sprinkle evenly over the pastry. Working lengthwise, cut the pastry into 6 long strips, each ¾ inch wide. Lightly twist the strips, keeping the

If you thought you had to give up taffy apples to be a real grown-up, we'll prove you wrong with this recipe. We took the whole thing apart, made each element fresh and delicious, and then put it back together into a familiar but newly enticing dessert. Now the apples are braised in a lemon-brandy caramel; the sticks are twisted from puff pastry dusted with cinnamon sugar; and the sauce is a rich, creamy brew sprinkled with freshly chopped peanuts.

The apples, twists, and sauce can all be made well in advance. Simply rewarm the apples and sauce before assembling the dessert on serving plates.

Photograph on page 134.

cinnamon sugar on the inside, to make long twisted "straws" with barber-pole stripes of plain pastry and cinnamon-sprinkled pastry. The finished straws should be about 8 inches long. Transfer to the pan, run your fingers along the twists to straighten them, and bake about 20 minutes, until puffed and golden brown.

MAKE THE SAUCE

Pour the sugar into the center of a saucepan. Carefully pour the water around the sugar, trying not to splash any sugar onto the sides of the pan. Do not stir; gently draw your finger through the center of the sugar, making an X, to moisten it. Bring to a boil over medium heat without stirring. Cook until light caramel in color and immediately remove from the heat. Carefully stir in the cream with a wooden spoon until smooth (it will bubble up and may splatter).

To serve, place an apple on each serving plate. Drizzle with caramel sauce, sprinkle with peanuts, and place a pastry straw in the hole of each apple so that it sticks up like a wooden stick.

MAKES 6 SERVINGS

At a grown-up party, pour a sweet Portuguese Madeira; its caramel flavor will harmonize with the taffy. But a frosty vanilla milkshake would be good, too!

plum crisp

8 to 12 large plums
½ cup all-purpose flour
¼ cup light brown sugar, packed
1 tablespoon granulated sugar
¼ teaspoon ground cinnamon
Pinch of ground nutmeg
4 tablespoons (½ stick) cold unsalted butter, cut into pieces
½ cup very coarsely chopped pecans
Ice cream, such as Sweet-Hot White Pepper Ice Cream (page 239), Lemon-
   Buttermilk Ice Cream (page 168), or store-bought ice cream of your
   choice

Heat the oven to 400 degrees. Butter a large, deep baking dish.

Quarter and pit 8 of the plums and put them in the baking dish. They should be at least 2½ inches deep. If not, quarter and pit the remaining plums and add to the dish.

Mix the flour, brown sugar, granulated sugar, cinnamon, and nutmeg together. Add the butter and, using your fingertips, pinch the ingredients together into a sandy, crumbly mixture. Add the pecans and mix. Sprinkle the mixture over the plums.

Bake until the plums are tender and the topping is browned, 25 to 30 minutes. Let cool slightly and serve warm, topped with ice cream.

MAKES 4 TO 6 SERVINGS

With a fruity-sweet farmhouse dessert like this one, we love a glass of cold, tangy buttermilk. Almond milk (milk with a few drops of almond extract and a pinch of superfine sugar) isn't bad, either.

A great big, juicy plum is one of our favorite things to eat. In addition to cool flesh and sweet juice, there is often the element of surprise on biting into it: Will the flesh be purple, white, red, or yellow? There are so many different varieties on the market now, from speckled "dinosaur eggs," shadowy "elephant hearts," and apricot-plum hybrid "plumcots," to traditional French varieties with lovely names like **Mirabelle** and **Reine Claude,** named half a millennium ago for a famously sweet queen of France. Any of them will make a delightful crisp; the light scattering of warm nuts and spice creates a fragrant crunch. You can even use the tiny purple-blue plums that are one of the first signs of fall, but you'll need a few more.

strawberry shortcake with brown sugar and sour cream

This irresistible creation is based on a classic biscuit shortcake, but it's also inspired by a memorable dessert Gale tasted when she was just starting out as a chef. In the 1980s, one of the most influential restaurants in New England was The Blue Strawbery, in Portsmouth, New Hampshire. John Haller, the restaurant's owner and chef, cooked only with fresh and seasonal ingredients—a radical idea at that time and place—and he put them together in unusually simple ways. A bowl of perfectly ripe strawberries with a dollop of sour cream and a sprinkling of brown sugar would have been laughed off the dessert cart at most "serious" restaurants, but that's just what he served, and it sent Gale into pure ecstasy. Sometimes it's great to be reminded of what we already know.

If your strawberries are utterly perfect, you could leave out the whipped-cream biscuits altogether and just dip the whole berries into the sour cream, but if not, their light, lemony sweetness and crumbly texture beautifully complete the experience.

With strawberry shortcake, lemonade is a must. Try our strawberry lemonade (see page 280), or add mint ice cubes.

FOR THE STRAWBERRIES
2 cups strawberries, green parts trimmed off, berries cut into chunks
2 tablespoons light brown sugar, packed

FOR THE BISCUITS
1½ cups all-purpose flour
¼ teaspoon salt
1 tablespoon granulated sugar
4 teaspoons baking powder
½ teaspoon freshly grated lemon zest
1 cup heavy cream, whipped

FOR SERVING
1 cup sour cream
¼ cup light brown sugar, packed

PREPARE THE BERRIES
In a bowl, toss the strawberries with the 2 tablespoons brown sugar, cover, and refrigerate until ready to serve.

Heat the oven to 400 degrees.

MAKE THE BISCUITS
Mix the flour, salt, sugar, baking powder, and lemon zest in a mixer fitted with a paddle attachment. Mix in the whipped cream until the mixture is moistened and just forms a ball. Turn out onto a lightly floured work surface and knead briefly just to bring the dough together.

Form the dough into a log, then use a rolling pin to roll the dough into a long rectangle about 1 inch thick and 3 inches wide. Using diagonal strokes of a sharp knife, cut into 4 or 6 large triangular biscuits. Arrange on a sheet pan and bake until golden brown, about 20 minutes. Let cool on a wire rack.

When ready to serve, split the biscuits in half horizontally. Place the bottoms on serving plates. On each, place a spoonful of strawberries with the syrup that has collected in the bowl, a dollop of sour cream, and a sprinkling of brown sugar. Place the top halves of the biscuits on top. Serve immediately.

MAKES 4 TO 6 SERVINGS

raspberry cream tart

4 cups raspberries

2 cups milk (not skim)

½ vanilla bean, split lengthwise

2½ teaspoons powdered gelatin

2 tablespoons cold water

6 egg yolks

⅔ cup sugar

1 recipe Crumbly Pie Crust, pressed into a 10-inch tart pan with a removable bottom and prebaked (page 33)

Pick over the raspberries, setting aside the best ones to make a circle around the edge of the finished tart. (You'll need about 1 cup.)

Heat the milk and vanilla bean in a saucepan over medium heat just until it boils. Immediately turn off the heat and set aside to infuse for 10 minutes. Combine the gelatin and water in a small bowl, and let dissolve, stirring occasionally, until no dry spots remain.

Whisk the egg yolks and sugar together in a medium bowl. Whisking constantly, slowly pour the still-hot milk mixture into the egg yolk mixture. Return the mixture to the saucepan and cook over medium heat, stirring constantly with a wooden spoon. At 160 degrees, the mixture will give off a puff of steam. When the mixture reaches 180 degrees it will be thickened and creamy, like eggnog. If you don't have a thermometer, test it by dipping a wooden spoon into the mixture. Run your finger down the back of the spoon. If the stripe remains clear, the mixture is ready; if the edges blur, the mixture is not quite thick enough yet. When it is ready, quickly remove it from the heat.

Meanwhile, half-fill a large bowl with ice water. Strain the mixture into a medium bowl to smooth it and remove the vanilla bean. Pour off 1 cup of the mixture into a large bowl and set aside. Place the medium bowl containing the remainder of the mixture in the ice water and let cool, stirring often. (You have just made an *anglaise*.)

Meanwhile, add the gelatin to the 1 cup of hot *anglaise* in the large bowl and mix until completely dissolved. (Now the mixture is a Bavarian cream.) Working quickly, fold the larger amount of berries into the Bavarian cream and spoon the mixture into the center of the tart shell. Spread until smooth and even (don't worry

In this super-easy tart, a pile of fresh berries is tumbled into the quickest crust you can imagine. Pour on a small amount of vanilla cream, just enough to caress the berries and barely bind them together; the fruit, not the cream, is dominant. The result is like a dessert of raspberries with cream and cookies—all in one voluptuously fruity bite. The cream flows around the berries in a most delicious way.

There's no actual cream in the "cream" here; it's what pastry chefs call a Bavarian cream, which is an **anglaise** with a little gelatin added. Get it? No? Well, anglaise is the most basic dessert sauce; it's a thin egg-yolk custard. An anglaise is where you start to make countless desserts: ice creams, custard, puddings, even zabaglione. Pastry chefs would be lost without it!

if the berries break up a bit). Before the filling cools completely, arrange the reserved berries around the edge of the tart to form a rim. Chill at least 2 hours and serve in slices, pouring a bit of the plain *anglaise* next to each slice.

MAKES 1 TART

↪ *This fruity, pretty dessert calls for flutes of not-too-dry Champagne—with a fresh raspberry dropped into each one. Lemon or orange tea would also taste great.*

chilled pear and pineapple soup

When Gale started making cold fruit soups as part of her popular "Blue Plate Specials," tiny servings of four or five desserts on one plate, she used pureed fruit for the liquid. But the textures seemed too thick, the flavor too one-dimensional, and she just could not rest until she perfected the method. She needed a dessert equivalent of soup stock to make her fruit soups flavorful but delicate, and she found it in tea! Now, many of Gale's recipes use different teas, like camomile, jasmine, and Earl Grey, to add liquid and flavor. If you don't like camomile tea here, you might substitute another flower tea like lemon verbena or rose hip.

You needn't bother to cut the eyes out when peeling the pineapple for this refreshing elixir; they'll be strained out later. Pineapple is a good choice in fruit soups because its acidity prevents them from turning brown. Try combining this with other desserts, such as Nutmeg Cheesecake, Lydia's Austrian Raspberry Shortbread, or Pumpkin Crème Brûlée.

1 large ripe pineapple, peeled, cored, and cut into chunks, leaves washed and reserved
3 pears, peeled, halved, cored, and cut into chunks
2 cups cooled camomile tea
½ cup Muscat de Beaumes de Venise, Sauternes, or another fragrant dessert wine
Honey
Fresh lemon juice

Combine the pineapple and pear chunks in a food processor. Puree until smooth, then strain through a fine sieve into a bowl. Add the tea and wine and mix. Add honey and lemon juice a little bit at a time, to taste. Chill until very cold. Serve in bowls or martini glasses, garnishing each bowl with 2 pineapple leaves, sticking up like rabbit ears.

MAKES 4 SERVINGS

↪
Sip chilled glasses of the dessert wine you used in making the soup for a seamless taste pairing.

blueberry hazelnut frangipane tart

5 ounces hazelnuts, toasted, peeled, and cooled (page 14)

⅔ cup sugar

10 tablespoons (1¼ sticks) cold unsalted butter, cut into pieces

2 eggs

¼ teaspoon pure vanilla extract

2 teaspoons all-purpose flour

1 recipe Sweet Pastry (page 35), rolled out to fit a 10-inch tart pan
  with a removable bottom, lightly pressed into the pan, and chilled at least
  30 minutes

1½ pints (3 cups) fresh blueberries, picked over

1 cup apricot jam

1½ tablespoons water

Heat the oven to 375 degrees.

Pulse the hazelnuts and sugar in a food processor fitted with a metal blade just until sandy. Do not overprocess, or the mixture will become pasty. Add the butter and process just until blended. Add the eggs and process until blended.

Scrape down the sides of the bowl, add the vanilla and flour, and process until smooth (you have just made a frangipane). Spoon into the unbaked tart shell. Spread 1 cup of the blueberries in a single layer over the frangipane.

Bake until the frangipane is golden brown and puffy and the crust is golden brown, 45 to 50 minutes. Let cool to room temperature.

Bring the jam and water to a boil in a medium saucepan. Immediately turn off the heat. Working quickly, add the remaining blueberries all at once and fold gently with a spatula until evenly coated. Pour into the center of the tart and gently spread over the entire surface of the tart. Let cool until set, then remove the sides of the pan. Serve at room temperature.

MAKES 1 TART

Hazelnuts and coffee are, of course, a naturally wonderful flavor combination. Pour a strong, bright-flavored Latin American coffee such as Colombian.

This is a truly spectacular dessert, covered with a thick layer of juicy blueberries, each one polished to a high gloss with a light jam glaze. And that's just the top: Underneath is a nutty-chewy layer of buttery hazelnut frangipane. Isn't that a great word? Frangipane (pronounced **fran-ji-PAN**) is a French cooking term that describes a pastry filling made with lots of ground nuts, usually almonds. The Marquis di Frangipani, an Italian aristocrat, created an almond-scented perfume for gloves that was all the rage in Paris for a time—in the sixteenth century! So take note; if you want to stay famous for five hundred years, persuade pastry chefs to name delicious things after you. We're open to suggestions.

bob's blueberry swirl ice cream

1 cup blueberries
1 cup sugar
2 cups heavy cream
2 cups half-and-half
½ vanilla bean, split lengthwise
9 egg yolks
½ teaspoon freshly grated orange zest

Along with root beer and chocolate chips, we had to import loads of blueberries to cook with when we moved to England for a few years. Our English customers called them "bilberries" and regarded them as quite exotic. We felt the same way about the fat green and red gooseberries they ate on a daily basis!

Our friend Bob Paylon, who was American, owned the country-house hotel where we cooked and lived, and he was a man with a mission: to introduce the English to the food of our people. We knew the English had really taken to blueberries when the country's foremost restaurant critic, Fay Maschler, wrote that this was the single best ice cream she had ever tasted. Do you agree?

Blueberries and lemon are a tasty combination. Try a tart spritzer of lemon syrup and seltzer to quench that ice cream thirst.

Heat the blueberries and ¼ cup of the sugar over medium heat, stirring occasionally, until the berries pop and begin to cook down, about 10 minutes. Set aside to cool, then refrigerate until ready to use.

Heat the cream, half-and-half, and vanilla bean in a saucepan over medium heat, stirring occasionally to make sure the mixture doesn't scorch on the bottom. When it reaches a fast simmer (do not let it boil), turn off the heat and set aside to infuse 10 to 15 minutes.

Whisk the egg yolks and the remaining ¾ cup of sugar together. Whisking constantly, slowly pour the still-hot cream mixture into the egg yolk mixture. Return the mixture to the saucepan and cook over medium heat, stirring constantly with a wooden spoon. At 160 degrees, the mixture will give off a puff of steam. When the mixture reaches 180 degrees it will be thickened and creamy, like eggnog. If you don't have a thermometer, test it by dipping a wooden spoon into the mixture. Run your finger down the back of the spoon. If the stripe remains clear, the mixture is ready; if the edges blur, the mixture is not quite thick enough yet. When it is ready, quickly remove it from the heat.

Meanwhile, half-fill a large bowl with ice water. Strain the mixture into a smaller bowl to smooth it and remove the vanilla bean. Whisk in the orange zest. Rest the smaller bowl in the ice water and let the mixture cool, stirring often, then freeze according to the directions of your ice-cream maker.

Put a large mixing bowl in the freezer to chill. When the ice cream is finished, transfer it to the frozen bowl. Using a sturdy rubber spatula, fold in the blueberry mixture until swirled. Freeze.

MAKES 1 QUART

marthe's rhubarb streusel pot pies

1 recipe Plain and Perfect Pie Crust (page 30), in 2 disks, chilled
½ cup all-purpose flour
¼ cup light brown sugar, packed
½ cup plus 1 tablespoon granulated sugar
¼ teaspoon ground cinnamon or ground ginger or a combination of
  the two
4 tablespoons (½ stick) cold unsalted butter, cut into pieces
6 cups rhubarb, leaves and brown edges trimmed off, cut into ½-inch dice
  (about 14 stalks)
¼ cup cornstarch

Roll out 1 disk of dough on a floured surface (following the directions on page 30) into a square large enough to cut 4 circles about 6 inches in diameter (the dough will be about ³/₁₆ inch thick). Using an individual (4-inch) pie pan as a guide, and leaving an extra 1 inch of dough all the way around, cut the dough into circles with the tip of a sharp knife. Line the individual pie pans with the dough circles as described on page 31, for a single-crust pie. Repeat with the remaining dough to make a total of 8 individual pie shells. Arrange the lined pie pans on a sheet pan and refrigerate, uncovered, 30 to 60 minutes.

Heat the oven to 400 degrees.

Mix the flour, brown sugar, the 1 tablespoon of granulated sugar, and the cinnamon together. Add the butter and, using your fingertips, pinch the ingredients together into a sandy, crumbly mixture. Do not overmix; as soon as the mixture is sandy, cover and refrigerate until ready to use.

Toss the rhubarb, the remaining ½ cup of sugar, and the cornstarch together. Divide among the pie crusts, mounding the filling high (it will cook down during baking). Sprinkle the topping over the pies, gently pressing the topping onto the rhubarb with your hand.

Bake until the rhubarb is tender and the topping is golden brown, about 30 minutes. Serve warm or at room temperature.

MAKES 8 SERVINGS

To smooth the sweet-tart flavors of the pie, pour glasses of cold milk, sweetened with drops of pure vanilla extract and a pinch of superfine sugar.

One of the first American food writers was Laura Ingalls Wilder, whose absorbing accounts of frontier life in the LITTLE HOUSE ON THE PRAIRIE books are full of details about how her family and neighbors procured, prepared, and ate their food. Pie is everywhere in these books, from pumpkin and mince to custard, vinegar, and even blackbird one memorable year. Laura's first pie as a married woman is a total disaster: She forgets to put any sugar in the rhubarb filling. So beware!

Gale's friend Marthe is like a modern-day Ma Ingalls. She bakes her own bread, pickles her own home-grown vegetables, makes her own jam, paints her own china, spins wool from her own sheep, and, miraculously, does it all without making you want to punch her. Gale and Marthe once devoted a whole memorable summer together to gardening, preserving, and baking. Rhubarb is a Marthe favorite.

A sweet streusel topping is perfect with the juicy, tart rhubarb; it releases the fruit's steam and absorbs its juices. Pot pies are irresistibly cute, but if you'd rather make one large pie, use half a Plain and Perfect Pie Crust recipe and roll it out for a single-crust, 10-inch pie; do not prebake it. Bake the large pie for 40 to 50 minutes.

peach-blackberry cobbler

FOR THE FILLING

8 to 12 peaches, peeled, pitted, and cut into 1-inch chunks

2 tablespoons cornstarch or flour

5 tablespoons light brown sugar, packed

1 teaspoon fresh lemon juice

Pinch of salt

2 cups blackberries

FOR THE TOPPING

2 cups all-purpose flour

½ teaspoon salt

¼ cup light brown sugar, packed

2 teaspoons baking powder

¼ teaspoon ground ginger

¼ teaspoon ground cinnamon

2 pinches of ground mace or nutmeg

6 tablespoons (¾ stick) cold unsalted butter, cut into pieces

¾ cup plus 1 tablespoon milk

1 tablespoon granulated sugar

At high summer, when every garden is awash with zucchini, tomatoes, and fruit that is just tipping into over-ripeness, the time is perfectly ripe for cobbler. Last summer, on a trip to our local farmer's market, a bushel of soft peaches and a quart of huge blackberries called out to us. Soft, sweet, bursting fruit is wonderful cooked down into a fruity mass topped with a not-too-sweet biscuit dough. We like to add a soft note of spice to the topping.

Peaches and berries of any kind are a glorious summer combination. This could be made with raspberries, huckleberries, blueberries, marionberries—you name it. Nectarines would make an excellent substitute for the peaches.

With these summer berry flavors, pour tall glasses of blackcurrant iced tea freshened with sprigs of mint.

MAKE THE FILLING

Combine the peaches, cornstarch, brown sugar, lemon juice, and salt, tossing gently. Carefully fold in the blackberries and transfer the mixture to a shallow 8-cup baking dish. Set aside.

MAKE THE TOPPING

Heat the oven to 350 degrees. Mix the flour, salt, brown sugar, baking powder, ginger, cinnamon, and mace together in a mixer fitted with a paddle attachment (or using a hand mixer). Add the butter and mix until coarse and crumbly. Add the ¾ cup of milk and mix just until combined.

Turn the dough out onto a lightly floured surface and knead a few times. Form into a ball and roll out into the shape and size of the baking dish, about ½ inch thick. Place on top of the prepared fruit.

Brush the top of the dough with the remaining 1 tablespoon of milk and sprinkle with the granulated sugar. Place the cobbler on a sheet pan to catch any juices that boil over. Bake until the top is golden brown and juices are bubbling, 30 to 40 minutes. Let cool slightly before serving. Serve warm or at room temperature.

MAKES 8 TO 10 SERVINGS

gingery cherry pie
with hazelnut crust

FOR THE CRUST

10 ounces (2¼ sticks) cold unsalted butter, slightly softened

1½ cups confectioners' sugar

2 eggs

3¼ cups all-purpose flour

½ cup finely ground peeled and toasted hazelnuts (page 14)

FOR THE FILLING

1¼ pounds fresh or thawed frozen cherries or two 16-ounce cans pie cherries

3 tablespoons cornstarch

¾ cup granulated sugar

¼ teaspoon freshly grated ginger

1 teaspoon fresh lemon juice

MAKE THE CRUST

Cream the butter in a mixer fitted with a paddle attachment (or using a hand mixer) until smooth. Add the confectioners' sugar and mix. Add the eggs and mix. Add the flour and mix until almost incorporated. Add the hazelnuts and mix just until smooth, being careful not to overmix the dough.

Form the dough into 2 disks and wrap in plastic wrap. Chill at least 2 hours or overnight. (If the dough is refrigerated overnight, remove it from the refrigerator 30 minutes before using.) Roll out both disks for a 2-crust 9-inch pie, according to the method on page 31, and chill.

MAKE THE FILLING

Heat the oven to 375 degrees.

Drain the cherry juices (see sidenote) into a medium saucepan; you should have about a cup of juice. Add the cornstarch, sugar, ginger, and lemon juice and bring to a simmer over medium heat, stirring to dissolve the cornstarch. When thickened, turn off the heat, stir in the cherries, and set aside to cool slightly.

Put the cherry filling in the unbaked pie shell. Brush the overhanging edges of the dough with water. Carefully place the rolled-out top crust on top and pinch the edges together, turning under all around to make a thick edge. To decorate the rim, just press it all around with the back of a fork. For a slightly more advanced

Every summer we try to play hooky from work long enough for a weekend in Wisconsin, where the cherries, though not as famous as the ones in Michigan, are fresh, sweet, and wonderful. As a kid, Rick used to spend hours up in a cherry tree near his house—eating and spitting out pits, and eating some more. It's his first "food memory." Cherries are so bright and sweet that it's no wonder people tend to fall for them young. Our son, Gio, learned to eat cherries last summer; he was wearing an all-white outfit at the time, which quickly became dramatically splattered with red. Another mom admired our son's tie-dyed outfit!

This fragrant, toasty crust has a beautiful golden color from the hazelnuts in the dough. You'll have plenty of dough scraps left over after you've made the crust; make cookies or little jam tartlets. If using fresh cherries, you'll need to squeeze out a cup of juice by pressing additional cherries in a strainer, or buy about a cup of cherry juice to make the filling. Use bright red or sour cherries, not the sweet, dark maroon varieties.

look, press the thumb and forefinger of one hand together. Use them to gently push the thick dough rim *inward*, while pushing *outward* with the forefinger of the other hand, so that they intersect in a "V" with the dough in between. Repeat all around the rim to make a zigzag edge. With the tip of a pair of scissors, snip 4 evenly spaced small vent holes in the top crust.

Place the pie on a sheet pan to catch any juices that boil over. Bake until the crust is golden brown and the juices are bubbling at the vents, 40 to 50 minutes. Let cool to room temperature. Serve at room temperature.

MAKES 1 PIE

Iced coffee, milk, or cherry cider would be delicious.

banana strudel with ginger-molasses ice cream

FOR THE ICE CREAM

2 cups heavy cream

2 cups half-and-half

¼ teaspoon ground ginger

½ vanilla bean, split lengthwise

½ cup molasses (not blackstrap)

9 egg yolks

½ cup granulated sugar

FOR THE STRUDEL

8 ounces cream cheese

1 egg yolk

½ cup confectioners' sugar

1 teaspoon pure vanilla extract

¼ teaspoon ground cinnamon

2 ounces bittersweet chocolate, chopped with a heavy knife

3 sheets phyllo pastry, thawed overnight in the refrigerator if frozen, kept moist (page 15)

6 tablespoons unsalted butter, melted

¼ cup granulated sugar

1⅓ cups walnuts (black walnuts if you can find them), lightly toasted and finely chopped (page 14)

2 large bananas

MAKE THE ICE CREAM

Heat the cream, half-and-half, ginger, and vanilla bean in a saucepan over medium heat, stirring occasionally to make sure the mixture doesn't scorch on the bottom. When it reaches a fast simmer (do not let it boil), turn off the heat and set aside to infuse 15 minutes. Whisk in the molasses.

Whisk the egg yolks and sugar together. Whisking constantly, slowly pour the still-hot cream mixture into the egg yolk mixture. Return the mixture to the saucepan and cook over medium heat, stirring constantly with a wooden spoon. At 160 degrees, the mixture will give off a puff of steam. When the mixture reaches 180 degrees it will be thickened and creamy, like eggnog. If you don't have a thermometer, test it by dipping a wooden spoon into the mixture. Run your finger down the back of the spoon. If the stripe remains clear, the mixture is ready; if the edges blur, the mixture

Albert Kumin, the legendary Swiss pastry chef who ruled the White House kitchen in the 1970s, fathered an entire generation of American pastry chefs through his cooking classes. Years later, Gale still remembers the sight of his huge hands gently spinning sugar into near-invisible threads, and stretching a single lump of strudel dough to cover an entire table. Strudel-making used to be a family affair, with all the women standing around the dining-room table, gradually pulling and smoothing the dough until it hung all the way to the floor!

These days, we have smaller families, working moms, and frozen phyllo dough to take the place of strudel dough. See page 15 for tips on working with the phyllo. We sprinkle nuts and sugar between the layers to let air in and to make a nice, crisp dough to surround the soft banana and chocolate. Cool ice cream with the warm flavors of ginger and molasses complements the strudel, which looks quite spectacular when whole. Roll it up tightly and neatly, as if you are rolling your hair up on curlers! You can serve the strudel with supermarket ice cream if you like.

Photograph on page 157.

is not quite thick enough yet. When it is ready, quickly remove it from the heat.

Meanwhile, half-fill a large bowl with ice water. Strain the mixture into a smaller bowl to smooth it and remove the vanilla bean. Rest the smaller bowl in the ice water and let the mixture cool, stirring often, then freeze according to the directions of your ice-cream maker.

MAKE THE STRUDEL

Heat the oven to 375 degrees. Line a sheet pan with parchment paper.

Cream the cream cheese in a mixer fitted with a paddle attachment (or using a hand mixer) until soft and smooth. Add the egg yolk and mix. Add the confectioners' sugar, vanilla, and cinnamon and mix. Add the chocolate and mix just until incorporated. Spoon the mixture into a pastry bag fitted with a large plain tip (or just set aside in a bowl).

Place 1 sheet of phyllo on the pan and brush generously with melted butter. Sprinkle evenly with 1 tablespoon of the granulated sugar and 3 tablespoons of the walnuts. Place another sheet of phyllo on top. Brush with melted butter, sprinkle with 1 tablespoon sugar and 3 tablespoons walnuts, and lay another sheet of phyllo on top. Brush the top with melted butter and sprinkle with 1 tablespoon sugar and 3 tablespoons walnuts. Reserve the remaining melted butter, sugar, and walnuts.

Pipe half the cheese filling in a line along one short end of the phyllo, leaving a 2-inch margin on the top, bottom, and side. Arrange the whole bananas next to the cheese. Pipe the remaining filling next to the bananas. Starting at the filled end, roll the phyllo up tightly to encase the filling.

Move the log to the center of the sheet pan and tuck the ends under to keep the filling from oozing out. Brush the surface with melted butter and sprinkle with 1 tablespoon sugar. You may not use up all the melted butter and walnuts.

Bake until golden brown, about 30 minutes. Let cool 10 to 15 minutes on the pan. Using a serrated knife, cut carefully into sections and serve warm, with the ginger-molasses (or another) ice cream.

MAKES 6 TO 8 SERVINGS

We have a weakness for the rich, malty flavor of Ovaltine; try it here cold or hot. Or, complete the chocolate-banana-cinnamon flavors with a cup of coffee.

apple-cranberry bolster

2 Granny Smith apples, peeled, cored, and coarsely chopped

½ teaspoon fresh lemon juice

¼ teaspoon freshly grated lemon zest

½ teaspoon pure vanilla extract

½ cup dried, fresh, or frozen cranberries, pulsed in a food processor until coarsely chopped

1 tablespoon cornstarch

¾ cup sugar

3 sheets phyllo pastry, thawed overnight in the refrigerator if frozen, kept moist (page 15)

6 tablespoons unsalted butter, melted

½ cup almonds, lightly toasted and ground (page 14)

Heat the oven to 375 degrees. Line a sheet pan with parchment paper.

Toss the apples, lemon juice, lemon zest, and vanilla together. Add the cranberries, cornstarch, and ½ cup of the sugar and toss.

Place 1 sheet of phyllo on the pan and brush generously with melted butter. Sprinkle evenly with 1 tablespoon of the sugar and 2 tablespoons of the almonds. Place another sheet of phyllo on top. Brush with melted butter, sprinkle with 1 tablespoon sugar and 2 tablespoons almonds, and lay another sheet of phyllo on top. Brush the top with melted butter and sprinkle with 1 tablespoon sugar and 2 tablespoons almonds. Reserve the remaining melted butter, sugar, and almonds.

Leaving a 1-inch border around the edges of the phyllo stack, spoon the apple-cranberry mixture onto the top layer and spread out to cover evenly.

Starting at one long edge, roll up the pastry into a log. Move the log to the center of the sheet pan and tuck the ends under to keep the filling from oozing out. Brush the surface with melted butter and sprinkle with 1 tablespoon sugar and 2 tablespoons almonds. (You may not use all the melted butter.)

Bake until golden brown and crisp, 25 to 35 minutes. Let cool 10 to 15 minutes on the pan. Using a serrated knife, cut carefully into sections and serve warm.

MAKES 6 TO 8 SERVINGS

Accentuate the autumnal flavors with spice tea and honey, stirred with cinnamon sticks.

A modern, chunky, and tangy reworking of a classic jelly roll, this dessert has the same beautiful pinwheel effect when sliced. It's easily accomplished with frozen phyllo dough and cranberries and firm, fresh Granny Smith apples. Both fruits have the tartness you want in a filling perfumed with vanilla, lemon, almonds, and sugar.

many-melon salad with yogurt sauce and lime

½ cup milk

1 cup good-quality plain yogurt, preferably not fat-free

1 cantaloupe or another orange muskmelon, such as Crenshaw, Charentais, or Cavaillon

½ green honeydew melon

½ small watermelon

2 to 3 tablespoons light brown sugar

1 or 2 limes, cut into wedges

Melons and yogurt (milk fermented by the natural bacteria in the air) are among the most ancient foods known to man; both are mentioned in the Old Testament. Together, they make a dessert that is both stunningly healthy and wonderfully refreshing.

Gale ate quantities of this calcium- and vitamin-rich combination when she was pregnant; not surprisingly, our son, Gio, loves it. The live cultures in real yogurt clean out your system by creating an environment in which other bacteria can't live. When choosing yogurt, remember that fat-free yogurt tends to contain quantities of thickeners and stabilizers, which do nothing for its flavor.

There are two broad categories of melons: watermelons, which originated in Africa (and are closely related to cucumbers), and muskmelons, from the Mediterranean. The latter category includes all those fleshy-sweet green- and orange-fleshed melons, such as cantaloupe, honeydew, Crenshaw, and Cavaillon; the first includes red- and yellow-fleshed watermelons. Aim for a mix of colors and textures.

Whisk the milk and yogurt together. Cover and refrigerate until ready to serve.

When ready to serve, peel and seed the melons and cut into 1-inch cubes. Combine them in a bowl, toss lightly, and divide the mixture among dessert bowls (preferably glass, so that you can see the melon colors). Drizzle the yogurt sauce on top of the fruit. Sprinkle each serving with about 2 teaspoons brown sugar and serve with lime wedges to squeeze over the fruit at the table.

MAKES 6 TO 8 SERVINGS

Citrus and melon is a terrific combination; sip a sweet-tart lime rickey, lime syrup with a squirt of seltzer.

nuts

"Nuts . . . add an uncommon dimension."
James Haller

marzipan torte with ginger

chocolate pecan pie

cashew-cinnamon brittle

walnut carrot cake with pineapple

sugared walnut sundaes in chocolate cups

oatmeal cake with broiled coconut

broiled pineapple with macadamia crunch

biscuit tortoni with amaretti and poached nectarines

roasted peanut ice cream

toasted hazelnut-almond biscotti

personality profile: With their rough exteriors, nuts can seem gnarled, difficult, and shy—but once you pry them open, they'll reward you for it. Often overshadowed by the more glamorous fruits, nuts are not the least bit temperamental; you can mix them with anyone and they'll always happily recede into the background. But with more attentive treatment, those stalwart nuts can step forward to understudy for flour or fruit, or even be spiffed up into a leading role of their own.

Crunchy, aromatic, simple but sophisticated, and endlessly versatile, nuts will never let you down. Whether they're busy lending texture to a homey fruit crisp, infusing ice cream with their sophisticated flavor, or nestling down in amber sheets of candy, nuts are there for you. When you think you have nothing in the house to bake with, go to the stash we know you have—the tossed-aside leftover walnuts from a batch of brownies, the peanuts your kids crave—and let them guide your imagination. Nuts generously bring flavor, texture, substance, oil, starch, and powerful aromas to baking, and they have the long-term popularity to prove it.

Long before milk, butter, oil, and flour were widely available, nuts provided milk, oil, and flour in a compact and nutritious package. Candied pine nuts and almonds were among the first desserts to appear when sugar first became available in medieval Europe, though long before that, the combination of honey and almonds is mentioned in the Old Testament. Medieval *blanc-manges*, ancestors of today's rice puddings, included rice cooked in almond milk, seasoned with sugar, salt—and shredded chicken! In Sicily, the ancient Arab tradition of marzipan (almond-sugar paste) confectionery is still kept alive by a few cloistered nuns: Legend has it that the secrets of creating the tiny, gorgeously colored sculptures of fruit, vegetables, fish, and even plates of spaghetti would be revealed by each Mother Superior to her successor only on her deathbed.

Nuts are a very international crowd, from the Fertile Crescent's robust walnut trees (now grown everywhere from England to India), to Hawaii's macadamias, America's own hard-shell pecans, and even Brazil's oddity the cashew nut, not a nut at all but the seed of a kind of apple. We like them all. Peanuts, of course, are a key flavor of an American childhood (though peanut butter was not, as many people believe, invented by George Washington Carver; it was a native American staple when the Jamestown colony was founded). In Provence, we saw almonds growing on trees, all green, fuzzy, and waxy.

Like the perfect little black dress, nuts can seem plain and even drab in themselves, but boy, do they make you look good. Chocolate and fruit, especially, benefit hugely from nutty pairings, in such satisfying desserts as Chocolate Pecan Pie, Broiled Pineapple with Macadamia Crunch, Plum Crisp (page 182), and Flourless Chocolate Walnut Torte (page 262).

Nuts are truly the most forgiving ingredient in baking, and that's probably why they tend to get forgotten and pushed around. But even nuts that have been hanging around in the back of the cupboard for a while can be polished right up with ten minutes in a hot oven; toasting them really refreshes the flavors of any packaged nuts. See the notes on page 14 for more on toasting and peeling. Nuts that have already turned rancid, however, cannot be saved. The oils in nuts are rather delicate and when they turn rancid the taste of the nuts becomes distinctly "off," almost like gasoline. Taste your nuts before you go to the trouble of cooking them; if they are rancid or stale, you will certainly know it. Harder nuts, like almonds and peanuts, take much longer to turn rancid. Roasted nuts will not turn rancid, but they may go stale. Again, taste them to see.

Nut desserts are especially appealing in the autumn and winter, when their substance and their affinity for spices make for comforting desserts that are luxurious but still homey. The built-in crunch of Toasted Hazelnut-Almond Biscotti and our cookie-spiked Biscuit Tortoni, the mellow moistness of our Marzipan Torte, and the mouth-filling savor of Roasted Peanut Ice Cream are just a few ways to use these humble-looking but extraordinary gifts of Nature.

marzipan torte with ginger

1¼ cups sugar

8 ounces marzipan (see sidenote)

10 ounces (2½ sticks) unsalted butter, slightly softened

1 teaspoon pure vanilla extract

6 eggs

1 cup all-purpose flour

1½ teaspoons baking powder

¼ teaspoon salt

½ teaspoon ground ginger

Confectioners' sugar

The secret ingredient that makes this cake so moist, so fragrant, and so sweetly long-lasting is an ancient treasure of cooks: almond-sugar paste, also known as marzipan. Like many sweets, marzipan traveled to Europe from the Middle East and was immediately, enthusiastically adopted by pastry cooks. You can buy marzipan in candy stores and in the baking section of many supermarkets.

This is a torte in the famous Austro-Hungarian baking tradition, flat and dense, with nuts replacing some of the flour (Linzer torte is the most famous example). A beautiful deep gold color, it is easily made from ingredients you are likely to have around the kitchen and is even better the day after it is made. Serve it in small slices, with fresh fruit, fruit compote, ice cream, or nothing but a sprinkling of powdered sugar.

Heat the oven to 350 degrees. Butter and flour a 9-inch springform pan.

Combine the sugar and marzipan in a food processor. Pulse until combined into fine crumbs.

Cream the butter in a mixer fitted with a paddle attachment (or using a hand mixer) until smooth. Add the sugar-marzipan mixture and mix. Add the vanilla and mix. Add the eggs two at a time, mixing after each addition.

Sift the flour, baking powder, salt, and ginger together. Working in batches, add the dry ingredients to the marzipan mixture, mixing after each addition just until combined.

Pour into the pan and bake until the cake is firm in the center and a toothpick inserted into the center comes out dry and almost clean (a few crumbs are okay), 60 to 75 minutes. Let cool in the pan. (*The torte can be made up to 24 hours in advance and stored at room temperature.*)

When ready to serve, remove the sides of the pan and dust the top with confectioners' sugar.

MAKES 1 CAKE

This is a perfect cake for afternoon tea or coffee. We'd drink a strong brewed leaf tea, such as Ty-Phoo.

chocolate pecan pie

1½ cups pecan halves, toasted (page 14) and cooled

2 eggs

½ cup sugar

½ cup light corn syrup

4 tablespoons unsalted butter, melted

1 recipe Pâte Brisée (page 34), rolled out, pressed into a 10-inch tart pan with a removable bottom, and prebaked

6 ounces semisweet chocolate, coarsely chopped or semisweet chocolate morsels

Heat the oven to 350 degrees.

Whisk the eggs in a medium bowl. Whisk in the sugar, corn syrup, and melted butter.

Place the prebaked crust on a cookie sheet. Sprinkle in the toasted pecans and chocolate pieces. Pour the egg mixture gently over the pecans and chocolate. Bake 45 to 50 minutes, until the filling is set and slightly risen. Let cool in the pan to room temperature. Remove the sides of the pan.

Refrigerate at least 2 hours. *(Or refrigerate until ready to serve, up to 24 hours.)* Slice the pie with a serrated knife when it comes out of the refrigerator, but let warm to room temperature before serving.

MAKES 1 TART

Hot coffee with a strong character, such as Mocha Java, would balance this mouth-filling dessert and melt its richness.

Pecans and blueberries were among the "exotic" American delicacies we served to our English friends at Stapleford Park Hotel in Leicestershire, where we in turn were introduced to English treats like real mince pie and gooseberries. Pecans are an indigenous American nut, in the hickory family. Pecan pie is, of course, a Southern classic (European explorers commented on the pecans growing wild all along the Mississippi), but chocolate and nuts are such a good combination that we felt no qualms about adding chunks of chocolate to this otherwise traditional recipe.

cashew-cinnamon brittle

Vegetable oil
½ cup water
2 cups sugar
¼ teaspoon cream of tartar
1 cup light corn syrup
2 teaspoons ground cinnamon
2 tablespoons unsalted butter
2 cups roasted, salted cashew nuts (if using unsalted cashew nuts, add ⅛ teaspoon salt with the sugar)
1 teaspoon baking soda

Who would think it possible to take a pile of sugar and a pile of cashews and spin them together into a shiny, chunky sheet of amber candy? If you've never made candy at home, try it and see how easy it is. Candymaking used to be a popular American recreation. Taffy pulls, fudge parties, and praline-making all turned into festive, social events, especially in winter, when the warmth of the stove was most welcome. With its light cinnamon flavor and handmade look, this candy makes a terrific Christmas present. If you want to be a real perfectionist, wear cotton gloves while breaking the candy to prevent fingerprints.

Generously oil a sheet pan (preferably one with sides), at least 11×17 inches, with vegetable oil.

Combine the water, sugar, cream of tartar, and corn syrup in a medium-size heavy saucepan and bring to a boil over medium heat. Using a candy thermometer to test it, boil the mixture until it reaches 350 degrees. Remove from the heat and, working quickly, whisk in the cinnamon. Whisk in the butter, cashews, and baking soda.

Pour the mixture onto the oiled pan and spread it out a bit with a wooden spoon, to about ¼- to ½-inch thickness. Don't spread it too thin. Let harden, uncovered, in a cool place, 30 to 45 minutes.

Using your hands, break the brittle into pieces. Store in an airtight container. (To wash the saucepan, soak it overnight.)

MAKES 1 SHEET

Intensely sweet nibbles of candy go nicely with strong drink: After-dinner coffee and liqueurs are perfect.

walnut carrot cake with pineapple

FOR THE CAKE

2½ cups freshly grated carrots

1½ cups coarsely chopped walnuts

1 cup fresh or drained canned pineapple chunks

1 cup golden raisins

1 cup packed shredded coconut

2 cups cake flour

2 teaspoons ground cinnamon

2 teaspoons baking soda

½ teaspoon salt

4 eggs

1½ cups sugar

1 cup vegetable oil

FOR THE FROSTING

1 pound cream cheese, preferably fresh

1 cup confectioners' sugar

¼ cup honey

Nuggets of walnut are only the beginning of the treasures hidden in this dark, rich classic cake. We like our carrot cake really loaded with treats: pineapple chunks, coconut shreds, walnuts, golden raisins, and bits of carrot. The cinnamon-spiked cake is really only there to bind the toothsome sweetmeats together.

Tossing moist ingredients like raisins and pineapple in flour helps keep them from "slipping" down into the bottom of the cake; it creates friction and increases their surface area just enough to hold them in place. This is less sweet than other carrot cakes, making the marriage of cake and smooth honey–cream cheese frosting that much better.

A floral tea like Darjeeling is perfumey and perfect here.

Heat the oven to 350 degrees. Butter and flour a 10-inch round cake pan. Cut a circle of parchment or wax paper to fit the bottom of the pan and press it in.

MAKE THE CAKE

Toss the carrots, walnuts, pineapple, raisins, and coconut with ½ cup of the flour in a large bowl. Sift the remaining 1½ cups flour, cinnamon, baking soda, and salt together.

Whisk the eggs and sugar in a large bowl until very fluffy and light. Still whisking, drizzle in the oil. Fold in the dry ingredients. Pour this mixture over the carrot mixture and fold together.

Pour into the pan and bake until the cake is firm in the center, 60 to 75 minutes. Let cool in the pan.

MAKE THE FROSTING

Cream the cream cheese in a mixer until smooth. Add the confectioners' sugar and honey and mix at low speed until combined. Increase the speed to high and beat until fluffy.

When the cake is cool, turn out onto a serving plate with the bottom side up. Peel off the paper and frost. Serve at room temperature.

MAKES 1 CAKE

sugared walnut sundaes in chocolate cups

FOR THE SUGARED WALNUTS
¾ cup sugar
⅓ cup water
Freshly grated zest of ¼ orange
Pinch of ground cinnamon
2 cups walnut halves
FOR THE CUPS AND SPOONS
½ cup walnuts, toasted and coarsely chopped (page 14)
4 ounces semisweet chocolate, melted (page 14)
TO MAKE THE SUNDAES
Ice cream of your choice (we suggest chocolate, vanilla, or coffee)
Hot espresso or strong brewed coffee (or decaf)
Whipped cream

What could be better than eating a chunky ice cream sundae? Eating a chunky ice cream sundae with a chocolate spoon. To put these fetching individual sundaes together, you'll dip the rims of the serving cups and the spoons in melted chocolate, then in chopped walnuts. People will gasp when they see them, but making them is child's play. In fact, without the espresso, these would make a sweet treat for a kids' birthday party, and the birthday boy or girl can help dip them up to 2 days in advance. With the espresso, they are quite sophisticated: We love the interplay of cold ice cream, hot coffee, smooth chocolate, and chunky glazed walnuts.

We must thank Patrick, one of our most faithful waiters at Brasserie T, for inspiring these.

Photograph on page 146.

The coffee in the dessert is all you need to complete the experience.

MAKE THE SUGARED WALNUTS

Combine the sugar, water, orange zest, and cinnamon in a deep saucepan and bring to a boil. Add the walnuts and simmer, stirring, as the water evaporates. The glaze will be shiny and transparent at first, then turn opaque as the water cooks away. When the nuts are completely coated with sugar crystals, they are done. Spread them out on a sheet pan to cool. (To wash the saucepan, soak it overnight.) *(The walnuts can be made up to 2 weeks in advance and stored in an airtight container.)*

COAT THE CUPS AND SPOONS

Spread the toasted walnuts out on a plate. Dip the rims of 6 coffee cups or mugs into the melted chocolate, then into the chopped walnuts. Turn them right side up and set aside. Dip 6 teaspoons in the chocolate until the bowls are covered and sprinkle with chopped walnuts. Set aside on wax paper to cool. Let the cups and spoons cool at room temperature until set, about 2 hours.

TO FINISH THE DESSERT

Scoop ice cream into each chocolate-dipped coffee cup and pour espresso over it. Top with a dollop of whipped cream and sugared walnuts. Place the cup on the saucer and rest a chocolate-dipped spoon alongside.

MAKES 6 SERVINGS

oatmeal cake with broiled coconut

FOR THE CAKE

1 cup rolled oats (not instant)

1¼ cups boiling water

8 tablespoons (1 stick) unsalted butter, slightly softened

½ cup granulated sugar

1 cup light brown sugar, packed

2 eggs

1 teaspoon pure vanilla extract

1½ cups all-purpose flour

1 teaspoon baking soda

1 teaspoon ground cinnamon

¼ teaspoon ground nutmeg

½ teaspoon salt

FOR THE TOPPING

10 tablespoons (1¼ sticks) cold unsalted butter, cut into pieces

⅔ cup light brown sugar, packed

¼ cup heavy cream

⅔ cup chopped walnuts or pecans (page 14)

1 cup packed shredded or flaked sweetened coconut

The nuttiness of rolled oats really works with sweet coconut and crunchy walnuts. Broiling the coconut cooks the sugars into a toasty caramel crust in just a few minutes, but it makes the cake seem much more impressive. The soaked oats keep the batter moist, so this cake lasts particularly well, too. It may be the ultimate after-school snack.

MAKE THE CAKE

Place the oats in a medium bowl. Add the boiling water, mix, and let stand 20 minutes. Heat the oven to 350 degrees. Lightly butter a 9-inch round or square cake pan.

Cream the butter in a mixer fitted with a paddle attachment (or using a hand mixer) until smooth. Add both sugars and mix until smooth and fluffy. Add the eggs and vanilla and mix just until combined. Add the rolled oats and mix just until combined.

Mix the flour, baking soda, cinnamon, nutmeg, and salt together. Working in 3 batches, add the dry ingredients to the butter-oat mixture, mixing just until combined after each addition. Pour into the pan. Bake until a tester inserted into the center of the cake comes out dry and almost clean (a few crumbs are okay), 40 to 50 minutes.

MEANWHILE, MAKE THE TOPPING

In a medium bowl, mix the butter, brown sugar, and cream. Add the nuts and coconut and mix just until combined.

When the cake comes out of the oven, preheat the broiler to high.

Spread the coconut topping evenly over the cake and broil until golden brown, about 2 minutes, watching carefully to make sure it doesn't burn. Let cool at least 10 minutes before serving.

MAKES 1 CAKE

This sweet and crumbly, lightly spiced cake, perfect for an autumn weekend, makes us crave big mugs of hot cider.

broiled pineapple with macadamia crunch

Broiling fruit is a great way to bring out its natural sugars, and a ripe pineapple has plenty of those. With the added crunch of macadamia nuts (they're geographically correct with pineapple, but you could also use pecans or pistachios if you like), this dessert is sophisticated but still simple, and the contrast of juicy fruit and firm nuts is wonderful in your mouth. To make sure that your pineapple is ripe, smell the bottom before you buy; it should have a clear, pungent pineapple scent.

The topping can be made well in advance and held at room temperature until you are ready to serve. You can also prepare the pineapple slices in advance, and the cooking happens very quickly.

1 whole ripe pineapple
1 cup coarsely chopped macadamia nuts
⅓ cup light brown sugar, packed
4 tablespoons (½ stick) unsalted butter, melted and slightly cooled
Pinch of salt

Heat the broiler to very hot.

Cut off the top of the pineapple. Cut a slice off the bottom to stabilize the pineapple, then peel from top to bottom with a sharp knife. Cut out any "eyes" remaining in the fruit. Cut into ½-inch-thick slices. Using a small cookie or biscuit cutter, cut the core out of each slice. Divide the slices on ovenproof plates and chill until ready to serve.

In a small bowl, toss together the macadamia nuts, sugar, butter, and salt. Spoon over the pineapple slices.

Broil (not too close to the heat) until the topping is caramelized and bubbly, 2 to 4 minutes. Serve hot.

MAKES 4 TO 6 SERVINGS

The warm softness and crunch of this fruity dessert calls for cold contrast—a chilled late-harvest Gewürztraminer has the perfect blend of fruit and spice.

biscuit tortoni with amaretti and poached nectarines

FOR THE TORTONI

1 cup small amaretti cookies plus 7 to 9 extra cookies, for garnish

2/3 cup whole almonds, toasted (page 14) and cooled

1 cup chilled heavy cream

7 tablespoons sugar

2 eggs, separated

1 tablespoon Amaretto liqueur

FOR THE NECTARINES

2 cups water

1 cup sugar

1 strip lemon zest, about 1 inch x 3 inches

1/2 vanilla bean, split lengthwise

3 nectarines

In 1798, when a spiffy new Italian ice cream parlor opened in Paris, even the notoriously picky Parisians had to admit that Signor Tortoni had a light hand with his **granitas, sorbettos,** and **semifreddos.** This signature dessert (which has long outlived the café; it closed in 1893) is a simple **semifreddo:** It is much less custardy than ice cream, is lightened with whipped egg whites, and never quite freezes hard.

This is the most wonderful use of toasted almonds imaginable. It is a sublime rendition of a Good Humor Toasted Almond Bar, accomplished with a combination of real toasted almonds and ground amaretti cookies —the sweet, hard little macaroons that come from Italy in red tins, labeled "Amaretti di Saronno." The finished tortoni has almonds both inside and on top.

With the cool, creamy semifreddo and the crunchy, toasty nuts, the soft tartness of a nectarine is wonderfully mouth-filling. Plain, very ripe peaches or apricots would also be wonderful.

MAKE THE TORTONI

Butter a medium bowl or a 6-inch springform pan. Line with plastic wrap, letting at least 3 inches of extra wrap hang over the sides.

Pulse 1 cup amaretti cookies and the almonds in a food processor until coarsely ground. Set aside.

Whip the heavy cream and 4 tablespoons of the sugar until stiff. Refrigerate until ready to use.

Whip the egg yolks and 1 tablespoon of the sugar until light and lemon-colored. Add the Amaretto and whip until incorporated. Set aside.

Whip the egg whites in a clean, dry bowl until soft peaks form. Add the remaining 2 tablespoons of sugar and continue whipping just until stiff and glossy, about 30 seconds more.

Fold half of the ground almond mixture into the egg yolk mixture. Fold the egg whites into the egg yolk mixture, then fold in the cold whipped cream. Spoon the mixture into the bowl or pan, pulling on the plastic wrap to eliminate creases. Freeze, uncovered, 3 to 4 hours (*or up to 1 week*).

PREPARE THE NECTARINES

Bring the water, sugar, lemon zest, and vanilla bean to a simmer in a saucepan. Cut the nectarines in half and unscrew the two halves to remove the pit. Cut each half in half again. Add the fruit to the simmering syrup and cook until slightly softened, 3 to 5 minutes. Remove from the heat and let the fruit and syrup cool in the pan.

When ready to serve, take the tortoni out of the freezer. Invert the bowl or pan on a serving plate. Remove the sides of the pan; or, if using a bowl and the tortoni doesn't come out, rub the out side of the bowl with a hot, wet sponge or cloth and pull gently on the overhanging plastic wrap. Peel off the plastic wrap.

Sprinkle the top of the tortoni with the remaining ground almond mixture. Place 6 or 8 whole amaretti cookies (depending on how many people you are serving) around the tortoni, on the plate. Place 1 cookie on the center of the top of the tortoni.

Surround the tortoni with poached nectarines, lifting them out of the liquid and shaking to remove any excess. Or, serve the nectarines at the table, placing them on the individual plates. Serve the tortoni immediately, cut into wedges.

MAKES 6 TO 8 SERVINGS

◗ *A cool glass of Prosecco, a sparkling white wine from Italy, is the perfect light and fruity accompaniment.*

roasted peanut ice cream

½ cup roasted peanuts
1½ cups heavy cream
2½ cups half-and-half
½ vanilla bean, split lengthwise
¼ cup smooth peanut butter
9 egg yolks
¾ cup sugar

Toast the roasted peanuts as described on page 14. Let cool. Pulse in a food processor just until coarsely chopped. Set aside.

Heat the cream, half-and-half, vanilla bean, and peanut butter in a saucepan over medium heat, whisking occasionally to make sure the mixture doesn't scorch on the bottom. When it reaches a fast simmer (do not let it boil), immediately turn off the heat. Set aside to infuse 15 minutes.

Whisk the egg yolks and sugar together. Whisking constantly, slowly pour the still-hot cream mixture into the egg yolk mixture. Return the mixture to the saucepan and cook over medium heat, stirring constantly with a wooden spoon. At 160 degrees, the mixture will give off a puff of steam. When the mixture reaches 180 degrees it will be thickened and creamy, like eggnog. If you don't have a thermometer, test it by dipping a wooden spoon into the mixture. Run your finger down the back of the spoon. If the stripe remains clear, the mixture is ready; if the edges blur, the mixture is not quite thick enough yet. When it is ready, quickly remove it from the heat.

Meanwhile, half-fill a large bowl with ice water. Strain the mixture into a smaller bowl to smooth it and remove the vanilla bean. Rest the smaller bowl in the ice water and let the mixture cool, stirring often, then freeze according to the directions of your ice-cream maker.

Put a large mixing bowl in the freezer to chill. When the ice cream is finished, transfer it to the frozen bowl. Using a sturdy rubber spatula, fold in the chopped peanuts. Freeze.

MAKES 1 QUART

Ice cream calls for something thirst-quenching and light, like lemonade. For especially pretty glasses, freeze ice cubes with whole blueberries in the center.

Those of us who like peanut desserts tend to **really** like peanut desserts, so here's an ice cream with a double peanut hit: smooth peanut butter and fresh chopped peanuts. Plain peanut is such an intense flavor that putting it in ice cream actually improves it; the cream tones it down deliciously. And, of course, your kids will think you are a genius.

This was the very first ice cream Gale ever made, as a Brownie at Camp Sacagawea. The Indian maiden the camp is named for probably ate plenty of peanuts herself—they were among the foods the native American population tried to persuade the Pilgrims to eat during those first hard years. But those Pilgrims were pretty stubborn, and peanuts didn't catch on in America until well into the nineteenth century.

toasted hazelnut-almond biscotti

Hazelnuts and chocolate have been an esteemed flavor combination since the seventeenth century, when chocolate was quite new to Europe. Chocolate was treated as a medicinal product, and cocoa powder mixed with water was prescribed as a digestive, rather like Alka-Seltzer. Its bitter taste was certainly medicinal. No wonder the aristocrats who could afford chocolate soon began to add sugar, cloves, and hazelnuts to the mixture!

Here the combination joins with chunks of almond in a crisp and airy cookie that is wonderful dunked into sweet wine, cold milk, or hot coffee. Biscotti have been made the same way for centuries: They are cooked twice, which is where they get their Italian name; **bis cuit** means the same thing in French. They are cooked dry so that they will last for a long time, until revived with a tasty liquid. These harmonize beautifully with spicy custards and ice creams, like our Cardamom-Coffee Custard (page 246).

Biscotti are baked dry so that they can be saved for a long time and, eventually, deliciously softened in liquid. Tradition in Tuscany, where biscotti originated, demands sweet vin santo *(holy wine), an amber-colored dessert wine that resembles sherry.*

2 cups sifted all-purpose flour
½ teaspoon baking powder
½ teaspoon baking soda
¼ teaspoon salt
1 cup sugar
⅓ cup blanched whole almonds, toasted (page 14)
12 ounces bittersweet chocolate, cut into small chunks with a heavy knife
1½ cups whole hazelnuts, toasted and peeled (page 14)
2 eggs
1 teaspoon pure vanilla extract
¼ teaspoon pure almond extract
2 tablespoons Amaretto liqueur

Heat the oven to 375 degrees. Grease a large sheet pan.

Sift the sifted flour, baking powder, baking soda, salt, and sugar together. Transfer ½ cup of the mixture to a food processor. Add the toasted almonds and grind until fine and powdery, about 45 seconds. Add to the dry ingredients. Add the chopped chocolate and whole hazelnuts and mix.

Whisk the eggs, extracts, and Amaretto together. Add to the dry ingredients and mix. The dough may seem dry, but it will come together as you work it. Turn the dough out onto a lightly floured work surface and divide into 2 equal pieces. Wet your hands and roll each piece of dough into a flattened log about 10 inches long, 3 inches wide, and 1 inch high.

Transfer the logs to the pan, leaving at least 3 inches between the logs (they will spread during baking). Bake until golden brown, 25 to 30 minutes, rotating the pan after 15 minutes to ensure even baking.

Let cool 30 minutes. Reduce the oven temperature to 300 degrees. Carefully transfer the logs to a cutting board. Wipe off the sheet pan and butter it again.

Using a serrated knife, cut the logs on the diagonal into ½-inch-thick slices, discarding the ends. Arrange the slices cut side up on the sheet pan. Bake until toasted, 20 to 25 minutes. Turn the oven off, prop the oven door open, and let cool completely in the oven to set the chocolate. Store in an airtight container.

MAKES ABOUT 30 BISCOTTI

cheese

"Poets have been mysteriously silent
on the subject of cheese."
G. K. Chesterton

coeur à la crème

cherry-cheese phyllo napoleon

tiramisù

noodle pudding with farmer cheese and lingonberries

montrachet cheesecake with winter fruit compote

dessert waldorf salad with roquefort

gruyère with pear confit

fontina val d'aosta with golden raisins
  and roasted chestnuts

farmhouse cheddar with oven-dried apples
  and toasted pumpkin seeds

fresh mozzarella with sweet strawberries
  and mint drizzle

fresh goat cheese with caramelized figs

personality profile: Young cheese is a placid and contented milkmaid, soothing and comforting everyone with her strong, milky-white arms. She can be a bit of a loner, but she has many personalities. Cheese shows her age: With time she grows less placid and more challenging, but also more complex and rewarding. Cheese is never stagnant or boring: She changes constantly, from sweet to salty, white to yellow, bland to tangy. Sometimes she even sings the blues.

Fresh. Creamy. Milky. Tangy. Soft. These are the words you'll see a lot of in this chapter, our tribute to an ingredient that we feel isn't included often enough on American dessert tables. From baby-fresh cheeses like cream cheese, mascarpone, mozzarella, and ricotta, through adolescent pleasures like tangy goat cheese, nutty Gruyère, and pillowy Fontina, to powerful adult experiences like sharp Roquefort and farmhouse Cheddar—we love them all. Because of their extraordinary range of flavor, texture, geography, and age, cheese as dessert is especially exciting; there's always a new one to discover, or a way to introduce an old friend to new companions in the friendly Fruit, Nuts, and Flour families.

There are two kinds of desserts in this chapter: desserts that use mild fresh cheeses as a key ingredient (think cheesecake), and desserts that present the complex flavors of some of the world's great aged cheeses, by combining them with our favorite complements.

Cheesecake is one American classic that really shows off the fresh-milk flavor of young cheese, and we've roamed the world for desserts that have the same marvelous mouth-filling effect. In this chapter, we zip across the Atlantic and bump smack into northern France's ultimate nursery dessert, *coeur à la crème,* a simple construction of cream, cheese, and berries that is pure dairy pleasure. Northern Italy's Tiramisù (literally "pick me up") contains cream cheese–like mascarpone showcased by chocolate and coffee, two bittersweet flavors that emphasize the mascarpone's thick creaminess. Dip south for a plate of pillowy mozzarella, fresh mint, and the surprise sweetness of strawberries macerated in a touch of balsamic vinegar and sugar. Back at home, noodle pudding is the homiest, most satisfying dessert casserole imaginable, with mild cottage cheese, golden raisins, and tender egg noodles sparked with tart preserves.

Some fresh cheeses, like ricotta and farmer cheese, are naturally very low in fat, despite their milky character. But when you are cooking with heavy cream, crème fraîche, or cream cheese, processed "low-fat" alternatives are not a good option. They contain thickeners, stabilizers, and preservatives, which do nothing for the flavor or texture. Even full-fat heavy cream has a cooked flavor when it has been ultra-pasteurized. In general, choose dairy products that have been processed as little as possible. Fresh cream cheese from a dairy is worlds away from the supermarket bricks.

Aged cheese, of course, could be a book in itself—or hundreds. We Americans are only just beginning to appreciate the great European cheese tradition, and to explore the possibilities offered by our homegrown dairy tradition. We absorbed the idea of cheese as a part of daily meals when we lived in England, where the "savory" course is part of fine-dining tradition; but the cheese plates in this chapter can actually stand in for dessert.

These plates are really only a jumping-off point for the ones we hope you'll create. We use only a few of the hundreds of excellent cheeses already available to you, not to mention the thousands still to come as we all become more knowledgeable and demanding about good cheese. More than any other dessert ingredient, cheese is a brilliant food to pair with wines. Sweet dessert wines, like fine aged cheeses, are little known in this country, but they can make stunning, mouth- and mind-filling pairings.

Cheese—"milk's leap toward immortality"—is full of tradition, but it also tastes new these days. Dairy-rich desserts are long out of fashion, but real cream is too wonderful an ingredient to ignore forever. We'll bet you already eat ice cream; now take the final step and plunge with us into the cool, creamy world of cheese.

coeur à la crème

We couldn't resist one heart-shaped dessert, and neither will whoever is lucky enough to eat your **coeur à la crème.**

We're delighted to see more and more American cheesemakers turning out the French-style dairy products **fromage blanc** and **crème fraîche**—so fresh and white that they barely qualify as cheese. They are combined in this classic French dessert: pure dairy in five different forms, sprinkled with sugar! Its simple flavor is best set off with a few perfect berries. In France, **coeur à la crème,** like Nutella sandwiches and hot chocolate with cream, is considered a children's dessert, but it's perfect for adults too, every so often. It's great for Sunday brunch.

In French kitchenware stores, you can buy special heart-shaped molds with draining holes just for making this dessert. If you have a heart-shaped mold **without** draining holes, such as a cake pan, you can still use it to drain the cheese. Just line it with a few extra layers of cheesecloth. If there's nothing heart-shaped in your kitchen, resort to a large colander. If you can get **fromage blanc,** substitute a pound of it for our blend of cottage and cream cheeses and begin the recipe by draining the **fromage blanc.**

8 ounces cottage cheese
8 ounces cream cheese
½ cup sour cream or crème fraîche
2 tablespoons confectioners' sugar
½ cup chilled heavy cream, whipped stiff
Heavy cream
Granulated sugar
Strawberries, raspberries, blackberries, or blueberries

Press the cottage cheese through a coarse sieve into a bowl. Cream the cottage cheese in a mixer fitted with a paddle attachment (or using a hand mixer) until as smooth as possible (it will remain a bit grainy, from the curds). Add the cream cheese and mix. Add the sour cream and confectioners' sugar and mix well. Fold in the whipped cream.

Lightly dampen a 12-inch square of cheesecloth. Use it to line a 3-cup heart-shaped mold with draining holes (or use a large colander; see sidenote). Spoon the cheese mixture into the mold, tapping the filled mold on the counter to pack it down. Place the mold on a plate (to catch any liquid) and refrigerate at least 2 hours or overnight.

Invert the mold on a serving plate. Lift off the mold and peel off the cheesecloth. Serve in small wedges, pouring a couple of teaspoons of cream and sprinkling granulated sugar over each serving at the table. Pass the berries.

MAKES 6 TO 10 SERVINGS

A light, fresh iced tea with berry or citrus flavors—and maybe an aromatic fresh mint sprig—would be ideal.

cherry-cheese phyllo napoleon

FOR THE PHYLLO

3 sheets phyllo pastry, thawed overnight in the refrigerator if frozen, and kept moist (page 15)

6 tablespoons unsalted butter, melted

6 tablespoons sugar

FOR THE CHERRY FILLING

1¼ pounds fresh or frozen pitted cherries (if frozen, use slightly thawed)

2 tablespoons cornstarch

½ cup sugar

1 teaspoon fresh lemon juice

FOR THE CHEESE FILLING

½ cup chilled heavy cream

½ cup ricotta cheese

8 ounces cream cheese

½ cup sugar

1 teaspoon pure vanilla extract

½ teaspoon freshly grated orange zest

Confectioners' sugar

PREPARE THE PHYLLO

Heat the oven to 350 degrees. Line a large sheet pan with parchment paper. Place 1 sheet of phyllo on the pan and brush with melted butter. Sprinkle evenly with 2 tablespoons of sugar, then place another sheet of phyllo on top. Brush with melted butter, sprinkle with sugar, lay another sheet of phyllo on top, brush with melted butter, and sprinkle with sugar. You may not use up all the melted butter.

With the tip of a sharp knife or a pizza cutter, cut the phyllo into 12 to 18 rectangles (you'll need 3 per serving). Cover with parchment paper. Place another, empty sheet pan on top. (This is to keep the phyllo from buckling during baking.) Bake until golden brown, about 15 minutes. Remove the top sheet pan and let cool. *(The recipe can be made up to this point up to 24 hours in advance. Store the rectangles in an airtight container.)*

MAKE THE CHERRY FILLING

Combine the cherries, cornstarch, sugar, and lemon juice in a medium saucepan, and mix well. Heat over medium heat until the cherries release their juices and the mixture has thickened, 3 to 5 minutes. Let cool to room temperature.

Cheesecake with cherry topping always seemed like a good idea—cherries are so dark and intense, great with a creamy backdrop—but we knew we could do better than those synthetic supermarket versions full of gelatin, cornstarch, and who knows what else. This fluffy stack is packed with real, direct flavors: ripe cherries, crisp wafers of phyllo dough, and fluffy orange- and vanilla-scented ricotta cheese. Like buttermilk, ricotta is really a by-product of another process. Just as churning butter leaves the buttermilk behind, making cheese leaves the whey behind. (The curds become the cheese, as Miss Muffet could tell you.) When whey is heated again (recooked, thus **ri cotta**), the remaining milk solids curdle into ricotta cheese, which is extremely low in fat and, when fresh, extremely delicious.

It's rare to see fresh Italian ricotta in American markets, but if you do see it, snap it up. Usually made from sheep's milk rather than cow's milk, it has a nuttier, tangier flavor than the domestic product (though fresh domestic ricotta is usually excellent).

MAKE THE CHEESE FILLING

Whip the cream until stiff and refrigerate. Mix the ricotta and cream cheese in a mixer fitted with a paddle attachment (or using a hand mixer) until as smooth as possible (it will remain a bit grainy, from the ricotta). Add the sugar, vanilla, and zest and mix. Fold in the whipped cream. Refrigerate until ready to serve.

To serve, put 1 phyllo rectangle on each of 4 to 6 dessert plates. Top with a spoonful of cheese filling, then a spoonful of cherry filling. Top with another phyllo rectangle, pressing lightly. Top with another spoonful of cheese, then one of cherries. Finish with a phyllo rectangle and dust with confectioners' sugar. Serve immediately.

MAKES 4 TO 6 SERVINGS

Cheesecake and coffee is a natural combination; or for a racier dessert course, pour a sweet German Scheurebe Trockenbeeren-auslese, a dessert wine with bright blackcurrant flavors.

tiramisù

7 egg yolks (see page 14 for a note on raw egg yolks)
1¼ cups sugar
26 ounces (3¼ cups) mascarpone cheese
1 cup chilled heavy cream
1 teaspoon powdered gelatin
2 tablespoons cool water
3 egg whites, at room temperature
2½ cups cooled espresso (instant is fine)
½ cup Kahlúa or another coffee liqueur
2 to 3 packages ladyfingers (about 72 ladyfingers)
1 cup semisweet chocolate shavings (page 14)

Whip the egg yolks and 1 cup of the sugar in a mixer fitted with a whisk attachment (or using a hand mixer) until thick, fluffy, and pale yellow. When you lift the beaters, the mixture should fall in a smooth, flat ribbon. Add the mascarpone and whip just until blended and stiff, being careful not to overmix (the mixture may separate). Cover and refrigerate.

Whip the cream until stiff in a clean, dry bowl. Cover and refrigerate.

Combine the gelatin and water in a small bowl or the top of a double boiler, and let soak about 10 minutes, stirring occasionally. Heat in a microwave or over simmering water until dissolved, stirring occasionally.

Whip the egg whites in a clean, dry bowl until soft peaks form. Add the remaining ¼ cup sugar and continue whipping until stiff and glossy. With the mixer running, slowly drizzle in the melted gelatin and continue whipping until incorporated. Fold into the mascarpone mixture, then fold in the whipped cream. Set aside.

Combine the espresso and Kahlúa in a shallow dish. One by one, dip about half of the ladyfingers in the espresso mixture, let soak 5 seconds, and transfer to a 9×13-inch baking dish, creating a single layer of ladyfingers. Pour half the mascarpone mousse over the ladyfingers and smooth the top. Sprinkle half the chocolate shavings over the mousse. Repeat with the remaining ladyfingers, mousse, and chocolate. Chill, lightly covered, at least 2 hours. *(Or refrigerate until ready to serve, up to 24 hours.)* Cut into squares and serve cold.

MAKES 8 TO 12 SERVINGS

This coffee-scented classic comes from the Lombardy region of northern Italy, where the cream and cheese are very good and very plentiful. It's a voluptuous dessert that you practically lie down in, and definitely a dessert for those who love cream.

Mascarpone, like cream cheese and clotted cream, which it resembles, isn't really a cheese (it is never curdled and is made from pasteurized milk). It is, however, smooth, naturally sweet, and delicious, with a texture that is very similar to buttercream frosting. Both are as rich as cream can be without tipping the scales into butter.

Mouthfuls of cool mascarpone contrast wonderfully with the dark, roasted flavor of espresso. What makes this version ours? We lighten the cheese with whipped cream and egg whites, we use coffee liqueur instead of the traditional rum or brandy, and we prefer a topping of grated dark chocolate to the usual cocoa powder. The cocoa always used to make us cough, like the powdered sugar on doughnuts!

Hot espresso, perhaps with a shot of anisette or rum, is a heady accompaniment that cuts through the richness.

noodle pudding with farmer cheese and lingonberries

8 ounces medium-wide egg noodles
3 eggs
8 ounces farmer cheese, pot cheese, or cottage cheese, crumbled (see sidenote)
¼ cup light brown sugar, packed
1 cup sour cream
⅓ cup milk
Pinch of salt
½ teaspoon pure vanilla extract
Pinch of ground cinnamon
Pinch of ground nutmeg
¼ cup thawed apple juice concentrate
4 tablespoons (½ stick) cold unsalted butter, cut into pieces
¾ cup lingonberry preserves, redcurrant preserves, or cranberry sauce
1½ teaspoons sugar mixed with 1 large pinch of cinnamon
Sour cream for serving (optional)

Noodle pudding (or **kugel,** in Yiddish) is a brilliant example of creative cooking, taking ingredients—cheese and pasta—that are usually used in savory dishes, then adding a bit of sugar and fruit to transform the dish into a satisfying dessert. We created this dessert after a vacation in Wisconsin, where the local cheeses are wonderfully fresh and the local population's fondness for lingonberries reveals their Scandinavian roots. Lingonberries are very closely related to cranberries.

Farmer cheese (like pot cheese) is simply a drier version of cottage cheese; all three are un-aged fresh cheeses made from pasteurized milk. If you substitute cottage cheese, use large-curd cheese and drain it in a colander lined with a coffee filter for about an hour before using.

Bring a large pot of water to a boil, add the noodles, and boil until cooked through but not mushy. Drain well and set aside.

Heat the oven to 350 degrees and butter an 8-inch square baking dish.

Whisk the eggs in a large bowl until frothy. Whisk in the cheese, brown sugar, sour cream, milk, salt, vanilla, cinnamon, nutmeg, and apple juice concentrate. Add the drained noodles, butter pieces, and lingonberry preserves and mix.

Pour into the pan, sprinkle with cinnamon sugar, and bake until the pudding is set and butter is bubbling around the edges, 30 to 40 minutes.

Let cool 10 minutes before serving. Serve warm or at room temperature, cut into squares and topped with a dollop of sour cream (if desired).

MAKES 6 TO 8 SERVINGS

A lemony cup of tea with a fat square of noodle pudding makes a wonderful old-fashioned snack.

montrachet cheesecake
with winter fruit compote

FOR THE CHEESECAKE

1 recipe Crumbly Pie Crust (page 33), pressed into the bottom of a
  9-inch springform pan

1 tablespoon unsalted butter, melted

1½ pounds fresh (not aged) goat cheese

8 ounces cream cheese

2 cups sugar

1 teaspoon pure vanilla extract

8 eggs

FOR THE COMPOTE

¼ cup dried cherries

½ cup dried apricots

½ cup prunes

¼ cup golden raisins

½ vanilla bean, split lengthwise

1 piece orange zest, about 1 inch x 3 inches

1 piece lemon zest, about 1 inch x 3 inches

2 tablespoons ruby or tawny port (see sidenote)

2 cups water

1 cup sugar

2 tablespoons orange juice

MAKE THE CHEESECAKE

Heat the oven to 400 degrees. Bake the crust until light golden
brown, 20 to 25 minutes. Remove the crust and reduce the oven
temperature to 325 degrees. When the pan is cool enough to
handle, brush the sides with melted butter.

Cream the goat cheese and cream cheese in a mixer fitted with a
paddle attachment (or using a hand mixer) until very smooth. Add
the sugar and vanilla and mix. Add the eggs two at a time, mixing
and scraping down the bowl after each addition. Pour into the pan
and smooth the top.

Place the springform pan on a double-layer sheet of aluminum
foil, with at least 3 inches of foil all around the pan. Fold the aluminum foil up around the sides of the pan. Fill a roasting pan
large enough to hold the cake pan with hot water to a depth of
about 1 inch, then lift the foil-wrapped cake into the roasting pan,
keeping the foil turned up so that it prevents water from

Fresh, un-aged goat cheese such as
French Montrachet adds a very subtle
tang to this cheesecake; it makes the
filling bold-flavored enough to stand
up to an intense dried-fruit compote.
Our friend Laura Chenel, a highly
skilled cheesemaker in northern
California's Sonoma County, makes
our favorite cheese. Laura has a herd
of 300 female goats, and she knows all
their names.

The glowing ruby-amber compote
and snowy cake make this a very beautiful plate. It's like a fruit and cheese
plate, but in cake form. Serve it in
small slices. Ruby port is young and
fiery, but it can have a good fruity
flavor; aged tawny port tastes more
like the wood it is aged in and is
silkier.

overflowing or seeping into the cake. Be careful not to make any holes in the foil as you do this!

Bake about 1 hour, until the top of the cake is golden and dry to the touch, though still a bit soft in the center. It should "shimmy" a bit when you shake the pan; it will firm up more as it cools. Lift the foil up to remove the cake from the water bath, remove the foil, and let cool 1 hour. Refrigerate at least 2 hours before serving.

MAKE THE COMPOTE

Combine all of the ingredients in a medium saucepan. Bring to a simmer, stir, and reduce the heat so that the mixture is barely simmering. Simmer 20 minutes, stirring occasionally. Turn off the heat, cover, and set aside to soften and infuse. If not using within a few hours, refrigerate until ready to serve.

When ready to serve, remove the sides of the cheesecake pan and, if desired, reheat the compote. Serve the cake in small wedges, with compote spooned around the sides.

MAKES 8 TO 12 SERVINGS

Sip the same port you used to make the compote, for a peerless flavor pairing.

dessert waldorf salad
with roquefort

¼ cup thawed frozen apple juice concentrate

1 tablespoon fresh lemon juice

¼ cup sour cream

Pinch of salt

1 sweet red apple (do not peel), cored and diced

1 tart green apple (do not peel), cored and diced

¼ cup diced fennel bulb

½ cup raisins

½ cup coarsely chopped walnuts

2 leaves fresh mint, shredded

¼ cup crumbled Roquefort or other strong blue cheese

4 slices cinnamon-raisin bread

Put 4 serving plates in the refrigerator to chill.

Whisk the apple juice concentrate, lemon juice, sour cream, and salt in a large bowl. Add the apples, fennel, raisins, walnuts, mint, and Roquefort and toss gently just until combined. Divide on serving plates.

Just before serving, toast the bread and cut each slice diagonally into quarters. Arrange around the salads and serve immediately.

MAKES 4 SERVINGS

The complex sweet and salty flavors and chunky texture call for a substantial fortified wine such as a cream sherry; the best bear the name Oloroso.

Back to the future, again. We've long had a sneaking fondness for chunky, sweet-salty Waldorf salad, but it was begging to be reinvented. Turns out it wanted to be a cheese plate all along! We realized that a firm, sharp blue cheese was the perfect match for the apples, walnuts, and fennel (instead of celery) that we wanted to keep on the plate. After much tinkering, this final version smooths out the blue cheese with sour cream, lemon juice, a sweet dash of apple juice concentrate, and fresh mint to brighten all the flavors. This makes a fun and very delicious fall or winter dessert.

Roquefort is a very strong and tangy blue cheese, as it is made from raw sheep's milk. English Stilton or Italian Gorgonzola **naturale** (stronger than the young Gorgonzola **dolcelatte**) are close in flavor and texture, but even a milder (and less pricey) Danish blue cheese would give a good effect.

gruyère with pear confit

2 large firm Anjou or Bartlett pears
4 tablespoons (½ stick) unsalted butter
½ cup light brown sugar, packed
1 tablespoon fresh lemon juice
2 slices fresh ginger, about ¼ inch thick
4 ounces Gruyère cheese
8 thin slices wholegrain bread, cut in half

Aged Gruyère is used most often in French cooking as a grating cheese, to create the melting mouthfuls that top hot onion soup or ooze from the layers of a potato gratin. But Gruyère, which is made in both the Swiss and French Alpine regions, is also a wonderful cheese in its own right, with a nutty, rich flavor and smooth texture. When it's time for dessert, the gentle, fruity tang of pears cooked soft with lemon and warmed with ginger makes this plate wonderfully satisfying. To really savor the tastes, try eating in alternating mouthfuls: pears-and-toast, pears-and-cheese, and cheese-and-toast.

Don't use the slender brown Bosc pears for this confit; their texture is too grainy. Fat, not-too-ripe Anjous or Bartletts are a better choice.

Peel the pears and cut them in half. Scoop out the seeds with a melon baller or cut them out with a knife. Slice thin and set aside.

Melt the butter in a medium skillet over medium heat. Add the sugar and cook, stirring, until the butter starts to separate, 3 to 5 minutes. Add the lemon juice and ginger and stir. Add the pears and reduce the heat to low. Cook uncovered, stirring occasionally, until the pear slices are tender and almost translucent and the mixture is thickened, about 30 minutes. Let cool to room temperature.

To serve, shave the cheese with a vegetable peeler or a cheese slicer into thin shards. Toast the bread. Spoon a mound of confit in the center of each serving plate. Fan four pieces of toast around the top of the plate, and pile the cheese shards around the bottom.

MAKES 4 SERVINGS

Hard pear cider is a wonderful sparkling wine, with a light sweetness and a faint echo of pear flavor.

fontina val d'aosta with golden raisins and roasted chestnuts

16 fresh whole chestnuts
⅓ cup golden raisins
2 tablespoons fresh orange juice
4 ounces Fontina Val d'Aosta

Heat the oven to 375 degrees. With the tip of a sharp knife, cut an X in the flat side of each chestnut. Bundle them up in foil and bake 35 minutes. Peel one chestnut to check for softness; continue baking if necessary, until softened.

Meanwhile, combine the raisins and orange juice in a bowl and let macerate at least 15 minutes. Thinly slice the cheese into 8 slices.

As soon as the chestnuts are cool enough to handle, peel 12 of them and divide the chestnuts on 4 serving plates, placing one unpeeled chestnut on each plate. Lay 2 slices of cheese and a spoonful of raisins next to the chestnuts.

MAKES 4 SERVINGS

Vin santo, *an aged dessert wine made in Tuscany, is traditionally offered to all guests in Tuscan homes; its oaky sweetness would be delightful here.*

The Fontina called d'Aosta, made from raw cow's milk in the Italian Alpine valley of Aosta, is the firmest and finest Fontina. It also has a stronger milk and herbal flavor than others. We tasted it first in Bologna and were staggered by how different it is from the flabby Scandinavian Fontinas at the supermarket. It's certainly the best choice when you're going to be eating it in thin slices rather than using it in cooking. If you can't find Fontina Val d'Aosta or another Italian Fontina (it may be called Fontanella or some such), choose another rich, butter-soft cheese such as Taleggio or Pont l'Évêque.

This is a great plate for nibbling, and for lingering over with a glass of wine or Cognac. Don't be daunted by the idea of roasting chestnuts at home; it's easy, and their toasty flavor is wonderful with the sweet raisins. It's a great way to welcome in the holiday season. Our friend Karen has a passion for roasting chestnuts; the foil wrapping is her method.

farmhouse cheddar with oven-dried apples and toasted pumpkin seeds

¼ cup fresh lemon juice

¼ cup sugar

2 medium green apples, cored and left whole (do not peel)

½ cup shelled pumpkin seeds

1 teaspoon olive oil

¼ teaspoon salt

2 grinds of the pepper mill

8 ounces farmhouse Cheddar cheese

Though European cheeses still grab most of the attention of cheese connoisseurs, a handful of great American-made cheeses have really transformed the domestic cheese scene. Laura Chenel's French-style Sonoma goat cheeses, and Grafton Village and Shelburne Farms' fine Vermont Cheddars, based on the classic English farmhouse cheese, are world-class. We developed a taste for real Cheddar during our time in England; there's just nothing like cheese made with real, unpasteurized milk. Any cheese labeled "farmhouse" is made with raw milk; they are well worth seeking out.

This is a very American plate, with Cheddar, apples, and nutty-salty pumpkin seeds you won't be able to stop eating. The apples are dry and crisp, with plenty of apple flavor and sweetness. Eat the sharp cheese with soft, toasted oat bread.

Heat the oven to 275 degrees.

Stir together the lemon juice and sugar in a bowl and set aside to dissolve into a syrup, stirring occasionally. Carefully slice the apples into very thin rings. One at a time, dip the rings into the lemon syrup and arrange in a single layer on a nonstick sheet pan. Bake until crisp, about 1 hour. Let cool. *(The apples can be made up to 3 days in advance and stored in an airtight container.)*

When ready to serve, heat the oven to 400 degrees. Toss the pumpkin seeds with the oil, salt, and pepper on a sheet pan. Spread in a single layer and toast until just beginning to brown, about 10 minutes.

Meanwhile, thinly slice the cheese and divide on 4 serving plates, keeping the cheese on one side of each plate. Place a stack of apple slices in the center. Sprinkle the hot pumpkin seeds on the remaining empty space on the plate.

MAKES 4 SERVINGS

Depending on the weather and the occasion, either hot spiced cider or chilled hard cider would beautifully complement this apple-perfumed plate

fresh mozzarella with
sweet strawberries and mint drizzle

2 balls (about 1 pound) very fresh mozzarella cheese, buffalo or
   cow's milk
2 cups strawberries, green tops removed and cut into chunks
1 tablespoon sugar
½ cup extra-virgin olive oil
8 fresh mint leaves
2 teaspoons best-quality balsamic vinegar

Slice the cheese ½ inch thick. Arrange in overlapping slices on
4 to 6 serving plates.

Toss the strawberries with the sugar in a bowl and set aside.

Puree the oil and mint leaves in a blender or food processor
until smooth and green.

Spoon the berries with their syrup alongside the cheese. Drizzle
both cheese and berries with mint drizzle and a little balsamic
vinegar and serve.

MAKES 4 TO 6 SERVINGS

A bubbly Prosecco at brunchtime leaves everyone feeling cheerful.

All good cheese plates live in the balance of sweet and savory elements. Many of our pairings are regional (Wisconsin Cheddar with apples, Swiss Gruyère with pears), and this one is uniquely Italian, based on a dessert we ate (Okay, inhaled) after lunch in Taggia, a town in the San Remo area. Having spent the morning tasting new olive oil on fresh bread at the Crespi family's plant, we didn't think we were hungry. We were wrong. As we ate, we discovered that soft, fresh mozzarella makes a deliciously soothing dessert, that sweet strawberries and fresh green mint combine beautifully with salad standbys olive oil and balsamic vinegar. Try it for brunch.

Of course, this plate also works as a sort of culinary joke: Substitute tomatoes for the strawberries and basil for the mint and you have the classic antipasto **insalata Caprese.**

Photograph on page 150.

fresh goat cheese
with caramelized figs

8 ounces young goat cheese

4 small bunches green seedless grapes

4 fresh purple or green figs, halved lengthwise

¼ cup coarse or raw sugar

16 whole almonds, toasted (page 14)

8 slices multigrain bread

This very Mediterranean combination takes us back to our first meal from the kitchen of the brilliant Provençal chef Roger Vergé. Eager to reach the warmth of Provence as we drove down from Paris, we arrived about three hours early—to find the great chef, amazingly, picking figs up in the tree outside the restaurant. We had never seen fresh figs on the tree before. On the tree, figs look like nothing special —until you open up those luscious pink-brown-gold centers.

Many artisanal American cheese makers are making fresh goat cheeses now—a world away in flavor and texture from the supermarket logs made from frozen milk. Either a good fresh cheese or a lightly aged one, with a bit more butteriness, would be terrific with these figs. Older cheeses will display yellower rinds, grading to brown, than chalky-white ones, which are completely fresh.

Heat the broiler to very hot.

Slice the goat cheese into ¼-inch-thick coins. Divide the slices on 4 serving plates, placing them on one side of the plate. Place a bunch of grapes next to the cheese.

Arrange the fig halves on a sheet pan and sprinkle with the sugar. Broil just until the sugar is golden brown and caramelized, about 2 minutes. Divide the broiled figs next to the grapes. Divide the almonds next to the figs.

Just before serving, toast the bread and cut each slice diagonally into quarters. Tuck the toast points around the other ingredients and serve.

MAKES 4 SERVINGS

This fruity plate is delightful with a fancy grape juice such as Zinfandel or white, or a light sparkling Moscato d'Asti.

spice

"Had I but a penny in the world,
thou shouldst have it for gingerbread."
Shakespeare

gingerbread people

nutmeg cheesecake

root beer–vanilla parfaits

moist ginger cake with orange icing

sweet-hot white pepper ice cream

saffron-pistachio ice cream

myrna's cinnamon raisin monogram pies

anisette mascarpone cake

vanilla panna cotta

five-spice tea cake

cardamom-coffee custard

allspiced apple butter

personality profile: Spice is a small but pushy individual with a strong personality—he demands *all* the attention at any gathering. But he's warm and fascinating and potent, with a whiff of the exotic. He exerts a strong spell, changing everything he comes in contact with. He doesn't have much substance, but we love him because he livens up the dullest gathering, and always keeps things interesting.

Every pinch of toasty nutmeg, every teaspoon of woodsy cinnamon, every whiff of ginger or saffron or pepper in your kitchen makes you part of the long and dramatic story of spices.

Your innocent-looking spice rack holds a dizzying history of exploration, ingenuity, survival, and determination in those neat little jars, as well as a breathtaking array of colors, flavors, and aromas. Spices play a unique role in cooking, for they are the only ingredient that exists for flavor alone. They come to us from all corners of the earth and even from under the earth itself: some are roots (ginger), some are seeds (cardamom), some are orchids (vanilla), some are flower stigmas (saffron) or tree barks (cinnamon). Even roasted coffee beans can be considered a spice. All are powerfully concentrated flavor sources, and they have to be treated with respect.

We take the array of Madagascar vanilla, Chinese cinnamon, and Tellicherry peppercorns in our markets for granted, but it took centuries to put them there. If not for the love of spices, our world would look completely different. For example, South Africa was settled by the Dutch only because it was a convenient stopover for spice traders sailing between Amsterdam and Java. And Ferdinand and Isabella of Spain might never have sent Cristoforo Colombo in search of the Spice Islands, only to run across the Americas instead. Spices represented wealth in sixteenth-century Europe, and a single ship with a hold full of cloves could make or break a nation's fortunes.

The Spice Islands! A wonderful phrase, evoking a fantasy world where the sun always shines, where the breezes themselves waft the scent of cinnamon among the palm fronds, and where nutmegs hang heavy on the tree, ripe for the picking. Of course, the expensive reality is that most spices are hard to come by, burying their flavor deep inside husks, shells, barks, petals, and roots. To get saffron, whole fields of crocuses must be picked at dawn, and then the stigmas must be painstakingly removed from the blossom, each one of which contains exactly three strands of the precious stuff. (No wonder chefs store it in the restaurant's safe.) Cinnamon must be gently pried off the trunk of an evergreen tree.

Vanilla is a special case in the spice world, and one of our favorites. Out of 20,000 varieties of orchids, vanilla is the only edible one. It is indigenous to the Americas, and is an important flavor component of the other great New World ingredient: chocolate. We love it all on its own. In the American baking tradition, two seasonings are found in virtually every dish, from chocolate chip cookies to yellow cake to apple pie: salt and vanilla. Gale calls them the "underwear" of baking—the invisible essentials that you put on before anything else. But vanilla itself rarely gets the respect we think it deserves, so we urge you to try our Vanilla Panna Cotta, made with real "vanilla caviar": the seeds inside of the bean. Vanilla beans are becoming widely available, and their cherry-creamy-sweet aroma is worlds away from vanilla extract.

We used ground spices from the supermarket to test the recipes. They were not freshly ground, but they were freshly bought. Preground spices can last for some time, but the fact is that their flavor starts to deteriorate as soon as they are ground. Buy them at a busy market and replace them as often as you can, at least once a year. Yes, we know it's hard to throw things out, but this is your cooking we're talking about. If you're going to the trouble of baking, you want the end result to be as good as it can be.

Spices are the jewelry of dessert-making—the alluring, decorative touches that give style to simplicity and add sensuality to seasoning. Choose them carefully, use them wisely, and you'll dazzle everyone.

gingerbread people

Ginger has been loved for its stimulating, medicinal powers for thousands of years. Pastes pounded from fresh ginger, honey, and other spices, then formed into pills prescribed to treat everything from broken bones to food poisoning are the true ancestors of gingerbread. But that's only the beginning of the gingerbread story.

In medieval Europe, gingerbread figurines in the shapes of churches and castles were created to honor the aristocracy. Visitors to the court of Queen Elizabeth I were presented with gingerbread shaped in their own likenesses. Later, the custom trickled down to the common folk: Lovers began to exchange gingerbread hearts; holidays were commemorated with gingerbread symbols and decorations; and parents gave gingerbread men to their children. Today, gingerbread boys and girls can be cut out of the sweet-spicy dough and decorated as anyone wishes. This is a great project for a snowy day.

FOR THE COOKIES

8 ounces (2 sticks) unsalted butter, slightly softened
¾ cup light brown sugar, packed
1 egg
½ cup dark molasses (not blackstrap)
½ teaspoon pure vanilla extract
3¼ cups all-purpose flour
½ teaspoon baking soda
¼ teaspoon salt
1 teaspoon ground cinnamon
2 teaspoons ground ginger
¼ teaspoon ground cloves
Raisins, currants, dried cranberries, or dried cherries

FOR DECORATING

White icing (page 99)
Colored sugar

MAKE THE COOKIES

Cream the butter in a mixer fitted with a paddle attachment (or using a hand mixer) until smooth. Add the sugar and mix. Add the egg and mix. Add the molasses and vanilla and mix.

Sift the flour, baking soda, salt, cinnamon, ginger, and cloves together. Working in batches, and mixing after each addition just until combined, add the dry ingredients to the butter-sugar mixture. Shape the dough into a thick disk, wrap in wax paper, and refrigerate 1 to 2 hours.

Heat the oven to 350 degrees. Grease one or two cookie sheets.

On a lightly floured surface, roll the dough out ¼ inch thick. Cut into boy and girl shapes with cookie cutters. Use dried fruit to make a line of buttons down the front of each figure. Bake 12 to 15 minutes, until firm. Cool on wire racks.

DECORATE THE COOKIES

Using a pastry bag, decorate the figures with icing and/or colored sugar.

MAKES ABOUT 18 LARGE COOKIES

➤ *Ice-cold milk, strong hot tea stirred with a hard butterscotch candy, or even a hot rum grog would all complement the spice.*

nutmeg cheesecake

3 tablespoons unsalted butter, melted
2 pounds fresh cream cheese, at room temperature
1 teaspoon pure vanilla extract
¼ teaspoon pure almond extract
1 teaspoon ground nutmeg
1¾ cups sugar
⅛ teaspoon salt
4 eggs
⅓ cup graham cracker crumbs (available at large supermarkets, or pulse
    whole graham crackers in a food processor)

Thickly brush a 9-inch springform pan with half of the melted
butter and place in the freezer to harden, about 10 minutes. When
hard, repeat to make a thick coating of butter. Adjust your oven
rack to the lowest position and heat the oven to 350 degrees.

Beat the cream cheese in a mixer fitted with a paddle attachment (or using a hand mixer) until fluffy and very smooth. Beat in
the extracts, nutmeg, sugar, and salt. Add the eggs one at a time,
scraping down the bowl after each addition. Pour into the pan.

Place the pan on a double-layer sheet of aluminum foil, with at
least 3 inches of foil all around the pan. Fold the aluminum foil up
around the sides of the pan. Fill a roasting pan large enough to
hold the cake pan with hot water to a depth of about 1 inch, then
lift the foil-wrapped cake into the roasting pan, keeping the foil
turned up so that it prevents water from overflowing or seeping
into the cake. The foil should not be closed over the top of the
cake. Be careful not to tear any holes in the foil!

Bake until the top of the cake is golden brown and dry to the
touch, though still a bit soft in the center, about 1½ hours. It
should "shimmy" a bit when you shake the pan; it will firm up
more as it cools.

Remove the pan from the water bath, remove the foil, and let
cool at room temperature 15 minutes. Refrigerate, uncovered, 2
hours before removing the cake from the pan.

To remove the cake from the pan, first remove the sides. Cover
the surface with plastic wrap. Place a large plate over the cake,
then flip the cake over and onto the plate, tapping if necessary to
help the cake come away from the pan bottom. Remove the pan
bottom and evenly sprinkle the exposed surface with graham
cracker crumbs. Place a serving plate over the crumbs and flip the

The cool creaminess of a basic cheesecake filling plays deliciously against
the warm toastiness of nutmeg.
Nutmeg is most often mixed with other
dessert spices like cloves and cinnamon, but here it stands beautifully on
its own. The quantity is small, but its
effect is big—almost "hot" from the
spice. Many chefs use nutmeg in
savory dishes like creamed spinach or
quiche, but Rick utterly refused to
cook with it. Gale gave him a slice of
this without telling him what the flavoring was, and he didn't recognize it—
but he loved it! And if you already
rather like nutmeg, imagine how much
you'll like this cake.

Since the nutmeg is the most potent
flavoring here, it's worth grating whole
nutmegs for the recipe, either with a
special nutmeg grater or against a fine
hand-held grater (but a fresh jar of
nutmeg from the supermarket will
make a great cake, too). It's also well
worth seeking out fresh cream cheese
at a cheese shop or deli, to avoid the
gums and additives of most supermarket versions.

The technique of adding the graham-
cracker crust at the **end** of the baking
belongs to our friend Maida Heatter, a
cook we adore as well as admire.

cake again so that the crumbs form the bottom crust and the top is covered with plastic. Refrigerate, lightly covered, at least 3 hours or overnight before serving.

MAKES 1 CAKE

Coffee and cheesecake are a natural; make it a strong, spicy coffee like Sumatra to stand up to the nutmeg.

root beer–vanilla parfaits

In this elegant dessert rendition of an all-American root beer float, the smooth flavor and texture of vanilla ice cream are a wonderful contrast to the aromatic crunch of granita, a chunkier Italian version of sorbet. The uniquely creamy, spicy flavor of root beer—traditionally a blend of roots and barks that includes sarsparilla, sassafras, wintergreen, maple, wild cherry, and ginger—has been a Gale Gand signature ever since she started making her own batches of the stuff in 1993.

Living and working in England, a root beer–free zone, meant that we had to make our own or go without! The terrier we adopted that year even got named after the wonderful brew. To this day, he's known as Rootie, and he appears on the label of Gale's Root Beer, which comes in several stimulating flavors. At Brasserie T, we serve this parfait with mini Tootsie Rolls on the side for a touch of chocolate and chew.

Photograph on page 156.

6 cups (1½ quarts) root beer
4 elbow straws
1 quart vanilla ice cream

The day before you plan to serve, pour 4 cups of the root beer into ice cube trays to a depth of no more than ½ inch. (Keep the remaining root beer refrigerated until ready to serve.) Freeze overnight, along with tall, thin glasses or parfait glasses for serving.

When ready to serve, unmold the cubes into a food processor fitted with the metal blade. Process, pulsing, just until crushed. Place a straw in each glass, leaning along the side. Layer the parfaits by alternating scoopfuls of the root beer granita and vanilla ice cream, ending with a scoop of ice cream on the top.

Serve with a pitcher of the remaining root beer, and pour root beer up to the top of each parfait at the table.

MAKES 4 SERVINGS; CAN BE DOUBLED

This dessert is its own refreshing drink!

moist ginger cake with orange icing

FOR THE CAKE

8 tablespoons (1 stick) unsalted butter, melted

1 large egg, lightly beaten

¾ cup granulated sugar

½ cup dark molasses (not blackstrap)

1 cup hot water

2¼ cups all-purpose flour

1 teaspoon baking soda

½ teaspoon salt

2 teaspoons ground ginger

1 teaspoon ground cinnamon

FOR THE ICING

2 cups confectioners' sugar

¼ cup fresh orange juice

1 teaspoon freshly grated orange or lemon zest, or a combination

Heat the oven to 350 degrees. Butter and lightly flour a 9-inch tube pan.

MAKE THE CAKE

Combine the melted butter, egg, and sugar in a mixer fitted with a paddle attachment (or using a hand mixer). Add the molasses and water and mix.

Sift the flour, baking soda, salt, ginger, and cinnamon together. Working in batches, and mixing after each addition, add the dry ingredients to the molasses mixture. Mix until smooth.

Pour into the prepared pan and bake in the center of the oven for about 35 minutes, until browned and the top of the cake feels dry and firm to the touch. Let cool in the pan for 10 minutes, then turn out onto a wire rack.

MAKE THE ICING

When the cake is completely cooled, whisk the icing ingredients together until smooth. Set the wire rack over wax paper to catch any drips. Spoon all the icing onto the top of the cake and spread it out, so that it runs down the sides. Set aside in a cool place until the icing has set, about 30 minutes.

MAKES 1 CAKE

Subtle desserts can be all very well, but when zingy ginger is the flavor at hand, you want to get maximum POW! Used in quantity, ginger has some of the heat of pepper and the zing of citrus. And like many spices, ginger is great in both sweet and savory dishes. Here it flavors an intensely spicy-sweet cake, like a gingerbread for grown-ups.

Molasses, made from sugarcane, has a strong affinity for ginger; together, they make a typically American flavor combination. (European bakers tend to use honey to flavor their gingerbread.) The orange icing freshens the flavors, but a dusting of plain powdered sugar and a cold glass of milk is all you really need.

Ginger cake is a British teatime favorite, so brew a pot of Earl Grey tea and serve with lemon or milk.

sweet-hot white pepper ice cream

2 cups heavy cream
2 cups half-and-half
½ vanilla bean, split lengthwise
9 egg yolks
¾ cup sugar
¾ teaspoon freshly ground white pepper

In the fifteenth century, European trading ships fanned out all over the world in search of pepper first, and gold second. The precious peppercorns were often used as a form of currency, and counterfeit peppercorns made of clay were already a problem. Since the overland route for pepper from India to Europe was a closely guarded secret known only to a few Arab merchants, Europeans were desperate to find an ocean route to India and the "Spice Islands." Despite fears of falling off the edge of the world, Spanish ships were finally driven to set out across the Atlantic.

White pepper is simply black pepper with its black skin removed, making it milder and sweeter. The heat of pepper and chili peppers (which are completely different species of plants) is certainly addictive. After a spicy meal, a plain dessert might taste bland, so this ice cream, with its soothing cold and creamy texture and tingly flavor, is perfect for those occasions.

Heat the cream, half-and-half, and vanilla bean in a saucepan over medium heat, stirring occasionally to make sure the mixture doesn't scorch on the bottom. When the cream mixture reaches a fast simmer (do not let it boil), turn off the heat. Set aside to infuse for 10 to 15 minutes.

Whisk the egg yolks and sugar together in a medium bowl.

Whisking constantly, slowly pour the still-hot cream mixture into the egg yolk mixture. Return the mixture to the saucepan and cook over medium heat, stirring constantly with a wooden spoon. At 160 degrees, the mixture will give off a puff of steam. When the mixture reaches 180 degrees it will be thickened and creamy, like eggnog. If you don't have a thermometer, test it by dipping a wooden spoon into the mixture. Run your finger down the back of the spoon. If the stripe remains clear, the mixture is ready; if the edges blur, the mixture is not quite thick enough yet. When it is ready, quickly remove it from the heat.

Meanwhile, half-fill a large bowl with ice water. Strain the mixture into a smaller bowl to smooth it and remove the vanilla bean. Whisk in the white pepper. Rest the smaller bowl in the ice water and let the mixture cool, stirring often, then freeze according to the directions of your ice-cream maker.

MAKES 1 QUART

The exotic spice and sweetness of this ice cream is even more exuberant when you complement it with tropical lemonade (page 280).

saffron-pistachio ice cream

2 cups heavy cream
2 cups half-and-half
½ vanilla bean, split lengthwise
12 saffron threads
1 strip orange zest, about 1 inch x 3 inches
9 egg yolks
¾ cup sugar
½ cup shelled green pistachio nuts (not the red-dyed ones), toasted
(page 14) and cooled

Heat the cream, half-and-half, vanilla bean, saffron, and orange zest in a saucepan over medium heat, stirring occasionally to make sure the mixture doesn't scorch on the bottom. When it reaches a fast simmer (do not let it boil), turn off the heat and set aside to infuse for 10 to 15 minutes. It will turn yellow.

Whisk the egg yolks and sugar together in a medium bowl. Whisking constantly, slowly pour the still-hot cream mixture into the egg yolk mixture. Return the mixture to the saucepan and cook over medium heat, stirring constantly with a wooden spoon. At 160 degrees, the mixture will give off a puff of steam. When the mixture reaches 180 degrees it will be thickened and creamy, like eggnog. If you don't have a thermometer, test it by dipping a wooden spoon into the mixture. Run your finger down the back of the spoon. If the stripe remains clear, the mixture is ready; if the edges blur, the mixture is not quite thick enough yet. When it is ready, quickly remove it from the heat.

Meanwhile, half-fill a large bowl with ice water. Strain the mixture into a smaller bowl to smooth it and remove the vanilla bean, saffron threads, and orange zest. Rest the smaller bowl in the ice water and let the mixture cool, stirring often, then freeze according to the directions of your ice-cream maker.

Pulse the pistachios in a food processor until coarsely chopped. Put a large mixing bowl in the freezer to chill. When the ice cream is finished, transfer it to the frozen bowl. Using a sturdy rubber spatula, fold in the chopped pistachios until swirled. Freeze.

MAKES 1 QUART

Quench your thirst with another Mediterranean tradition: iced peppermint tea.

Perhaps because of its rarity, its delicacy, and the rich golden hues that it imparts to whatever it touches, Spanish saffron is the gentle queen of the spice world. Orange, an equally sun-filled Mediterranean ingredient, is often used to enhance saffron's sweet flavor.

For as long as ships have sailed the Mediterranean, yellow saffron, bright oranges, and crunchy green pistachio nuts have been traded back and forth across its waters. Saffron threads are the stigmas of the crocuses that grow abundantly in Spain (though each flower yields only three strands of saffron); orange trees cluster thickly along Italy's Amalfi coast; and pistachio trees grow in the volcanic soil on the slopes of Mount Etna in Sicily. The flavors and colors of this ice cream always take us back to the warm, fruitful lands of the Mediterranean.

myrna's cinnamon raisin monogram pies

1 recipe Plain and Perfect Pie Crust (page 30), in 2 disks, chilled
2 cups raisins
1 cup light corn syrup
2 tablespoons fresh lemon juice
2 tablespoons all-purpose flour
2 tablespoons cold unsalted butter, cut into pieces
2 tablespoons sugar
½ teaspoon ground cinnamon
Cold cream or milk

Gale's mother, Myrna, often seemed to be in the middle of making a pie—mixing, rolling, filling, crimping, or baking. Gale loved to hang out in the kitchen and watch. If she stuck around long enough, sometimes she'd be rewarded with extra pie dough rolled out into a miniature crust and decorated with a big "G."

Monogramming individual pies is an extremely easy and affectionate way to make anyone feel special, even the most dignified grown-ups. These spicy little raisin bundles are like simplified mince pies; in England, they'd be called "Eccles cakes," pronounced **ecklz**. The cinnamon and lemon flavors lighten the dark raisin filling. If you're feeling deluxe, serve a pitcher of cold cream (milk is good, too) at the table for each person to pour into the hot pie.

On a floured surface, roll out 1 disk of dough (following the tips on page 000) into a rectangle large enough to cut 6 circles about 6 inches in diameter (the dough will be about ⅛ inch thick). Using an individual (4-inch) pie pan as a guide, and leaving an extra 2 inches of dough all the way around, cut the dough into circles with the tip of a sharp knife. Line the individual pie pans with the dough circles as described on page 31, for a single-crust pie. Arrange the lined pie pans on a sheet pan and refrigerate, uncovered.

Roll out the second disk of pie dough and cut 6 more dough circles, slightly smaller, to use for top crusts. Transfer to another sheet pan lined with parchment or wax paper and refrigerate. Reserve the remaining dough.

Heat the oven to 400 degrees. Mix the raisins, corn syrup, lemon juice, and flour together.

Divide the filling among the pie shells and dot with the butter. Brush the overhanging edges of the dough with water. Place the top crusts on the pies and crimp the edges according to the method on page 31.

Mix the sugar and cinnamon together. Brush the tops of the pies with water and sprinkle thickly with cinnamon sugar. Using your hands, roll pieces of the remaining dough into "worms," then shape the worms into initials on the top of each pie.

Bake the pies on the sheet pan until light golden brown, 20 to 30 minutes. Serve hot. After the top crust has been broken, pour cold cream or milk into each pie, passing a pitcher around the table.

MAKES 6 SERVINGS

The spicy sweetness of the filling is wonderful with strong tea with plenty of milk.

anisette mascarpone cake

FOR THE CAKE

3 eggs

1 cup sugar

½ cup vegetable oil

½ teaspoon pure vanilla extract

1½ cups all-purpose flour

1½ teaspoons baking powder

½ cup milk

FOR THE TOPPING

4 egg yolks

½ cup sugar

1 pound mascarpone

¼ cup Sambuca or another anisette liqueur

TO FINISH THE CAKE

½ cup sugar

½ cup water

2 tablespoons Sambuca or another anisette liqueur

2 tablespoons semisweet chocolate shavings (page 14)

A simple but festive cake for a family gathering—especially an Italian family gathering. Dark chocolate and creamy mascarpone (an Italian cheese similar to cream cheese) balance out the combination of light vanilla-scented cake juiced up with a sweet anise syrup. Anise is related to fennel, parsley, and licorice; in liqueur form, anisette, it has an aromatic licorice effect that Italians adore with coffee. Even people who don't like licorice love anisette—and this cake. On Christmas mornings in Rochester, the Tramonto clan moves from house to house, nibbling Christmas cookies and sipping warming espresso and anisette at each house.

MAKE THE CAKE

Heat the oven to 350 degrees. Line a 9×13-inch baking pan with parchment paper.

Whip the eggs and sugar in a mixer fitted with a whisk attachment (or using a hand mixer) until light and fluffy. With the mixer running, drizzle in the oil, then the vanilla.

Sift the flour and baking powder together. Working in alternating batches, and mixing after each addition, add the dry ingredients and the milk to the egg mixture until the batter is just mixed. Pour into the pan. Bake until firm and springy to the touch, and a tester inserted into the center comes out clean (a few crumbs are okay), 35 to 40 minutes. Let cool in the pan on a wire rack.

MEANWHILE, MAKE THE TOPPING

Whip the egg yolks and sugar in a mixer fitted with a whisk attachment (or using a hand mixer) until light and fluffy and the sugar is almost dissolved. Add the mascarpone and anisette and whip *just* until stiff and frosting-like, being careful not to overmix. Overmixing may cause the mascarpone to separate. Refrigerate until ready to use.

MAKE THE ANISETTE SYRUP

Bring the sugar and water to a boil in a small saucepan over medium-high heat. Turn off the heat and add the anisette. Set aside to cool slightly.

Turn out the whole cake onto a large sheet pan and peel off the parchment paper. Brush the surface of the cake with the anisette syrup until it is all absorbed. Cover the surface of the cake with the mascarpone cream, using all of the cream and spreading it all the way out to the edges. Chill, lightly covered, at least 2 hours. *(Or refrigerate until ready to serve, up to 24 hours.)*

When ready to serve, sprinkle the chocolate shavings over the surface, cut into squares, and serve cold.

MAKES 1 CAKE

The clear choice: espresso or strong coffee, laced with anisette.

vanilla panna cotta

3 tablespoons cold water
1 tablespoon powdered gelatin
4 cups heavy cream
½ vanilla bean, split lengthwise
½ cup sugar
Mixed berries

Combine the water and gelatin in a small bowl and let soak about 10 minutes (do not stir).

Meanwhile, heat the cream, vanilla bean, and sugar to a simmer in a medium saucepan over medium heat, stirring occasionally to dissolve the sugar. As soon as it simmers, turn off the heat and add the gelatin mixture, stirring to dissolve the gelatin. If the gelatin doesn't completely dissolve in 3 minutes, return the mixture to the heat and warm gently until dissolved.

Strain the mixture into 6 to 8 ramekins or dessert cups. Chill, uncovered, 2 hours. Dip the cups in hot water for 10 seconds, then turn the panna cottas out onto dessert plates (or, serve in the cups). Surround each panna cotta with berries.

MAKES 6 TO 8 SERVINGS

With smooth, silky, cool panna cotta, hot, robust, dark espresso makes an addictive contrast.

Vanilla doesn't get any respect. It's the most essential flavoring in American baking; chocolate chip cookies and apple pie and butterscotch pudding wouldn't taste at all the same without it. Vanilla is **everywhere.** But vanilla itself is considered a starter flavor, almost like training wheels; you eat vanilla ice cream until you graduate to chocolate.

We're out to change that. We love the flowery, spicy, creamy flavor of vanilla so much that we named our first bakery the Vanilla Bean as a tribute. And when you do use real vanilla beans in baking, you'll see what we mean. Real vanilla has an exotic, spicy undertone that balances its sweet smoothness; vanilla extract is sweeter and gives a pleasant but blander flavor to desserts. Different vanilla beans have different flavors: Madagascar, the most plentiful, are the creamiest-tasting. Indonesian beans give a light woody flavor, and Tahitian beans, if you can find them, have the most wonderful aroma of ripe cherries.

Panna cotta, or "cooked cream," is a perfect venue for the flavor of vanilla. A simple custard-like dessert served in fetching individual pots, it is on the menu at virtually every **trattoria** in northern Italy—the equivalent of chocolate mousse in French bistros. But chocolate mousse is a bear hug of flavor; vanilla panna cotta is a soft, sweet caress. You don't exactly eat it; you absorb its softness through all your senses.

five-spice tea cake

The beautifully named star anise – related to the magnolia flower—is one of the five spices; the others are warm cinnamon, pungent cloves, mild fennel, and punchy Szechuan peppercorns. Five-spice is a basic Chinese flavoring mixture, with an aromatic, faraway quality that is wonderful in a plain cake such as this. Chinese cinnamon is lighter in color and flavor than what we call cinnamon, which is really cassia; connoisseurs generally consider it superior. With the spicy-sweet cake, we love the gentle bite of the peppercorns. (By the way, Szechuan peppercorns aren't really peppercorns; these spices are so troublesome!) If you wanted to make your own five-spice powder, star anise and Chinese cinnamon can be ordered from the wonderful Penzey spice company in Wisconsin. You can also order their five-spice powder at 1-414-679-7207.

The applesauce and tea give the cake a lovely moistness and color. You can use another strong tea if you like, but using jasmine adds to the Asian flavors.

¼ teaspoon baking powder

1 teaspoon baking soda

½ teaspoon salt

1½ cups all-purpose flour

1½ teaspoons Chinese five-spice mixture (available at Asian food shops and some supermarkets)

¼ teaspoon ground ginger

½ cup cooled, very strong jasmine tea (use 1 teabag)

1 cup applesauce

2 eggs

1½ cups sugar

½ cup vegetable oil

Heat the oven to 325 degrees. Butter a 6-cup loaf pan and line it with wax or parchment paper.

Sift together the baking powder, baking soda, salt, flour, five-spice mixture, and ginger. In a medium bowl, mix the tea and applesauce.

Whip the eggs and sugar in a mixer fitted with a whisk attachment until very light and fluffy. With the mixer running at medium speed, drizzle the oil into the egg mixture and mix. Add one third of the dry ingredients and one third of the tea-applesauce mixture and mix. Repeat twice more, using up all the ingredients. The batter will be somewhat thin.

Pour the mixture into the prepared pan and bake until firm to the touch and split on the top, and a toothpick inserted into the center comes out clean, 70 to 90 minutes. Set the pan on a wire rack and let cool 30 minutes, then turn the cake out onto the rack, peel off the paper, and let cool.

MAKES 1 CAKE

Strong jasmine tea will gracefully echo the flavors of the cake.

cardamom-coffee custard

2 cups milk
½ vanilla bean, split lengthwise
**2 tablespoons dark-roast coffee beans, coarsely ground in a coffee grinder
 or crushed with a heavy skillet**
4 green cardamom pods, crushed
6 egg yolks
⅔ cup sugar
Pinch of salt
¼ cup cornstarch
1 tablespoon unsalted butter
4 whole coffee beans, for garnish

Bring the milk, vanilla bean, coffee, and cardamom to a simmer in a saucepan over medium heat. Immediately turn off the heat and set aside to infuse for 15 minutes.

Meanwhile, whip the egg yolks, sugar, and salt in a mixer fitted with a whisk attachment (or using a hand mixer) until pale yellow and fluffy. With the mixer running at low speed, mix in the cornstarch, then very gradually pour in the hot milk mixture, mixing it in as you go.

Strain the mixture through a fine sieve back into the saucepan, to smooth it and to remove the spices. Whisking constantly, cook over medium-high heat until thick and just boiling. When the mixture thickens, the whisk will leave trail marks on the bottom of the pot and the mixture will have a few large bubbles boiling up to the top. Cook just until no starchy taste or feeling remains. Remove from the heat and stir in the butter until melted.

Pour into 4 custard cups, ramekins, or mugs and chill, uncovered, at least 2 hours or overnight. Serve chilled, with a whole coffee bean placed in the center of each serving.

Lime-green cardamom pods contain the dark, sweetly scented seeds that were long, and appropriately, known in the West as "grains of paradise." Cardamom was used in ancient Greece and Rome as incense, perfume, and even mouthwash (it magically neutralizes the pungent oils of garlic). From its native India, cardamom traveled around the world during the years of the spice trade and for some reason became hugely popular in Sweden; to this day, most Swedish cookies and cakes contain a warming pinch of ground cardamom.

When used as an ingredient in desserts, coffee beans behave just like a spice; along with the cardamom pods here, they are crushed and infused into a delectable custard. Cardamom is best known as the mysterious spice in the sweet, black, thick brew we call Turkish coffee. This dessert is a cool, creamy echo of that heady drink.

MAKES 4 SERVINGS

Small cups of strong coffee are a must; serve with strips of lemon zest to freshen the spice of the cardamom.

allspiced apple butter

5 pounds any kind of apples, peeled, cored, and cut into ½-inch chunks
1 pound light brown sugar
2 teaspoons cinnamon
1 teaspoon allspice, preferably freshly ground

Put the apples in a large, heavy-bottomed pot. Turn on the heat to low and cook, uncovered, 1½ hours, stirring every 15 minutes or so. Add the brown sugar and spices and continue cooking over low heat, stirring occasionally, until very thick, about 30 minutes more.

To test for doneness, place a spoonful of the mixture on a white plate and let sit 20 seconds. If a ring of liquid forms around the apples, there is still too much liquid in the mixture. Continue cooking and testing until no ring forms.

Let cool to room temperature and refrigerate in an airtight container.

MAKES ABOUT 5 CUPS

Gale spent a lot of time at folk music festivals as a child (playing the mandolin and singing with her father and brother), and though she never dreamed that desserts would be her destiny, she was deeply interested in the food. There was a homespun quality to the festivals, and churning, baking, and preserving were in the air. Often cauldrons of apple butter, simmering away all day, scented the whole fair with their sweetness and spice. Apple butter with spoon bread, baked beans, hominy, and ham were something to look forward to all year.

Allspice, a Caribbean berry, bears an uncanny flavor resemblance to a combination of cloves, nutmeg, cinnamon, and pepper. Only a strong fruit flavor can stand up to that intense spice, and a concentrated apple jam like this— utterly simple to make—is perfect. This is wonderful with strong cheese like Cheddar and even Roquefort. You can serve it as a topping for waffles or simple cakes or ice cream, or with toast and cheese, or swirled into hot cereal.

holidays

"What calls back the past,
like a rich pumpkin pie?"
John Greenleaf Whittier

valentine chocolate kisses

birthday cupcake tree

hot cross buns

martine's easter ricotta cheesecake

passover lemon sponge cake with strawberries

s'more baked alaska for independence day

mother's day passionfruit pound cake

flourless chocolate walnut torte

pumpkin pie to be thankful for

jewish new year's honey–almond crunch cake

thanksgiving cranberry angel food cake

halloween boo!scotti

tart holiday gooseberry tartlets

mrs. essam's mince pie

eggnog bavarian cream with butter-rum sauce

holiday cookie projects: snowflakes, dreidel trios,
  and ornaments

italian almond-iced christmas cookies

christmas tree linzer cookies

new year's eve venetian mask cookies

personality profile: Just as you gather people together to create a mood or to celebrate, holidays gather flavors, with their distinct personality profiles, together. Some flavors are elegant; Chocolate and Butter, for example, lend tone to any gathering. But for summertime cookouts, you might invite a down-to-earth pairing of Fruit and Flour. Spice lends a warm feeling in the cool months. We love to develop traditions by inviting certain flavors to the same party each year. You create a family of desserts, with all the different personalities of a real family!

For us, holidays are all about being with friends and family around a table. And if that table is adorned by a particularly beautiful, festive, and appropriate dessert, so much the better. There's nothing more fun than dreaming up desserts to tie into the holidays, and sometimes nothing more challenging than finding a dessert that everyone likes, that no one is allergic to, and that doesn't violate anyone's dietary or religious principles. We've tried to cover many bases, from those of you who are just trying to feed maximum people with minimum fuss, to those who want to take the opportunity to show off a little bit. After all, it's your party!

Though holidays can seem like extra work sometimes, we appreciate the way they mark the passage of time, forcing everyone to slow down, stay home, and pay attention to the seasons. Many holiday recipes reflect the seasonality of ingredients: Strawberries at Passover and pumpkin pie at Thanksgiving only make sense.

Holidays also show a strong tendency to attach themselves to certain desserts and never let go. Every member of our family has his or her own birthday cake tradition. Once we make the same dessert for Thanksgiving just two years in a row, we find that it's an indelible part of the celebration. Memories are created around it, you establish a continuity, and you find yourself having conversations in which you compare this year's pie to the one you made two years ago, and the one you made two years before that, and then there was the year you ran out of vanilla, and the year the power went off in the middle of the baking . . . and you've got yourself a tradition!

Anything that you make for your holiday party becomes your holiday tradition, even if you don't follow our recipes exactly. What's most important is to develop a collection of recipes that make you happy in the planning, the making, and the eating. You needn't have the perfect cookie cutters, or just the right colors of icing sugar. Although we are professional chefs, we know that sometimes it's more important to make your aunt's Christmas cookies the same way she's been making them for forty years than it is to make the finest, fanciest gourmet Christmas cookies we can dream up. It's not about skill; it's about love.

We also realize that these recipes cover only a very few of all the holidays you might conceivably be celebrating. They reflect our own large families (with their collective Italian, Catholic, Jewish, Hungarian, New York, Chicago, Midwestern, and Rochester backgrounds) and our own global circle of friends, which includes the many people we've cooked with and for over the years. When we cook their recipes, it's as though they are with us in the kitchen. When we make Mrs. Essam's Mince Pie, or the Passionfruit Pound Cake (which reminds Gale of her mother's favorite perfume), or the Birthday Cupcake Tree for our son Gio's annual birthday party, we are reconnecting with our past—and staking a claim in the future. It seems amazing that a dessert can do that, but it can. Maybe that's what cooking is all about.

Happy holidays!

valentine chocolate kisses

1 miniature (about 7 ounces) pound cake, marble pound cake,
  or chocolate cake (or half of a regular-size cake)
2 tablespoons unsweetened cocoa powder
1 cup confectioners' sugar
1½ tablespoons honey
¼ cup dark rum
30 frozen pitted cherries (do not thaw)
1 pound white chocolate, coarsely chopped (see page 14)
3 ounces semisweet chocolate, coarsely chopped

These are a double kiss: They are kisses themselves, and you're guaranteed to get kisses from anyone you give one to. Smoothly coated in white chocolate, they hide a real cherry heart at their center, with a layer of rum-moistened cake crumbs in between.

Cake crumbs, of course, are always available in bakeries (in fact, it's a challenge to bakers to use them creatively; see the Brooklyn Blackout Cake on page 110 for another solution) but you can make your own from any plain cake. We use white and dark chocolate to create a pretty paint-spattered effect, but you could stop at a single coating of chocolate, white or dark. Note that white chocolate, which contains a very high percentage of cocoa butter, melts at a lower temperature than dark chocolate. See page 14 for melting instructions. Melted white chocolate is hot, but not hot enough to burn you; that's why you can dip the kisses with your fingers. In either case, be careful not to let the chocolate scorch.

Kirschwasser, or "cherry water," is a powerful fruit brandy whose aroma alone is highly seductive. Pour the best one you can find, very cold, alongside hot dark coffee and a plate of these kisses. Wow!

Heat the oven to 400 degrees.

Pulse the cake into fine crumbs in a food processor. You should have about 2 cups. Spread them out on a sheet pan and bake them just until toasted and dry, about 10 minutes. Let cool.

Toss the cake crumbs, cocoa powder, and confectioners' sugar together in a large bowl. Drizzle in the honey and rum and mix until blended. The mixture should be moist enough to pack with your hands; if not, add more rum a little at a time.

Take a cherry and, using your hands, pack the chocolate crumb mixture around it until it is completely encased in crumbs. Smooth the surface, then set aside on a plate. Repeat with the remaining cherries and refrigerate, uncovered, for 30 minutes, until slightly dried.

Meanwhile, melt the white chocolate in a bowl set over very hot tap water, stirring often. Keep warm by replenishing the hot water as it cools. Melt the semisweet chocolate in the top of a double boiler or in a bowl set over barely simmering water, stirring often. Keep warm.

Line a sheet pan with parchment or wax paper. Using your fingers and working quickly, dip a kiss in the melted white chocolate to coat, shake off any excess, and place on the lined sheet pan to set. Repeat with the remaining kisses, leaving ½ inch between them.

Once all the kisses are coated, drizzle them with semisweet chocolate. Dip a fork in the chocolate and let it drip off the tines, holding the fork well above the pan. Refrigerate uncovered until firm, about 30 minutes. Serve or refrigerate in an airtight container. Let warm at room temperature for 1 hour before serving.

MAKES 20 KISSES

birthday cupcake tree

FOR THE CUPCAKES

Paper cupcake liners

3 cups sifted cake flour

1 tablespoon baking powder

½ teaspoon salt

8 ounces (2 sticks) unsalted butter, slightly softened

2 cups granulated sugar

4 eggs

1 teaspoon pure vanilla extract

1 teaspoon pure almond extract

1 cup milk

FOR THE FROSTING

11 tablespoons unsalted butter, slightly softened

2 ounces unsweetened chocolate, melted (page 14)

4 cups confectioners' sugar

1 teaspoon pure vanilla extract

2 to 4 tablespoons half-and-half or whole milk

FOR THE TREE

Mixed colored sprinkles

3 colors of curling ribbon

About 14 lollipops, in assorted colors

One 8-inch styrofoam cone (you can get this at a craft shop or in the craft department of a large discount store)

20 to 30 toothpicks

Birthdays mean parties at any time of the year, and the fact is that everybody just loves a cupcake. More than a messy, crumbly slice of cake, a perfect golden cupcake with chocolate buttercream frosting and bright sprinkles is just what you want at a birthday party—whether it's a fourth or a fortieth. Serving them stacked up in a festive cone with colorful lollipops, ribbon, and a candle on top will earn you an unshakable reputation as an extraordinary hostess, with remarkably little effort.

MAKE THE CUPCAKES

Heat the oven to 375 degrees. Line the cups of 1 or 2 muffin tins with paper liners (you can bake the cupcakes in batches if necessary).

Sift the flour, baking powder, and salt together three times and set aside.

Cream the butter in a mixer fitted with a whisk attachment until smooth and fluffy. Add the granulated sugar and mix until blended. Add the eggs one at a time, mixing after each addition. Add the vanilla and almond extracts and mix. With the mixer running at low speed, and working in alternating batches, add the dry ingredients and the milk to the butter mixture, mixing just to combine after each addition. Mix just until smooth. Fill the lined muffin cups about ⅔ full, using about ¼ cup of batter for each.

Bake until risen, golden, and firm to the touch, about 20 minutes. Let cool in the pans.

MEANWHILE, MAKE THE FROSTING
Cream the butter in a mixer fitted with a paddle attachment (or using a hand mixer) until smooth. Drizzle in the chocolate and mix. Working in batches, and mixing after each addition, add the confectioners' sugar and mix until smooth. Add the vanilla and 2 tablespoons half-and-half and mix. Add more half-and-half a little at a time until the frosting is thick and spreadable.

Use a pastry bag fitted with a large star tip or a flexible spatula to frost the tops of the cooled cupcakes. Refrigerate at least 1 hour before assembling the tree.

ASSEMBLE THE TREE
Spread a thick layer of sprinkles out on a plate. Dip the tops of the cupcakes in the sprinkles and set aside. Tie curling ribbon around the necks of the lollipops and curl with scissors.

Beginning 1 inch up from the bottom of the styrofoam cone, stick toothpicks into the cone 2 inches apart, making a circle around the cone and leaving them sticking out at least 2 inches. Place the cone on a serving platter. Make the bottom ring of cupcakes by spearing the bottom of a cupcake onto one of the toothpicks in the cone, with the frosting facing out and with the side of the cupcake resting on the plate. Between every *two* cupcakes (not between *each* cupcake), stick the lollipop sticks into the cone.

Place another row of toothpicks, 2 inches apart, 1 inch above the tops of the first row of cupcakes all around the cone, positioning them so that the second row will rest between the tops of the first row. You will fit fewer cupcakes on the second row; feel free to cut a cupcake in half if necessary to fit into the space available. Spear the cupcakes onto the toothpicks and add the lollipops as before. Continue up the cone to form a tree of cupcakes, ending with a single cupcake on top. Place a candle in the top cupcake. Serve within 1 hour, or refrigerate up to 24 hours. If refrigerated overnight, remove from the refrigerator 1 hour before serving.

MAKES ABOUT 25 SERVINGS

Tall frosted glasses of very cold root beer (with or without scoops of vanilla ice cream) and elbow straws make the party fizz.

hot cross buns

FOR THE DOUGH

1¼ cups milk, at room temperature

1 ounce active dry yeast

6 tablespoons honey

2 tablespoons unsalted butter, melted

3½ cups bread flour

1 teaspoon ground cinnamon

¾ teaspoon ground nutmeg

¼ teaspoon ground cloves

¾ teaspoon salt

Freshly grated zest of ½ lemon

¼ cup dried currants

¼ cup golden raisins

FOR THE ICING

2 tablespoons orange juice

1 tablespoon egg whites

1¾ cups confectioners' sugar

These lightly sweet, lightly spiced little buns are really too good to keep for Eastertime; they make terrific breakfast fare, especially in the winter. The classic combination of spices—nutmeg, cinnamon, and cloves—reveals the English origin of the recipe. If by some strange chance you don't want icing on your hot cross buns, you can also make the cross by slashing the top of each bun with a very sharp knife before baking. Serve warm, of course!

The spice and fruit of these buns is wonderful with smoky Irish coffee: coffee stirred with whiskey and topped with whipped cream. Mulled red wine with honey and spice is also delicious with the fresh buns.

MAKE THE DOUGH

Combine the milk, yeast, and honey in the bowl of a mixer fitted with a dough hook. Set aside and let proof for 5 minutes.

Add the butter, flour, cinnamon, nutmeg, cloves, salt, and lemon zest to the yeast mixture. Blend at low speed for 7 minutes. Add the currants and raisins and mix 1 minute more. Turn out onto a floured surface, knead for 1 minute, then transfer to an oiled bowl. Cover with a damp towel and let rise 1 hour in a warm place.

Line 2 sheet pans with parchment or wax paper. With your hands, pull off large handfuls of dough and shape them into balls. Place on the baking sheet and cover with a damp kitchen towel. Let rise 1 to 2 hours in a warm place, until doubled in bulk.

Heat the oven to 400 degrees.

Uncover the buns. Bake until golden, 15 to 20 minutes. Let cool slightly on wire racks.

MEANWHILE, MAKE THE ICING

Stir together the orange juice, egg whites, and sugar until smooth. Using a pastry bag fitted with a plain tip, pipe a cross over the top of each bun while the buns are slightly cooled but still warm. Serve immediately or let set 30 minutes at room temperature.

MAKES 15 TO 20 BUNS

FOR THE CRUST

1¼ cups graham cracker crumbs (pulse whole crackers in the food
    processor or use store-bought crumbs)

4 tablespoons (½ stick) unsalted butter, melted

½ cup pine nuts, toasted (page 14), cooled, and pulsed in the food
    processor until coarsely ground

½ teaspoon freshly grated lemon zest

FOR THE FILLING

2 pounds fresh ricotta cheese

1⅓ cups sour cream

6 eggs, separated, whites at room temperature

2 tablespoons all-purpose flour

1 cup sugar

4 tablespoons fresh lemon juice

1 teaspoon pure vanilla extract

1 cup raisins

The Mediterranean seasonings of this cake—lemon zest, pine nuts, and raisins—are a signpost to its Italian origin. Ricotta cheesecakes are part of Italian dessert tradition wherever cheese is made (ricotta is a by-product of cheese-making). When Gale married into Rick's family, she realized that ricotta cheesecake was going to be part of her life for a long time to come; the problem was that she loathed the stuff! All-ricotta cheesecakes tend to be heavy and grainy, so she created a smooth filling that combines ricotta and sour cream, lightened with egg. The flavors and textures of the seasonings are reminiscent of the sweet filling for traditional **cannoli.**

🌶 *Hot espresso with lemon zest deliciously echoes the aroma of the cake. So would* limoncello, *a sweet lemon liqueur that is drunk after special dinners in southern Italy, where lemons grow plentifully.*

Heat the oven to 350 degrees.

MAKE THE CRUST

Mix the ingredients together. Thickly butter a 9- or 10-inch springform pan and press the mixture into the bottom of the pan. Refrigerate, uncovered.

MAKE THE FILLING

Mix the ricotta cheese, sour cream, egg yolks, and flour in a mixer fitted with a paddle attachment (or using a hand mixer) until smooth (the mixture will remain a bit grainy from the ricotta). Add the sugar, lemon juice, and vanilla and blend until creamy. Fold in the raisins.

Whip the egg whites in a clean, dry bowl until stiff but not dry. Fold them into the filling mixture. Pour into the pan and bake until the top of the cake is set and dry to the touch, though still a bit soft in the center, 70 to 80 minutes. It should "shimmy" a bit when you shake the pan; it will firm up more as it cools.

Let cool in the pan. The cake will deflate a bit as it cools. Remove the sides of the pan, cover, and refrigerate at least 2 hours. *(Or refrigerate until ready to serve, up to 48 hours.)* Serve cold.

MAKES 1 CAKE

passover lemon sponge cake with strawberries

FOR THE CAKE

9 eggs, separated, whites at room temperature

¾ cup sugar

1 cup ground almonds (page 14)

½ cup chopped almonds (page 14)

¼ cup sifted matzoh cake meal, plus extra for flouring the pan

1½ teaspoons fresh lemon juice

Freshly grated zest of 1 lemon

FOR THE GLAZE

¾ cup confectioners' sugar

¼ teaspoon pure vanilla extract

¼ teaspoon freshly grated lemon zest

1 to 2 tablespoons fresh lemon juice

TO FINISH

1 cup apricot jam

1½ tablespoons water

2 cups strawberries, green parts trimmed off, cut into chunks

MAKE THE CAKE

Heat the oven to 350 degrees. Butter a 9- or 10-inch springform pan and line the bottom with parchment paper. Dust the sides of the pan with sifted cake meal.

Whip the egg whites in a mixer fitted with a whisk attachment (or using a hand mixer) until soft peaks form. Add ½ cup of the sugar and continue whipping just until stiff and glossy, about 30 seconds more.

In another bowl, whip the egg yolks with the remaining ¼ cup of sugar until light and fluffy. Fold in the egg whites. Gently fold in the ground almonds, chopped almonds, matzoh meal, lemon juice, and lemon zest. Pour the batter into the pan and bake until dry and spongy in the center, 35 to 40 minutes. Let cool for 15 minutes in the pan, then remove the sides of the pan and let cool completely on a wire rack. The cake will fall somewhat.

MAKE THE GLAZE

In a small bowl, stir the ingredients together until smooth, adding lemon juice as needed until the glaze is pourable. Set the wire rack holding the cake on a sheet pan. Drizzle the glaze generously

Passover and Easter both celebrate the coming of spring, and what could be a more delectable reminder than the first strawberries of the season? The marvelous thing about this cake is that your strawberries need not be at their prime, as they are glazed with sweet jam before topping the cake.

This is essentially an angel food cake with egg yolks added, making a pretty yellow crumb. Leavening comes only from whipped egg whites; flour is replaced by matzoh cake meal and ground almonds. Chopped almonds add a great texture with the soft strawberries, sugary lemon glaze, and light cake.

Note that there is no dairy in this cake, making it appropriate for meat meals. However, there is confectioners' sugar in the glaze, which some do not consider kosher for Passover because of the cornstarch it contains.

over the top of the cake, letting it trickle down the sides. Using a flexible spatula or pastry brush, gently spread the glaze over the sides of the cake, reusing any glaze that drips onto the sheet pan. Let set for at least 30 minutes before serving, or until the glaze is hardened. Transfer the cake to a serving platter, removing the pan bottom and parchment paper if desired.

FINISH THE CAKE

Bring the jam and water to a boil in a medium saucepan, stirring to break up any lumps. Working quickly, add the strawberries all at once and fold together with a spatula until evenly coated. Pour into the sunken center of the cake and gently spread into a circle on the surface, leaving a 1½-inch border all around. Let cool until set, about 30 minutes. Use a very sharp knife for slicing the cake.

MAKES 1 CAKE

A pot of herb tea with lemon wedges is the ideal complement after a family meal.

s'more baked alaska for independence day

½ gallon chocolate ice cream, in a single brick (do not thaw)
¼ cup milk chocolate shavings (page 14) or chips
2 packs graham crackers, about 20 whole crackers
1 cup egg whites (from about 8 eggs), at room temperature
1 cup sugar
Sparklers
½ recipe warm Satin Chocolate Sauce (optional; pages 90–91)

Make enough room in your freezer for a sheet pan to lie flat, and have a sheet pan at hand. Working quickly, remove the cardboard from the ice cream and lay it on a sheet of wax paper. Cut it in half horizontally to create 2 layers, as you would a cake. Lift off the top layer and lay it on another sheet of wax paper. Transfer both layers on the wax paper to the sheet pan and put them back in the freezer to harden. When hardened, remove them from the freezer and sprinkle the chocolate shavings over the tops. Put them back in the freezer.

Arrange a layer of graham crackers the same size as the ice cream brick on a flat, ovenproof serving platter. Working quickly, use a spatula to place one layer of ice cream on top of the crackers. Cover with a layer of crackers, then top with the other layer of ice cream. Cover the top and sides of the block with crackers. Cover with plastic wrap and freeze for at least 2 hours or up to 2 days.

Whip the egg whites in a clean, dry bowl until soft peaks form. Add the sugar and continue whipping until stiff and glossy.

As soon as the meringue is ready, remove the dessert from the freezer. Using a spatula, smoothly cover the entire cake with meringue until it looks like a big rectangular marshmallow. Make swirl patterns in the meringue with an icing spatula. Return to the freezer to set for at least 3 hours or up to 2 days.

When ready to serve, heat the oven to 500 degrees. Take the dessert out of the freezer and place it directly in the oven. Bake 3 to 4 minutes, until browned.

To serve, stick the sparklers in the cake, light them, and bring to the table (preferably in the dark!). Serve in slices, topped with warm chocolate sauce, if desired.

MAKES 8 TO 12 SERVINGS

Our dear friend Karen has the perfect backyard fireplace for toasting (and tasting) S'mores. We made them the traditional way—sandwiches of graham crackers, melted marshmallows, and chocolate bars—every July Fourth for years. Then came the year we started thinking about how to make them even better.

We took the S'mores apart, put them back together with a brick of ice cream—and wound up with a Baked Alaska! Marshmallows are just meringue with gelatin added, so the meringue coating was a natural. Its fluffiness hugs a layered "cake" of ice cream, graham crackers, and pure chocolate. The great thing about Baked Alaska is that it only improves if you make it up to a week ahead; you brown it at the very last minute. Serve this out in the backyard to get the full effect of the sparklers.

After a long day of parades, fireworks, and barbecues, a refreshing glass of seltzer, ice, and lime or lemon is just what you want with a sweet dessert to send everyone home happy.

1½ cups all-purpose flour

1 teaspoon baking powder

½ teaspoon salt

8 ounces (2 sticks) butter, slightly softened

1⅓ cups sugar

4 eggs

2 teaspoons pure vanilla extract

¼ cup plus ⅓ cup passionfruit juice or canned or frozen passionfruit puree (available in Latin and Caribbean markets)

There's a feminine simplicity to pound cake that makes it perfect for Mother's Day—or maybe it's the sweet scent and handmade quality that make us think of Mom. Passionfruit always reminds Gale of her mother, Myrna, who once brought back passionflower perfume from a trip to Bermuda and wore it on special occasions. Passion-fruit, though sweet and perfumey, has an almost citric tartness that we love. The tropical flavors of passionflower and vanilla blend beautifully in this cake.

Heat the oven to 350 degrees. Butter a 6-cup loaf pan and line it with parchment or wax paper. Mix the flour, baking powder, and salt together.

Cream the butter in a mixer fitted with a whisk attachment (or using a hand mixer) until smooth. Add 1 cup of the sugar and mix. With the mixer running at low speed, add the eggs one at a time. Add the vanilla. Working in alternating batches, and mixing after each addition, add the dry ingredients and the ¼ cup of passion-fruit juice to the butter mixture. Mix just until smooth.

Pour into the pan and bake until raised in the center and a tester inserted into the center comes out dry and almost clean (a few crumbs are okay), 65 to 75 minutes.

Meanwhile, make the glaze. Stir the remaining ⅓ cup of sugar and the remaining ⅓ cup of passionfruit juice together until the sugar is dissolved.

When the cake is done, let cool in the pan 15 minutes (it will still be warm). Set a wire rack on a sheet pan with sides (to catch the glaze) and turn the cake out onto the rack. Peel off the paper. Using a turkey baster or pastry brush, spread glaze all over the top and sides of the cake and let it soak in.

Repeat until all the glaze is used up, including any glaze that drips through onto the sheet pan. Let cool at room temperature or, wrapped in plastic wrap, in the refrigerator. *(Well wrapped, the cake will last up to a week)*. Serve at room temperature, in thin slices.

MAKES 1 CAKE

Earl Grey tea, with its note of citrusy bergamot, is perfect. Put a pretty pitcher of milk at Mom's elbow.

flourless chocolate walnut torte

FOR THE CAKE

8 ounces (2 sticks) unsalted butter

8 ounces semisweet chocolate

5 eggs

3 egg yolks

3 tablespoons sugar

½ cup matzoh cake meal, plus extra for flouring the pan

7 ounces finely ground walnuts (about 2⅓ cups)

FOR THE FROSTING

½ cup egg whites (from about 4 eggs)

½ cup sugar

8 ounces (2 sticks) cold unsalted butter, cut into pieces

1 ounce unsweetened chocolate, melted (page 14)

2 teaspoons cold brewed coffee

MAKE THE CAKE

Heat the oven to 350 degrees. Butter a 10-inch round cake pan and line the bottom with parchment or wax paper. Dust the sides of the pan with matzoh cake meal.

Melt the butter and chocolate together in the top of a double boiler set over barely simmering water, stirring frequently. Set aside to cool slightly.

Whip the eggs, egg yolks, and sugar in a mixer fitted with a whisk attachment (or using a hand mixer) until very light yellow and fluffy. Fold in the hot chocolate mixture.

Mix the matzoh meal and ground walnuts together. Fold into the chocolate-egg mixture. Pour into the pan and bake until firm and dry on the top and a toothpick inserted into the center comes out almost clean (a few crumbs are okay), 35 to 40 minutes. Let cool 20 minutes in the pan, then turn out onto a rack and let cool to room temperature. Transfer to a serving plate and refrigerate 1 hour. Peel off the parchment paper.

MEANWHILE, MAKE THE FROSTING

Whisk the egg whites and sugar together in the top of a double boiler set over barely simmering water until the mixture is very hot and the sugar has dissolved somewhat. Remove from the heat and whip the mixture in a mixer (or using a hand mixer) until cooled, smooth, and fluffy. Whipping, gradually add the butter and whip until smooth; the mixture might look broken at this point,

This deep, dark cake is flourless (for Passover purposes), but not wheatless (for allergy or health purposes). It contains matzoh cake meal: ground matzohs that are made from flour and water, but considered kosher for Passover because they are unleavened.

No one could turn down a piece of this double-chocolate cake, at any time of year. Fine matzoh meal and ground walnuts make the cake densely fudgy, almost brownie-like; a lighter, classic coffee–chocolate buttercream frosting is the crowning touch. Of course, in kosher households, this cake may be served only with a dairy meal.

but keep whipping and it will smooth out. Drizzle in the melted chocolate and coffee and whip until smooth and fluffy.

Using a flexible spatula, frost the chilled cake on the top and sides. Serve immediately or refrigerate up to 24 hours. Remove from the refrigerator 1 hour before serving.

MAKES 1 CAKE

A small wedge of this cake and a cup of strong coffee is wonderfully brightening to the spirits after a big holiday meal.

pumpkin pie to be thankful for

It's true that pumpkin pie is a controversial and divisive issue, but even those who generally turn up their noses at the stuff eat huge slices of this at our Thanksgiving table. The creamy, spicy filling goes over well with both pumpkin-haters and pumpkin-eaters. Maybe that's because the pumpkin flavor is just one of many in this pie: Cinnamon, nutmeg, cloves, and ginger are just as evident. As you can see from a glance at the recipe, this is a really, really easy pie. Whip chilled heavy cream and a sprinkling of light brown sugar together for the top, if you like

Cold milk tastes great with the spice of the pie, but if you're in need of a digestif, knock back a shot of Calvados (apple brandy), as they do in Normandy after a big meal. We also call it applejack.

One 15-ounce can pumpkin puree (not pumpkin pie mix)

3 eggs

½ **cup granulated sugar**

½ **cup light brown sugar, packed**

1 teaspoon ground cinnamon

½ **teaspoon salt**

¼ **teaspoon ground nutmeg**

¼ **teaspoon ground cloves**

¼ **teaspoon ground ginger**

½ **cup milk**

½ **cup heavy cream**

½ **recipe (1 crust) Plain and Perfect Pie Crust (page 30), rolled out, pressed into a 9-inch pie pan (do not prebake), and chilled**

Heat the oven to 350 degrees.

Mix the pumpkin puree and eggs in a mixer fitted with the whisk attachment (or using a hand mixer) until well blended. Add the sugars and mix. Add the remaining ingredients and mix until blended.

Pour into the pie crust and bake until dry and lightly browned on the top. (A knife inserted into the center should come out almost completely clean.)

Let cool and serve immediately, or chill overnight.

MAKES 1 PIE

jewish new year's honey–almond crunch cake

7 tablespoons unsalted butter, melted
1 cup light brown sugar, packed
½ cup plus 2 tablespoons honey
½ cup sliced almonds, toasted (page 14)
1 egg
1 cup buttermilk
2 cups all-purpose flour
1 teaspoon baking powder
½ teaspoon baking soda
½ teaspoon salt

Heat the oven to 350 degrees.

Thickly butter a 6-cup loaf pan. Pour in 3 tablespoons of the melted butter, swirl to coat the bottom, and sprinkle in ¼ cup of the brown sugar. Drizzle in the 2 tablespoons of honey and sprinkle the almonds evenly over the bottom.

Whisk the egg in a large bowl. Add the remaining ¾ cup of brown sugar and mix. Add the remaining 4 tablespoons of melted butter and ½ cup of honey and mix. Gradually mix in the buttermilk.

Combine the flour, baking powder, baking soda, and salt. Working in batches, and mixing after each addition, add the dry ingredients to the buttermilk mixture. Mix until smooth.

Pour the batter into the pan. Bake until a tester inserted into the middle of the cake comes out dry and almost clean (a few crumbs are okay), 50 to 60 minutes. Let cool in the pan for no more than 5 minutes, then turn out onto a wire rack and let cool until the topping is firm.

MAKES 1 CAKE

Squeeze a shot of lemon in your tea for a tart note that zips through the sweetness and crunch.

The Jewish New Year is always celebrated with honey, to ensure a sweet year to come. But most traditional honey cake recipes are not very sweet or very appealing; they are based on dark, heavy German gingerbreads, called **lebkuchen.** This one is light yellow, fluffy, and infinitely more festive. Honey and almonds are combined as a toasty and crunchy topping for tangy, moist buttermilk cake that's much too good to eat only once a year. There's a little bit of honey in the cake, and lots of it on the top. The honey-almond mixture, which loses its stickiness as it sets, is reminiscent of the popular old-fashioned Jewish dessert called **taiglach.**

thanksgiving cranberry angel food cake

Angel food cake, appropriately to its name, is a godsend when it comes to big family gatherings. Everyone likes it (even perennial dieters), almost no one is allergic to it (it contains no nuts or dairy), and it provides a light, sweet ending to what is too often a sloth-inducing meal. Nuggets of fresh cranberries color the cake pink and a citrusy glaze makes it festive.

Cranberry and orange is a flavor combination that has taken American palates by storm, and we think it's great: Anything that balances tang and sweetness is popular around our house (see the Citrus chapter for further proof). Gale's dad, Bob Gand, particularly loves this cake.

With this light dessert, a touch of luxury: coffee with real cream.

FOR THE CAKE
1½ cups egg whites (from about 1 dozen eggs), at room temperature
1¼ teaspoons cream of tartar
½ teaspoon salt
1½ cups sugar
1⅛ cups sifted cake flour
1 teaspoon pure vanilla extract
Freshly grated zest of 1 tangerine or orange
1 cup fresh or thawed frozen cranberries, coarsely chopped (pulse whole berries in the food processor)

FOR THE GLAZE
2 tablespoons fresh tangerine or orange juice
2 tablespoons cranberry juice
1 tablespoon egg whites
1½ cups confectioners' sugar

MAKE THE CAKE

Heat the oven to 375 degrees.

Whip the egg whites in a mixer fitted with a whisk attachment (or using a hand mixer) until foamy. Add the cream of tartar and salt and continue whipping until soft peaks form. With the mixer running, gradually add 1 cup of the sugar and continue whipping until stiff and the sugar has dissolved, about 30 seconds more.

Sift the remaining ½ cup of sugar with the sifted cake flour 3 times, to aerate the mixture. Fold into the egg whites, then fold in the vanilla, zest, and cranberries.

Spoon the batter into an ungreased tube pan. Bake until light golden brown, 30 to 35 minutes. Cool by hanging the cake (in the pan) upside down around the neck of a bottle until it cools to room temperature. Run a long, sharp knife blade around the cake to loosen, then knock the cake out onto a plate. The outside of the cake will remain in the pan.

MAKE THE GLAZE

Stir the ingredients together until smooth. Pour over the top of the cake and spread with a spatula, letting the glaze trickle down the sides. Let set for at least 30 minutes before serving, or until the icing is hard. Cut with a serrated knife, using a sawing motion.

MAKES 1 CAKE

halloween boo!scotti

2 cups sifted all-purpose flour
½ teaspoon baking powder
½ teaspoon baking soda
¼ teaspoon salt
1 cup sugar
⅓ cup plus 1½ cups blanched almonds, toasted (page 14) and cooled
2 eggs
1 teaspoon pure vanilla extract
¼ teaspoon pure almond extract
2 tablespoons Grand Marnier or thawed orange juice concentrate
2 teaspoons freshly grated orange zest
12 ounces white chocolate, coarsely chopped
Candy corn, licorice buttons, chocolate chips, raisins, sprinkles, and
  colored sugar, for decorating

Heat the oven to 375 degrees. Butter a large sheet pan.

Sift the sifted flour, baking powder, baking soda, salt, and sugar together into a large bowl. Transfer ½ cup of the mixture to a food processor. Add the ⅓ cup of toasted almonds to the food processor and pulse until fine and powdery, about 45 seconds. Return this mixture to the dry ingredients, stir in the whole almonds, and mix.

Whisk the eggs, vanilla, almond extract, Grand Marnier, and orange zest together. Stir into the dry ingredients. The dough may seem dry, but it will moisten as you work it. Mix until smooth. Turn the dough out onto a lightly floured work surface and knead it a few times just to bring the dough together. Divide into 2 equal pieces. Wet your hands and use them to shape each piece of dough into a flattened log about 8 inches long, 3 inches wide, and 1 inch high.

Transfer the logs to the pan, leaving at least 3 inches between the logs (they will spread during baking). Bake until light golden brown, 25 to 30 minutes, rotating the pan after 15 minutes to ensure even baking.

Let cool 15 minutes on the pan. Reduce the oven temperature to 300 degrees. Carefully transfer the logs to a cutting board. Wipe off the pan and butter it again.

Using a serrated knife, cut the logs into ½-inch-thick slices, discarding the ends. Arrange the slices on the sheet pan cut side up. Bake until toasted, 20 to 25 minutes. Turn the oven off, prop the oven door open, and let cool completely in the oven.

These are so cute that you'll risk being tricked rather than give them out as treats; we bet you'll want to save them all for your own crowd of goblins.
  Photograph on page 154.

Meanwhile, in the top of a double boiler (or in a bowl) set over hot (not boiling or simmering) water, slowly melt the white chocolate, stirring often. Line a sheet pan with parchment or wax paper and transfer the melted white chocolate to a small bowl.

Dip 2 inches of the end of each cookie into the white chocolate and turn chocolate side up so that the chocolate drips unevenly down the cookie. The chocolate-covered end of the biscotti is its head; the uneven edge is the bottom edge of the ghost's "sheet." Lay them on the wax paper as they are dipped.

While the chocolate is still warm, decorate the chocolate-covered ends with little ghost faces, using small candies, licorice, candy corn, chocolate chips, raisins, or sprinkles (see photograph). If necessary, snip the candies to make them smaller. Sprinkle orange, yellow, or black sugar on the top edges of the biscotti for hair or all over the ghost's face. Let cool on wire racks until set. Store in an airtight container.

MAKES ABOUT 20 COOKIES

For a Halloween party, rest a pot of hot cider inside a big jack-o'-lantern. Pour it into mugs with red-hot candies, cinnamon sticks, or cinnamon schnapps.

tart holiday gooseberry tartlets

1 recipe Sweet Pastry (page 35), chilled
8 ounces whole almonds
1 cup granulated sugar
½ pound (2 sticks) cold unsalted butter, cut into pieces
3 eggs
¼ teaspoon pure vanilla extract
1 tablespoon all-purpose flour
3 cups fresh gooseberries, tails and stems removed
Confectioners' sugar

Heat the oven to 400 degrees.

On a lightly floured work surface, using the rolling method on page 31, roll out the pastry dough into a large rectangle about ⅛ inch thick. Cut out 6 circles of dough, 6 inches in diameter, and use them to line six 4-inch tart pans. Refrigerate, uncovered, until ready to use.

Pulse the almonds and sugar in a food processor fitted with a metal blade until sandy. Add the butter and process until incorporated. Add the eggs and process until smooth (the texture will remain slightly grainy from the almonds).

Scrape down the sides of the bowl, add the vanilla and flour, and process until smooth. This is the frangipane. Divide it among the unbaked tart shells and smooth the tops. Divide the gooseberries on top of the frangipane, in a single layer. Arrange the tarts on a sheet pan with sides, to catch any juices.

Bake until the frangipane is golden brown and puffy and the gooseberries have sunk in and cooked, 30 to 35 minutes. Let cool on a wire rack. Dust with confectioners' sugar before serving.

MAKES 6 SERVINGS

Consider this traditional English recipe for "Cider Cup": 1 Flagon Cider, 1 Syphon Soda, Half Pint Lemon Squash, 2 Wineglasses Cyprus Sherry, 1 Tot Brandy, a Good Quantity of Ice, and Slices of Lemon or Orange. Or see our Drinks chapter for a recipe for hot rum grog, warming and heartwarming at the holidays.

We became addicted to gooseberries when we lived in England. Sweet, tart, fat, and juicy, they are a very satisfying fruit to cook with. We were delighted when they started turning up at local markets in Chicago. They are grown in Australia and New Zealand, so we get them in the middle of our winter, in time for the holidays. There's an Englishness to lots of American Christmas traditions, and gooseberries are as English as it gets.

Much like string beans, gooseberries must have their stems and tails nipped off before cooking (in England this process is called "topping and tailing"). Green gooseberries are sweeter than the red variety but either is fine for this recipe. If you prefer to make a single 10-inch tart, simply bake it for 40 to 50 minutes. See page 186 for an unscientific discussion of frangipane.

mrs. essam's mince pie

We met Mrs. Essam, one of many great home cooks who have shared their secrets with us over the years, at Stapleford Park, the luxurious English hotel in Leicestershire where we lived and worked for two years. Mrs. Essam told us wonderful stories of life at Stapleford, especially at Christmastime, when she used to make hundreds of tiny mince pies with this savory-sweet, aromatic filling. The English tradition is to attempt to eat twelve at one sitting, to ensure twelve sweet months to come.

This recipe is for one large pie rather than the tiny doll-size ones that are annoying to make. Traditional recipes for mincemeat, of course, include beef; this one does not. We do, however, use suet (purified beef fat) for making the filling. If you prefer, you can use an equivalent amount of solid palm shortening (available in blocks at many supermarkets) or even chilled butter instead.

Try hot ruby port spiked with a pinch of cloves along with your mince pie.

FOR THE MINCEMEAT

1 pound tart firm apples, such as Granny Smith

1½ cups raisins

1 cup golden raisins

1½ cups currants

1 cup candied citrus rind (lemon, orange, citron, or grapefruit, or a combination)

1½ cups chilled grated beef suet or 1 cup solid palm shortening or 2 sticks cold butter (see sidenote)

Freshly grated zest and juice of ½ lemon

Freshly grated zest and juice of ½ orange

½ teaspoon ground cinnamon

½ teaspoon ground mace

¼ teaspoon ground nutmeg

2 cups light brown sugar, packed

½ teaspoon salt

¼ cup dark rum

¼ cup apple juice concentrate

FOR THE CRUST

1 recipe Plain and Perfect Pie Crust (page 30), in 2 disks, chilled

MAKE THE MINCEMEAT

Peel, core, and coarsely chop the apples. Place in a large heavy pot. Coarsely chop the raisins, golden raisins, currants, and candied rind and add to the pot. Add the remaining filling ingredients and bring to a simmer. Cook, uncovered over very low heat, for 1 hour until thickened, stirring occasionally. Set aside to cool to room temperature, then refrigerate overnight. *(Or refrigerate, tightly covered, up to 1 month.)*

Heat the oven to 450 degrees.

PREPARE THE CRUST

Roll out the dough for a 2-crust, 10-inch pie, line the pan, and chill the crusts as directed on page 31. Fill the unbaked pie shell to the top with mincemeat. Finish the pie as directed on page 31.

Place the pie on a sheet pan. Bake 10 minutes, then reduce the heat to 350 degrees. Bake about 30 minutes more, until the crust is golden brown and the filling is bubbling at the vents. Let cool slightly. Serve warm.

MAKES 1 PIE

eggnog bavarian cream
with butter-rum sauce

FOR THE BAVARIAN CREAM

2 teaspoons powdered gelatin

3 tablespoons cold water

1 cup chilled heavy cream

3 cups milk

½ vanilla bean, split lengthwise

¼ teaspoon ground cinnamon

⅛ teaspoon nutmeg, preferably freshly grated

8 egg yolks

1 cup sugar

FOR THE BUTTER-RUM SAUCE

4 tablespoons unsalted butter

½ cup light brown sugar, packed

2 tablespoons dark rum

½ cup fresh orange juice

½ cup heavy cream

MAKE THE BAVARIAN CREAM

Combine the gelatin and water in a small bowl and let soak, stirring occasionally.

Whip the cream until stiff in a mixer fitted with a whisk attachment (or using a hand mixer). Refrigerate until ready to use.

Heat the milk, vanilla bean, cinnamon, and nutmeg in a saucepan, over medium heat, stirring occasionally to make sure the mixture doesn't scorch on the bottom. When it reaches a fast simmer (do not let it boil), turn off the heat and set aside to infuse for 10 to 15 minutes.

Meanwhile, whisk the egg yolks and sugar in a medium bowl. Whisking constantly, slowly pour the still-hot milk mixture into the egg yolk mixture. Return the mixture to the saucepan and cook over medium heat, stirring often, until the mixture is thick enough to coat the back of a spoon. Immediately remove from the heat and stir in the gelatin mixture until dissolved.

Meanwhile, half-fill a large bowl with ice water. When the gelatin is completely dissolved, pour the mixture through a fine sieve into a smaller bowl and rest in the ice water. Let the mixture cool, stirring frequently, just until it begins to thicken and jell. Working quickly, fold in the whipped cream. Pour into a 6-cup

This creamy yellow mold lends any holiday table a traditional, festive, European air. We know that many of you have cut eggnog out of your holiday plans for one reason or another, so we decided to create a dessert that brings back the flavor if not all of the fat of that creamy, once-a-year treat. The egg yolks are fully cooked when you make the custard that, with gelatin added, becomes Bavarian cream. The butter-rum sauce is a bit spicy from the rum and tangy from the orange juice. This is a truly voluptuous dessert.

mold or individual cups or ramekins and refrigerate, covered, overnight. *(The custard can be made up to 3 days in advance and refrigerated, covered, until ready to serve.)*

MAKE THE SAUCE

Melt the butter in a medium skillet, over medium heat. Add the brown sugar and cook, stirring, until bubbly. Slowly stir in the rum. Add the orange juice and cook, stirring, 2 minutes. Let cool to room temperature. If a skin forms on the top, strain the mixture through a sieve. Set aside until ready to serve

To serve, half-fill a large bowl with hot water. Dip the mold in the hot water for 10 seconds, then invert onto a serving platter. If necessary, run the tip of a knife around the edge of the mold to break the suction and shake the mold to release the Bavarian cream. If using individual molds, dip the bottoms in hot water to release the custards, or serve in the cups.

In a blender or food processor, or using a hand blender, process the room-temperature butter-rum sauce with the heavy cream until smooth. Pour around the Bavarian cream and serve, or transfer to a pitcher and pour over each serving at the table.

MAKES 8 SERVINGS

Strong coffee with a dash of rum would keep Santa going even at the end of his rounds.

holiday cookie projects:
snowflakes, dreidel trios, and ornaments

8 ounces (2 sticks) unsalted butter, slightly softened

¾ cup light brown sugar, packed

1 egg

½ cup dark molasses (not blackstrap)

½ teaspoon pure vanilla extract

3¼ cups cake flour

½ teaspoon baking soda

¼ teaspoon salt

1 teaspoon ground cinnamon

2 teaspoons ground ginger

¼ teaspoon ground cloves

FOR DECORATING

White icing (page 99)

Food coloring

Colored sugar

Cream the butter in a mixer fitted with a paddle attachment (or using a hand mixer) until smooth. Add the sugar and mix. Add the egg and mix. Add the molasses and vanilla and mix.

Sift the flour, baking soda, salt, cinnamon, ginger, and cloves together. Working in batches, and mixing just until combined after each addition, add the dry ingredients to the butter-sugar mixture. Shape the dough into a thick disk, wrap in wax paper, and refrigerate 1 to 2 hours.

Heat the oven to 350 degrees. Grease one or two sheet pans.

On a lightly floured surface, roll the dough out ¼ inch thick.

TO MAKE SNOWFLAKES

Use a snowflake-shaped cookie cutter to cut out the cookies, rerolling the scraps as needed. If you plan to hang the cookies, use a toothpick to make holes in the handles about ⅛ inch wide, keeping in mind that the holes will shrink as the cookies bake. Bake until firm, 12 to 15 minutes, and let cool on the pan. Using only white icing and a pastry bag fitted with the smallest plain tip, pipe thin lines from the center of the cookie out to the points, like spokes of a wheel. Connect the spokes with thin lines in between them, making a spiderweb effect to make it look like a snowflake.

Whether you're decorating a tree, a room, or a table during the holidays, these long-lasting ginger cookies bring into your house a sparkle, color, and feeling of warmth that no store-bought ornament can provide. Making them is an ideal Saturday project to usher in the holidays. String the finished cookies on stout wire and run them along your banisters and mantels, or coil them up into a wreath or centerpiece. Light candles to catch the twinkle in the sugar crystals.

One batch of dough will give you about 2 dozen cookies; if you plan to double the recipe, make two separate batches. You can add color to the cookies either by coloring the icing or by using white icing, then dusting the icing with colored sugar before it sets. After it sets, knock off the excess. The latter gives a prettier, more sparkly effect.

Photograph on page 155.

Let the icing harden before threading the cookies onto wire, string, or yarn for hanging.

TO MAKE DREIDEL TRIOS

Use a dreidel cookie cutter and cut out 3 cookies. Lay one on a greased sheet pan. Fanning out at an angle, with the handles overlapping at the top, lay two more dreidels next to the first one (it will look like a paper-doll effect). The handle is now three layers thick; press on it gently to thin it slightly and make it larger. Repeat with the remaining dough, rerolling the scraps as needed. If you plan to hang the cookies, use a toothpick to make a hole in the handle about ⅛ inch wide, keeping in mind that the hole will shrink as the cookies bake. Bake until firm, 12 to 15 minutes, and let cool on the pan. Color some of your icing blue with food coloring, or use blue colored sugar and white icing together. Using a pastry bag fitted with a small plain tip, pipe Hebrew letters or stars of David on the cookies' faces. Sprinkle the sugar on the icing while the icing is still wet. Let the icing harden before threading the cookies onto wire, string, or yarn for hanging.

TO MAKE ORNAMENTS

Use any holiday-themed cookie cutter to cut out the cookies, rerolling the scraps as needed. If you plan to hang the cookies, use a toothpick to make holes in the handles about ⅛ inch wide, keeping in mind that the holes will shrink as the cookies bake. Bake until firm, 12 to 15 minutes, and let cool on the pan. Meanwhile, color some of your icing in festive colors with food coloring, or use colored sugars. Using a pastry bag fitted with the smallest plain tip, pipe a few colorful borders and decorations on the cookies. When set, add more lines of icing in white. Let the icing harden before threading the cookies onto wire, string, or yarn for hanging

MAKES ABOUT 24 COOKIES

Strangely, both cold milk and hot whiskey toddies go perfectly with spicy gingerbread.

italian almond-iced christmas cookies

FOR THE COOKIES

3 cups all-purpose flour

1 tablespoon baking powder

½ teaspoon salt

3 eggs

½ cup sugar

½ cup vegetable oil

1 teaspoon pure vanilla extract

½ teaspoon pure almond extract

FOR THE ICING

2 tablespoons milk

1 tablespoon egg white

1¼ cups confectioners' sugar

¼ teaspoon pure almond extract

2 colors of food coloring, of your choice

MAKE THE COOKIES

Heat the oven to 350 degrees. Butter 2 sheet pans. Mix the flour, baking powder, and salt together.

Mix the eggs and sugar in a mixer fitted with a paddle attachment (or using a hand mixer) until pale yellow and fluffy. With the mixer running, drizzle in the oil, vanilla, and almond extract, and mix. Add the dry ingredients and mix just until combined.

Turn the dough out onto a lightly floured work surface. Using your hands, form into logs 1 inch in diameter. Working in batches if necessary, cut into ¾-inch-thick slices and arrange the cookies on the sheet pans. Bake until light golden brown, 12 to 15 minutes. Let cool on wire racks.

MAKE THE ICING

Whisk the milk, egg white, confectioners' sugar, and almond extract together until smooth. Divide the icing into one large and two smaller batches. Leave the large batch of icing white; color the two small batches to your liking.

When the cookies are cool, dip the tops into the white icing. To drizzle the cookies with the other colors, dip the tines of a fork into the icing and wave it over the cookies. Let set in a cool place 1 hour.

MAKES ABOUT 6 DOZEN COOKIES

Although we've been cooking professionally for years, we always leave the making of Christmas cookies to Rick's talented aunts, who dazzle us with their seemingly endless variety of recipes. Sisters Liz, Fran, Dot, Annie, Teresa, Flo, and Tootsie launch the Christmas cookie project in November, when they each make quantities of the basic dough and freeze it while they plan the staggering cookie trays to come. (These amazing women are also crochet champions.)

This recipe replicates the flavor and texture of our favorite cookies, though you'll have to be very creative with the icing to come up with something to match the aunts' colorful platters. They are thicker than most cookies, almost like nuts of dough.

Dunking is part of Tramonto family tradition: Try dunking these crisp cookies first in Grand Marnier, then espresso. Rick's dad, Frank, makes his own coffee liqueur for dunking.

christmas tree linzer cookies

12 ounces (3 sticks) unsalted butter, slightly softened
1½ cups confectioners' sugar, plus extra for dusting
3 eggs
½ teaspoon pure vanilla extract
1½ pounds ground almonds (page 14)
⅛ teaspoon salt
⅛ teaspoon ground cinnamon
1 cup all-purpose flour
1¼ cups raspberry jam

Linzer Torte is an imposing-sounding classic from the Viennese pastry tradition, but it's actually the perfect cop-out for exhausted hosts. The raspberry jam filling comes straight out of a jar, and the mixer does the work of creating the buttery-nutty crust. Our version shrinks the classic into sandwich cookies, with a cut-out on top for the glowing ruby jam to peek through. Cookie cutters are such a wonderful combination of bakers' tools and children's toys! Bring them all out at holiday time: You can use any shape you like for the cut-out.

Cream the butter in a mixer fitted with a paddle attachment (or using a hand mixer) until smooth. Add the 1½ cups of confectioners' sugar and mix. Add the eggs one at a time, mixing between each addition. Add the vanilla, ground almonds, salt, and cinnamon and mix well. Add the flour and mix at low speed just until a dough forms. Shape into a ball and wrap in plastic wrap. Chill at least 3 hours or overnight.

Heat the oven to 350 degrees. Turn out the dough onto a lightly floured work surface. Roll out to ¼-inch thickness and, using a cookie cutter, cut into rounds. Transfer to sheet pans and chill 30 minutes. Working on half the rounds, and using a small Christmas tree or other cookie cutter, cut out shapes from the center. Form all the scraps into a ball and wrap in plastic wrap. Chill 30 minutes, then roll out to make more cookies.

Bake the whole and cut-out cookies until golden brown, 10 to 12 minutes. Let cool completely on wire racks.

Place a spoonful of raspberry jam on each whole cookie round. Place a cut-out round on top and press gently to make a sandwich. The jam will hold the two cookies together and will show through the cut-out. Dust with confectioners' sugar and let set for at least 1 hour before serving. (Or, store in an airtight container for up to 5 days.)

MAKES 2 TO 3 DOZEN COOKIES

As a tribute to the great Viennese tradition of afternoon coffee and pastries, drink Kaffee mit Schlag—coffee with whipped cream—which is wonderful at Christmastime.

new year's eve venetian mask cookies

6 tablespoons unsalted butter
2 egg whites
¼ cup sugar
½ cup all-purpose flour
¼ teaspoon pure vanilla extract
White icing (page 99)
Colored sugar

MAKE THE STENCIL

On the lid of a large plastic container or a shirt cardboard (about 8 inches across), trace the outline of a domino mask (the kind that covers just your eyes and nose). With your pen, extend the top corners, making them flare up into points, like eyeglasses from the 1950s. Cut the mask shape out of the lid and set the lid aside. This is the stencil. Discard the mask shape.

MAKE THE COOKIES

Heat the oven to 350 degrees.

Melt the butter in a heavy skillet over medium heat. After it melts, continue to cook the butter, watching carefully. It will foam and subside, then separate into golden butterfat and cloudy white milk solids. The milk solids will begin to brown. When they are lightly browned and the butter smells nutty and toasted, remove from the heat and set aside to cool.

Whip the egg whites and sugar in a mixer fitted with a whisk attachment (or using a hand mixer) until stiff and glossy. Add the flour, vanilla, and brown butter and mix at low speed until blended. The batter will become thicker as the egg whites lose volume.

Hold the stencil firmly on a nonstick sheet pan (or a sheet pan lined with parchment paper). Using an offset spatula, an icing spatula, or the back of a spoon, spread batter through the stencil in a very thin, smooth layer. The batter should be so thin that you can see the pan through it, only about as thick as the stencil; and as even as possible. Carefully lift off the stencil and move it to another part of the sheet pan to make another cookie (you will probably be able to fit only a few cookies per batch). Using your index finger, make eye holes by gently clearing the batter away from the appropriate place on the mask with a circular motion.

Bake until light golden brown, 8 to 10 minutes. If possible, have

The masks worn by residents of Venice during **Carnavale,** the period of fun and frolic that comes before Lent, are the inspiration for these super-elegant cookies. The last day of carnival is Mardi Gras ("Fat Tuesday"), everyone's favorite party. We have had Mardi Gras–themed parties at other times of the year; the masks and costumes make any party more glamorous and mysterious. For those of us who don't live in New Orleans or Venice, New Year's Eve is an ideal Mardi Gras substitute.

You don't actually wear these delicate masks, but they look spectacular curled around scoops of ice cream or Milk Chocolate–Orange Mousse (page 109), the colored-sugar tips winking in the light.

Photograph on page 147.

a large rounded surface, such as the side of a clean 1-gallon paint can, at hand. When the masks come out of the oven, immediately lift them off the sheet pan with your fingers or a spatula and drape them over the rounded surface to cool. (You can cool them on a flat surface, but the masks will be flat.)

Repeat with the remaining batter. The batter will probably start to stiffen up as the butter cools; you can reheat it in the microwave, or set the bowl over hot water to keep the batter warm.

When the cookies are cooled, use white icing and colored sugar to decorate the masks. If necessary, store the masks in an airtight container, placing sheets of parchment or wax paper between them.

MAKES ABOUT 10 MASKS

There's no substitute for real Champagne on New Year's Eve; try a demi-sec *style, with a little sweetness, at dessert time.*

DRINKS, WE KNOW, ARE OFTEN AN AFTER-THOUGHT WHEN IT COMES TO SERVING DESSERTS AND SWEETS AT HOME; a last-minute pot of decaf, a handful of herb tea bags, the end of the wine you drank with the roast chicken. On very special occasions, you might dig the brandy out of the closet, or take down the bottle of grappa your uncle gave you last Christmas. But a special drink, or even just one that shows the tiniest bit of forethought, can truly enhance the whole finale. In fact, with many of the concoctions below, the drink actually becomes another dessert. And what could be better than that?

drinking quantities of whole milk, but can't abide the flavor of skim, both 1% and 2% are good "drinking milks." If you are lucky enough to live near a dairy or a good farmer's market, try to get hold of dairy-farm skim milk, which has a much richer flavor than the supermarket variety. **Chocolate milk,** if mixed not too sweet, is great with cookies, coffee-flavored desserts, puddings, and chocolate cake; chocolate syrup gives the best flavor. You can also transform milk into **almond milk** with a bit of superfine sugar and some almond extract; a few drops in a glass of milk give it a lovely nutty-sweet flavor.

drinks

Instead of *asking* your guests if they want coffee or tea, *tell* them you've whipped up a spicy Mexican hot chocolate to go with that mango flan, or bring out a pitcher of frosty cold lemonade to have with the ginger cake. Do you really think they'll say no? And for occasions like afternoon tea or a birthday party, where the sweet is the main food event, something a bit festive to drink makes all the difference. Here are just a few ideas.

We confess to a special fondness for **milk** with many of the treats in this book, and of course it's what kids will usually drink. Cake and milk, cookies and milk, pie and milk, even pudding and milk all sound great to us—as long as the milk is very cold. If you don't like the idea of

Vanilla milk, milk with a few drops of vanilla extract, tastes like milk but better. With some sweet desserts, especially fruity ones, we like an occasional glass of very cold, tangy **buttermilk.**

Hot chocolate is often saved for special occasions, but we love to serve it with winter desserts: It's like getting an extra treat and a warming after-dinner drink in one cup. To make an approximation of toasty, fragrant **Mexican hot chocolate,** melt an ounce of semisweet chocolate with $\frac{1}{4}$ to $\frac{1}{2}$ teaspoon ground cinnamon, a few drops of vanilla extract, and a few drops of almond extract for about 2 cups of hot milk. Whisk the milk into the chocolate mixture. **Chocolate phosphate,** a Myrna Gand favorite, is an old-time drink of chocolate syrup with a squirt of soda water; with milk added, it becomes a **chocolate egg cream.**

The aromatic intensity of **coffee,** of course, partners wonderfully with any number of desserts and most breakfast baking. For elegant occasions, choose dark roast coffees like Italian or espresso roast. If you are lucky enough to have an espresso machine, make **espresso** after a dinner party; but if not, simply use your usual method and apply it to fresh-ground espresso roast or Italian roast coffee. Brew the coffee strong and serve it in small cups, with a bit of lemon zest for aroma. Or, in the Italian manner, serve it with a shot of grappa, Sambuca, or another clear brandy, either in the cup or alongside (this is a favorite with Rick's family). Try adding a drop of real cream or a scoop of ice cream to coffee when you serve it with a spicy or strong-flavored dessert.

If you're interested in coffee, you may want to consider geography as a factor when choosing a coffee for specific desserts. Coffee is grown in tropical climates around the globe, and they have distinct regional characteristics in flavor and body. The three loose groupings are Latin American coffees, such as Guatemala, Costa Rica, Panama, Honduras, and Mexico; South Pacific coffees, such as Indonesia, Java, Sumatra, and Sulawesi; and East African and Arabian coffees, such as Kenya, Ethiopia, Yemen, and Sanani. Generally speaking, **Latin American coffees** are ideal morning coffees with bright acidity and lively flavors that hint at nuts, pepper, and cocoa; **Pacific coffees** are smooth and full-bodied, not very acidic, but with strong coffee flavor and earthy botanic undertones. **African coffees** have medium body, light sweetness balanced with acidity, and even fruity and exotic floral aromas. Mocha coffees are in this group, as are some others that have distinct wine or berry scents. Most coffee sold at Starbucks and other gourmet coffee shops is

not a single variety, but an export blend of the three.

Café au lait, cappuccino, café con leche, and **caffè latte** (all combinations of strong coffee and hot milk) are filling and best in the morning or afternoon, with muffins, scones, and the like. Without a special machine, you can still get good results by vigorously whisking the milk occasionally as it heats in a saucepan, then pouring the hot frothy milk into the coffee.

In the summer, nothing is more cooling and invigorating than **iced coffee;** decaffeinated iced coffee can be a wonderful dessert drink. We like to make **coffee ice cubes** to put in our iced coffee, so that it doesn't become diluted as it melts. Again, vanilla or chocolate ice cream is a nice addition for special occasions. You can add a squirt of carbonated water to strong, sweet iced coffee and milk for a great **coffee soda** that is particularly good with crisp cookies.

Having lived in England, we appreciate the ritual of **tea.** A pretty teapot (a tea cozy is optional) with a pitcher of milk, a sugar bowl, and a plate of lemon slices is an easy way to dress up any gathering, from morning muffins with a friend to a swanky tea party. Classic **British tea** blends like English Breakfast, Ty-Phoo, Darjeeling, and Irish Breakfast have a strong tea-leaf flavor and a refreshing, acidic quality. Jasmine, Earl Grey, and Seychelles teas are very perfumey; Earl Grey is scented with the oil of the citrus fruit called bergamot. **Herb teas** like peppermint and French style **flower teas**—called *tisanes*—are floral and soothing; these include camomile, verbena *(verveine),* rose hip, lemon blossom, orange blossom, and linden *(tilleul).* **Spice teas** like cinnamon and ginger are warming and good for the stomach.

Iced tea can be dressed up or down. Fruit teas like blackcurrant and raspberry make wonderful iced tea, even though they are often too sweet and fruity when hot. Make ice cubes special by dropping a few mint leaves, a tiny lemon wedge, a raspberry or strawberry, or an allspice berry or star anise pod in each cube before you freeze them. Pour iced tea over the frozen cubes and serve with sprigs of mint. **Lemonade ice cubes** or **iced tea ice cubes** are a wonderful addition to iced tea; just pour them into freezer trays.

Supplying a pitcher of **sugar syrup,** instead of a sugar bowl, is thoughtful when serving iced tea; one batch lasts indefinitely in the refrigerator. To make it, combine sugar and water in a saucepan, at a ratio of 2 to 1 (for example, 1 cup sugar to ½ cup water), bring to a simmer, and simmer just until dissolved. Let cool and refrigerate in an airtight container. To make **ginger syrup** to add to drinks, add a few peeled thin slices of fresh ginger to the mixture while it simmers, then strain them out after cooling. To make **lemon syrup,** wonderful for making refreshing lemon soda, boil 1 cup sugar, ½ cup water, the zest of 1 lemon, and a pinch of salt for 5 minutes. Let cool and add the juice of 3 lemons. Strain and refrigerate in an airtight container. To add berry flavors to drinks, dilute good-quality raspberry jam with boiling water, strain, and let cool into **raspberry syrup.** All these syrups are wonderful in teas, punches, and lemonades, or even with just a squirt of carbonated water, making very special sodas.

Lemonade or **limeade** can be dressed up and served at any daytime gathering, especially now that it's possible to buy frozen unsweetened lime and lemon juice at the supermarket. For 5 cups, you'll want a cup of fresh or reconstituted frozen juice, a cup of superfine sugar, and just over a quart of cold water, all stirred together in a pitcher until the sugar dissolves and always served over ice. Add more water to taste. For fresh **berry lemonade,** add about ¼ cup of pureed, strained fresh or frozen raspberries or strawberries. For **tropical lemonade,** add ¼ cup mango or passionfruit juice. For **mint lemonade,** add 6 mint sprigs, putting them in the pitcher first and crushing the leaves with a wooden spoon. For **ginger limeade,** add 5 peeled thin slices of fresh ginger, and let the drink steep at least 1 hour before serving. **Pink lemonade** is simply made by adding grenadine to lemonade, but you can also use cranberry juice for the purpose.

If you can make or get fresh-squeezed **citrus juices,** blend them to taste and serve them over crushed ice, with mint sprigs and elbow straws just for fun. Tangerine is an especially sweet and refreshing juice. Blend cantaloupe, honeydew, watermelon, crushed ice, and lemon juice to make light **melon coolers;** cucumber and honeydew are lovely in the hot months. For large gatherings, remember that **punch** is simply fruit juice spiked with fizzy water and ice cubes. A delightful English summer drink called **Pimm's Cup** is like fruit salad in a glass: For each glass, pour 1 part Pimm's No. 1 (available at large liquor stores) to 3 parts citrus soda over ice, then add 1 slice each of lemon, orange, cucumber, and green apple, mint sprigs, and a few mixed berries. Or mix the whole thing in a clear punch bowl.

When fall comes, **apple cider** is great with whole-grain desserts like banana bread or oatmeal cake. As winter sets in, make **mulled cider** by heating (but not boiling) apple or pear cider with a few cloves, a strip of orange or lemon zest, cardamom or star anise pods, even black peppercorns and cinnamon sticks. **Mulled red wine** is made exactly the same way as mulled cider; again, do not boil. Instead of eggnog, these days you might make **rum grog** or **hot toddies** for a holiday party. For grog, put 1 teaspoon of sugar or sugar syrup, 1 tablespoon of lemon juice, and 1 shot of rum in a mug and fill with hot water or tea. Hot toddies are made the same; just use a teaspoon of sugar or sugar syrup, a cinnamon stick, and shots of whiskey, rum, or brandy. If you like, put wedges of lemon studded with cloves on the top. Or spoon on a little **brown-sugar whipped cream,** made by whipping cold cream with light brown sugar.

Ice cream drinks really get people excited about dessert. We make miniature **root beer floats** as part of our dessert plates: Place a scoop of vanilla ice cream in each glass, fill with very cold root beer, and don't forget the elbow straws. For 4 small, rich **chocolate malteds,** blend 1 cup vanilla ice cream, 2 tablespoons Satin Chocolate Sauce (pages 90–91) or chocolate syrup, 2 teaspoons malt powder, and 1 cup very cold cream or whole milk until thick and smooth. Blender-whipped fruit **smoothies** can also be festive, if they are delicious enough; our favorite combination is fresh lime juice, fresh raspberries, orange juice, vanilla yogurt or frozen yogurt, and honey. Or never mind the yogurt and blend a ripe banana with orange juice, strawberries, and a squeeze of lime. If your smoothies taste flat, remember that sugar, lime juice, and lemon juice are all wonderful for bringing out the flavors of other fruits.

Matching wine and liqueurs to desserts is both a fine art and a complex business. Red or white table wine is rarely a good choice with sweet food; any wine served with dessert should have at least a strong hint of sweetness. **Dessert wines** such as Sauternes and Muscat de Beaumes de Venise, or late harvest Gewürztraminers and Rieslings from Alsace, Germany, and Austria, are naturally fermented to be sweet, and most have fruity overtones that can beautifully perfume a fruity, peachy, or berry dessert, or a dessert that combines fruit and nuts. Custardy desserts with delicate cream or fruit flavors are perfect with **demi-sec** and **light rosé Champagnes,** and **sparkling Moscato d'Asti** is wonderful with fruit. Champagne and other sparkling wines are often too

dry for desserts, but they can be made sweeter with a drop of raspberry or blackcurrant liqueur, transforming them into dessert sparklers that complement a range of desserts. **Vintage port** is one of the few wines that can stand up to a chocolate dessert and is wonderful with nut desserts, as is **oloroso sherry.**

Brandies, including Cognac, Armagnac, Calvados, and **fruit eaux-de-vie,** and **liqueurs** like Grand Marnier or Sambuca are best served after dessert, perhaps with an intensely sweet nibble like a tuile or a morsel of chocolate-covered grapefruit rind.

index

conversion chart

EQUIVALENT IMPERIAL AND METRIC MEASUREMENTS

American cooks use standard containers, the 8-ounce cup and a tablespoon that takes exactly 16 level fillings to fill that cup level. Measuring by cup makes it very difficult to give weight equivalents, as a cup of densely packed butter will weigh considerably more than a cup of flour. The easiest way therefore to deal with cup measurements in recipes is to take the amount by volume rather than by weight. Thus the equation reads:

1 cup = 240 ml = 8 fl. oz.   ½ cup = 120 ml = 4 fl. oz.

It is possible to buy a set of American cup measures in major stores around the world.

In the States, butter is often measured in sticks. One stick is the equivalent of 8 tablespoons. One tablespoon of butter is therefore the equivalent to ½ ounce/15 grams.

LIQUID MEASURES

fluid ounces	u.s.	imperial	milliliters
	1 teaspoon	1 teaspoon	5
¼	2 teaspoons	1 dessertspoon	10
½	1 tablespoon	1 tablespoon	14
1	2 tablespoons	2 tablespoons	28
2	¼ cup	4 tablespoons	56
4	½ cup		110
5		¼ pint or 1 gill	140
6	¾ cup		170
8	1 cup		225
9			250, ¼ liter
10	1¼ cups	½ pint	280
12	1½ cups		340
15		¾ pint	420
16	2 cups		450
18	2¼ cups		500, ½ liter
20	2½ cups	1 pint	560
24	3 cups		675
25		1¼ pints	700
27	3½ cups		750
30	3¾ cups	1½ pints	840
32	4 cups or 1 quart		900
35		1¾ pints	980
36	4½ cups		1000, 1 liter
40	5 cups	2 pints or 1 quart	1120

SOLID MEASURES

u.s. and imperial measures		metric measures	
ounces	pounds	grams	kilos
1		28	
2		56	
3½		100	
4	¼	112	
5		140	
6		168	
8	½	225	
9		250	¼
12	¾	340	
16	1	450	
18		500	½
20	1¼	560	
24	1½	675	
27		750	¾
28	1¾	780	
32	2	900	
36	2¼	1000	1
40	2½	1100	
48	3	1350	
54		1500	1½

OVEN TEMPERATURE EQUIVALENTS

fahrenheit	celsius	gas mark	description
225	110	¼	cool
250	130	½	
275	140	1	very slow
300	150	2	
325	170	3	slow
350	180	4	moderate
375	190	5	
400	200	6	moderately hot
425	220	7	fairly hot
450	230	8	hot
475	240	9	very hot
500	250	10	extremely hot

Any broiling recipes can be used with the grill of the oven, but beware of high-temperature grills.

EQUIVALENTS FOR INGREDIENTS

all-purpose flour — plain flour
coarse salt — kitchen salt
cornstarch — cornflour
eggplant — aubergine

half and half — 12% fat milk
heavy cream — double cream
light cream — single cream
lima beans — broad beans

scallion — spring onion
unbleached flour — strong, white flour
zest — rind
zucchini — courgettes or marrow